The Dumb Type Reader

PSi

Performance Studies international

In Between States

Published by Museum Tusculanum Press in collaboration with Performance Studies international
General Series Editors: Rune Gade and Edward Scheer

Vol. 1: *Performing Archives/Archives of Performance*
Edited by Gunhild Borggreen and Rune Gade

Vol. 2: *Visions and Revisions: Performance, Memory Trauma*
Edited by Bryoni Trezise and Caroline Wake

Vol. 3: *The Dumb Type Reader*
Edited by Peter Eckersall, Edward Scheer and Fujii Shintarō

The series *In Between States* comprises edited volumes and single authored books addressing the "unconditioned," that which is literally in between states, thus not yet fixed or formed by established learning or by institutionalized behavior, but nonetheless characterized by performing and producing effects at a cultural level. The interdisciplinary approach of performance studies, combining fields such as visual culture, cultural studies, drama and theatre studies, and anthropology, facilitates dynamic and innovative scholarship and new forms of knowledge. The themes addressed by the series are various forms of "cultural performatives" that fall between already established categories.

The Dumb Type Reader

Edited by
Peter Eckersall,
Edward Scheer
and Fujii Shintarō

Museum Tusculanum Press

The Dumb Type Reader
Peter Eckersall, Edward Scheer and Fujii Shintarō (eds.)

Copy editors: Nicola Gray and Jordy Findanis
Layout and cover design: Pernille Sys Hansen, Damp Design
Typesetting and composition: Janus Bahs Jacquet
Set in Reminga and Aptifer Sans
Printed on Munken Lynx 120 g by Tarm Bogtryk
ISBN 978 87 635 4493 1

Cover: Dumb type, *S/N*, 1994. Many of the illustrations reproduced in this book are available on the website epidemic.net, which has a section on dumb type.

This volume is published with generous financial support from
The Australian Research Council

Museum Tusculanum Press
Dantes Plads 1
DK – 1556 Copenhagen
www.mtp.dk

Contents

Acknowledgments 9

Introduction 11

Peter Eckersall and Edward Scheer

MOVEMENTS

Dumb Type as Dance 19

Reflections on the Politics of Gesture

Sara Jansen

The Historical Position of Dumb Type in Japanese Theatre 49

The Birth and the End of the Politics of New Media Dramaturgy

ŌTORI Hidenaga

Dumb Type Women 61

Where Corporeal Precarity Meets Media Terror

Katherine Mezur

Dumb Type Technology 79

Man and Machine in Japanese Art and Society

Gunhild Borggreen

S/N

The Creation of *S/N* and the Debate about Sexuality in 1990s Japan 97
Wim Lunsing

Teiji Furuhashi: On "Coming Out" in *S/N* (1994) 109
Keiko TAKEDA

Dumb Type's *S/N* and the Archive of Kyoto in the 1990s 121
Shinya YAMAKI (Archive for the Creation Project)

Amateurism 123
Inside Dumb Type
YOSHIDA Miya

NEW MEDIA DRAMATURGY

Dumb Type's *XD* 145
A Case Study in New Media Dramaturgy
Edward Scheer

Whiteout Dumb Type 159
Postmodernism and the Birth of New Media Dramaturgy
Peter Eckersall

Re-thinking the Audience 173
Dumb Type, New Media, New Dramaturgy and the Spectator
Andreas Regelsberger

Two Memoranda 179
Was That a Question Thrown to Us?
KUMAKURA Takaaki

BRIDGES

Lovers 191
Corporeal Projections and Ocular Demands
Stephen Barber

Turning Catastrophe into Art 203
On Dumb Type's *S/N* and Tadasu Takamine's *Cool Japan*
Shintarō FUJII

Bodies that Matter 215
S/N and the Art Activism of BuBu de la Madeleine and Akira the Hustler/Yukio Cho
Fran Lloyd

INTERVIEWS

"I don't see a difference between machine-time and human-time" 237
Interview with TAKATANI Shirō, Kyoto, 15 December 2013
Peter Eckersall, Edward Scheer, FUJII Shintarō

Punch Cards, *Pleasure Life* and *pH* 249
Interview with FUJIMOTO Takayuki, Kyoto, 15 December 2013
Peter Eckersall, Edward Scheer

Chronology of Works 256

Contributors 267

Acknowledgments

The Dumb Type Reader began as a symposium in April 2013 at the International Research Centre "Interweaving Performance Cultures," at the Freie Universität in Berlin. The symposium, titled "Dumb Type – The Birth of New Media Dramaturgy," was organised by Peter Eckersall while he was a fellow at the centre. The centre was deeply supportive of the project and we are grateful to Prof. Erika Fischer-Lichte, Prof. Gabriele Brandstetter, Dr. Christel Weiler, Holger Hartung, Claudia Daseking, and the centre's many research associates and student assistants who helped organise the symposium. The research for this book has also been supported by a grant from the Australian Research Council (ARC) on the theme of "New media dramaturgy: how new media transform the composition and reception of live performance." Our thanks to the ARC and to the members of the team: Helena Grehan, Edward Scheer, Peter Eckersall, Maaike Bleeker and Marin Blažević. This book would not be possible without the generous work of the contributors and to those who were present at the symposium and contributed ideas to the book's formation. We would also like to thank Museum Tusculanum Press for their enthusiasm and commitment to this project. Thank you also to Naomi Ota for translation help and to Eylül Fidan Akinci for editorial assistance. Finally, our deep gratitude is extended to the former members of dumb type, especially to Takatani Shiro, Takatani Yoko and Fujimoto Takayuki: your creativity and generosity are the inspiration for this book.

Japanese names are normally written surname first. However, some writers now prefer to reverse this convention when writing in English. We have not unified the order of names in these essays but, rather, let each author use their chosen approach. To avoid any confusion, the family names of each of the Japanese authors is written in small-caps in the table of contents and essay bylines. The name "dumb type" was often written in lower case and we have followed the convention here.

Introduction

Peter Eckersall and Edward Scheer

Dumb type is a remarkable example of the development of new media performance at the beginning of the digital era. Founded in 1984 in Kyoto, Japan, and active in art and cultural politics until the early 2000s, dumb type developed groundbreaking performances, art installations, community forums and even cafés with the aim to interweave art, politics and an increasingly media-saturated daily life. The work of these artists embraced postmodern theory and gender politics while also revelling in a radically inclusive if highly technical aesthetics, infused with references to drag performance and fantasy nightclub acts. Their works toured to many cities around the world and they were perhaps the first globalised contemporary performance group to emerge from Japan. Memorable performances such as *pH* (1990), *S/N* (1994), *OR* (1998) and *memorandum* (1999) mixed postmodern dance with *karaoke* and created performance environments made of designer machinery, outsize screens, bespoke lighting and immersive soundscapes. Their work revealed a future of performance as an intermedium between theatre, dance, visual arts and sonic experiment, informed by contemporary theoretical debates in the arts and humanities and marked by a cultural activist politics. They developed inclusive and interdisciplinary ways of working and invented new ways of using technology and media in the production of live events. In these and other ways that are discussed in this book, dumb type's impact in all these areas has been transformational.

The Dumb Type Reader began as a project to try and bring some perspective on the important legacy of this group. Despite a profusion of notable essays and discussions about their work, there had not been a publication solely focusing on dumb type until now. Given the great influence of their work on the development of new media performance and on their expanded oeuvre of cultural events and activism, the lack of such a book is an oversight we hope to address. Given the great diversity of their interests and practice, there can never be a monologic interpretation of dumb type. Instead, we propose a collection of viewpoints as the best way to present an account of their work.

To this end, *The Dumb Type Reader* offers a substantial rethinking of dumb type and their pivotal contribution to the development of new media dramaturgy, dance and installation practices, and arts based activism. Research essays in the book are accompanied by interviews with members of the group, personal accounts from collaborating artists and performance documentation. The images are themselves semiotically rich and expressive of dumb type's artistic and cultural practice. Important moments of the life of the company are discussed along with the images, sounds and sensations from dumb type's oeuvre that have stayed close to those of us who have been fortunate enough to experience their work.

Many contributions reflect on the life and work of Furuhashi Teiji (1960–1995), a founding member of dumb type whose death of HIV/AIDS-related illness deprived the international art world of a unique talent. Furuhashi's brilliant artistic vision and deep compassion touched the lives of many people in dumb type and beyond, and the memory of his life is strongly present in many of the contributions in this collection. There is also considerable discussion here of the extraordinary *S/N,* widely regarded as their masterpiece, which premiered at the Adelaide Festival of the Arts in 1994 and toured extensively on the international festival circuit. *S/N* combined reflective moments on the need for broader social inclusion with a critical investigation of the politico-scientific apparatus surrounding HIV/AIDS, the first time such issues were raised so forthrightly in a major Japanese artwork. Its futuristic scenography, with extensive use of digital projection techniques, and its distinctive sound design by collaborating artist Ikeda Ryoji, became emblematic of the company's aesthetic.

Reflecting the company's own desire to exemplify diversity, and our desire to gather provocative accounts and reflections of the work of dumb type, the book is organised into six thematic interventions: Movements,

S/N, New Media Dramaturgy, Bridges, Interviews, and Images. In "Movements," we aim to reflect on dumb type's place as a dance-media performance group and as part of a movement of contemporary performance in the 1980s and 1990s. For instance, Sara Jansen reconsiders the importance of dance in dumb type. The choreographic work of dumb type has not received serious critical attention until now and Jansen's essay is a timely intervention that shows the complexity of dance in the company's artistic and cultural practice. Ōtori Hidenaga takes an altogether different approach in contextualising dumb type's work in the history of contemporary theatre in Japan. This essay quixotically considers dumb type in connection to a field of performance that dumb type always rejected, that is, the post-*angura* theatre of the 1980s and 1990s. Ōtori's essay is a counter-history of Japanese theatre that rightly considers dumb type's wider influence in Japan. Katherine Mezur focuses on the question of women's labour in dumb type. The choreographic work of dumb type was conspicuously gendered, as Mezur's essay shows, and her contribution is a much-needed intervention into considering the relationship between the production of dance and the company's media arts practice. Finally, Gunhild Borggreen considers the machinic aspects of dumb type's work in the context of narratives of technological progress and robotics in Japan. Her work shows how dumb type exemplifies a deep concern in the Japanese arts with the politics of technology that produces both elements of dystopia and utopia in equal measure.

The experience of *S/N*, whether from the company's own perspective or that of a spectator, resonated with many people, not least because it featured Furuhashi Teiji in his last performance. The status of *S/N*, with its unique combination of radical dramaturgy and inclusive cultural politics, was a watershed moment for late twentieth-century theatre. Its significance is reflected in the selection of essays devoted to the work in this book. Wim Lunsing gives an insightful account of being a part of the process of making the work and his reflection deeply connects these experiences with a sense of the importance of *S/N* and how it is remembered. Takeda Keiko gives insights into the political resonance of the work and its times. Her reading shows how the work reconfigures the idea of "coming out" in its production of images that recontextualise queer culture. It shows that the need for witness of the AIDS epidemic is linked to a renewed visibility for subaltern sexualities in Japan and elsewhere. Yamaki Shinya considers the legacy of *S/N* as a cultural moment and links the memory of *S/N* with the lives of young people in Japan today. Finally, Yoshida Miya uses the idea of amateurism to consider aspects of dumb type's work. Dumb type members came from diverse backgrounds and did not always have professional training in the tasks they undertook. Yoshida shows how this enabled a spirit of experimentalism to thrive in dumb type and especially in *S/N*.

The third section on New Media Dramaturgy (NMD) concerns the immense influence of dumb type's new media performance aesthetic. New media dramaturgy is a concept developed by Helena Grehan, Edward Scheer and Peter Eckersall to describe the imbrication of visuality, intermediality and dramaturgy in the movement to mediatised performance that dumb type were so influential in developing. As dumb type's work demonstrates, NMD is a field of performance in-between theatre, dance, music and the visual arts. These concerns are addressed in Edward Scheer's essay where he takes the concept of "experience design" (XD), normally associated with industrial design and human computer interaction, to investigate dumb type's practice of NMD and its exacerbation of spectatorial sense experience. Peter Eckersall looks back at some of the contextual moments of the development of dumb type's work in exploring how postmodernism was received in Japan and how it influenced their work. Andreas Regelsberger recalls key moments in dumb type's work and indicates the importance of their approach to the development of NMD, while also giving insights into the reception of dumb type's work in European settings. Finally, Kumakura Takaaki gives a deeply critical reading of the politics of new media in arguing that the media technologies that came to dominate the later works of dumb type represented a shift away from their previous practices of radically inclusivity.

The section entitled "Bridges" considers how dumb type were always part of something larger and functioned more as a network of artists, technicians and activists than a formal or traditional company structure. Stephen Barber's essay considers one of Furuhashi's projects called *Lovers* (1994), the only moving-image installation that Furuhashi made. Barber's essay reads this work within the framework of the histories of immersive moving-image projection environments involving human figures and connects the work not only to video art practices in the 1980s but also to earlier media performance experiments. Fujii Shintarō explores the recent work of Takamine Tadasu, who worked with dumb type on *S/N* and has since developed his own media and visual arts practice. Fujii shows how Takamine's multi-dimensional artworks address social and ethical concerns also present in the work of dumb type, and how Takamine has found new ways of exploring these themes more suited to contemporary times. Another bridge from dumb type is the work of artist and activist BuBu de la Madeleine. Fran Lloyd explores BuBu's work with Akira the Hustler, both members of the performance activist group The Biters. Lloyd's essay shows how the gender and sexual politics that were introduced in dumb type's *S/N* have been influential in developing an expanded visual arts and performance practice featuring the work of BuBu and other artists.

The "Interviews" section of the book includes voices from former members of dumb type who reflect on their experiences and contributions to works which became sites of extensive collaboration. Takatani Shiro, as one of the founding members of dumb type who continues to work in new media and performance contexts, discusses the material and aesthetic philosophies behind some of the group's most iconic scenographies. Fujimoto Takayuki, a designer who was involved in developing the technical interfaces for the company, outlines his and Takatani's contributions to the development of dumb type's intermedial performance practice.

Finally, the book includes images of dumb type's work in different media. These compelling images are a record of the extraordinary inventiveness of dumb type and capture many of the landmark moments from the history of their work. They are also profoundly revealing artworks in their own right that remediate the complexity and sophistication of dumb type's aesthetic.

The Dumb Type Reader is an indicative rather than exhaustive record of one of the most inventive and seminal artistic practices of the digital age. These images, essays and stories mark the significance of a company that triggered a paradigm shift in twentieth-century culture through the interweaving of a fearless aesthetic experimentalism, a hacker's media sensibility let loose in the risky arena of live performance and an urgent cultural politics responding to the needs of the time. Finally, this book is an effort towards generating an understanding of this singular moment in culture and celebrating the unique confluence of skills and visions, techniques and obsessions that came together in the career of dumb type.

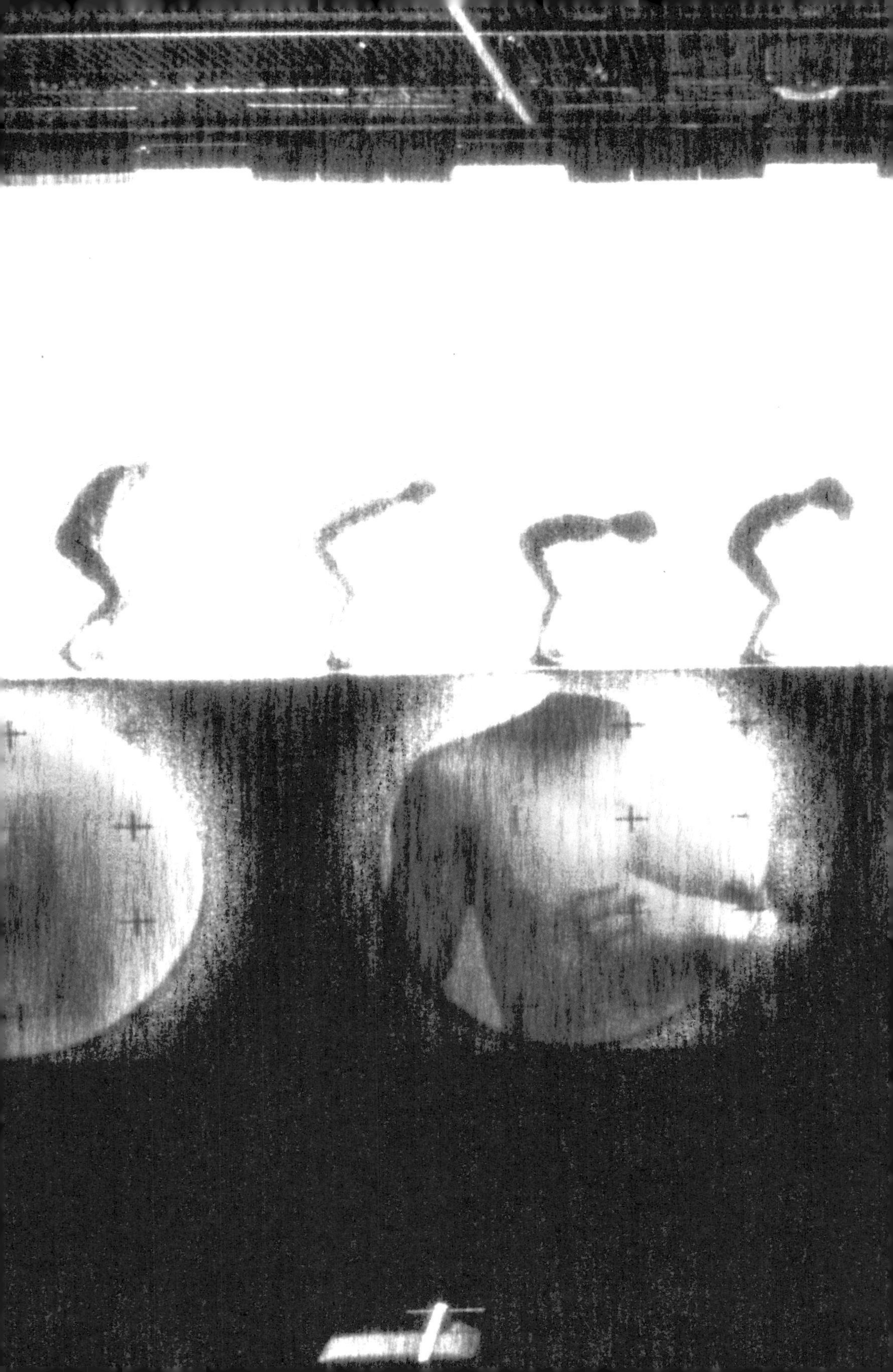

Movements

Dumb Type as Dance

Reflections on the Politics of Gesture

Sara Jansen

Dance/Not Dance

Initially, this essay set out to examine dumb type "as dance." Dumb type was founded in the mid-1980s, around the time when "contemporary dance" (or *kontenporarii dansu*) emerged in Japan and also began to make a name for itself on the international dance scene.[1] Having encountered this work for the first time in Belgium in the mid-1990s, dumb type was always, for me, part of this scene.[2] It was not until recently that I became aware of the fact that the Kyoto-based collective has largely been omitted from dance history. Its core members were trained in the visual arts and the work is almost exclusively discussed from that angle, and in the context of the theatre.[3] The collective's performances were, however, not only part of a move towards interdisciplinary practice in the visual arts, but also left their mark on Japanese contemporary dance, and continue to do so to this day.[4]

Part of my initial project was to account for the important role dumb type played in this context, not that it was ever my intention to define dumb type's work in this way or that, or to box it in or label it. It is clear that this would run counter to the very nature of this oeuvre, which rapidly gained international recognition precisely for its attractive merging of a wide range of artistic media—from photography, film and print, to performance art, theatre, architecture and design—and its innovative experiments with cutting edge audio, visual and digital technology. My main purpose was, rather, to move corporeality and the body-in-motion to the centre of my analysis of dumb type's performances, and to explore this work through dance. It was my contention that particularly choreography, as the practice of writing time and space, could offer an alternative lens to examine dumb type's artistic practice, accounting both for the ways in which it integrates different media in order to radically transform theatrical time and space, and the strategies the collective employs to write the broader socio-political and cultural context into its work, and the other way around.

From its very beginnings, dumb type showed itself to be extremely masterful in manipulating and expanding the time and space of performance. Consider, for example, how, beginning in the 1980s, the company developed spectacular multi-sensorial environments in order to visualise the impact on the individual body/subject of the accelerating speed and the unrelenting onslaught of visual and other stimuli characteristic of the present-day information society, mass-consumerism and the cosmopolitan lifestyle—or how the artist collective continues to extend its activities far beyond the conventional (temporal and spatial) scope of the theatre (and the visual arts) and into political activism and subculture.

It appears, then, that choreography, as it concerns itself not only with the movement of bodies in time and space but also with the interaction between bodies, and between the body and its immediate surroundings, is a particularly apt tool here. It provides a way in to explore some of the boundaries pushed by dumb type, beyond its pioneering role in introducing the latest technology into the theatre or in exploding tenacious borders between artistic disciplines. The company also aimed to break open the insular world of Japanese theatre of the 1980s, and set out to incorporate the edges of performance, its margins, its context and its audience. In turn, in the process it also pushes the boundaries of choreography, opens it up and redefines it.

Incarnation/Intextuation

The performer's body, its corporeality, undeniably plays a pivotal role in all of dumb type's activities. Actors and dancers are often put in situations that pose a threat to their bodies or place them under stress or duress. Indeed, while *Pleasure Life,* a work from 1987, celebrates, as its title indicates, the easy accessibility of novel technologies and consumer goods, and shows dancers prancing around televisions and personal computers, the relationship between the body and technology becomes increasingly strained in subsequent productions. In performances such as *pH* (1990), *S/N* (1994) and *OR* (1998), we observe how spectacular high-tech devices (low moving beams, oversized screens, blinding strobes, unrelenting slide projections, multi-channel video installations and overwhelming soundscapes) act on and/or capture the bodies of the performers. In this manner, the collective's spectacular pieces aim to represent the extent to which the human body, as well as its actions, gestures and behaviours, are shaped by their environment and by social practices and institutional and discursive powers (including law, medicine, politics, mass-media and urban space). Michel de Certeau, referencing Foucault's notion of the *dispositif,* fittingly refers to this as "mute processes."[5] Dumb type explores this by staging immediate, physical confrontations between the performer's body and the impressive scenery it finds itself in. The dancers move through these spaces, inhabit and resist them, are formed, marked and even wounded by them.

While the images produced in this way are often extraordinary, aesthetically as well as technically, they also reveal the insidious violence of the way in which the body is, in de Certeau's terms, always "defined, delimited, and articulated by what writes it."[6] The stunning ways in which the body is drawn and redrawn, written and overwritten in dumb type's work evokes what de Certeau refers to as the process of "intextuation." In *The Practice of Everyday Life,* he describes "two complementary operations" according to which "living beings are 'packed into a text' (in the sense that products are canned and packed), transformed into signifiers of rules (a sort of 'intextuation') and, on the other hand, the reason of *Logos* of a society 'becomes flesh' (an incarnation)."[7] The dynamic/movement between these two operations informs all of the collective's performances.

Dumb type inscribes itself into the debates on new media, visual culture and postmodernism of the late 1980s and early 1990s. On the one hand, it takes on identity politics and questions around race, gender, sexuality and AIDS; on the other, it addresses the effects of mass communication and the proliferation of digital technology, which company members exploit to the maximum in their performances and visual art installations. Quoting liberally from theorists including Michel Foucault, Paul Virilio, Jean Baudrillard and Marshall McLuhan, the artists investigate how reality, representation and processes of subjectivisation operate, and speak to the "always already mediated nature of embodied subjectivity."[8] Their work reflects an historical moment when, in Jonathan Crary's words, subjectivity has become "a precarious condition of interface between rationalised systems of exchange and networks of information."[9]

While *S/N* (also) makes a case for "real" bodies and raw, slow communication, performances such as *pH* and *OR* show young men and women walking the borderline between human and "post-human."[10] Moving alone through virtual landscapes, defined, numbed and disembodied by the sheer overload of images, codes and signs that they are incessantly inundated with, they become mere interfaces. Consequently, the physical presence of the dancers on the stage in dumb type's productions is both fundamental and precarious. While they are essential to bringing these stunning environments to life, the performers' bodies are often shown on the verge of erasure. They are inscribed and moved; they undergo. However, they are also shown in the act of revealing, exposing and resisting these so-called "mute processes." The movements, gestures and actions of dumb type's performers always embody this tension/duality as they are simultaneously triggered by the situations and environments in which they find themselves, and by powerful "gestures of refusal and dissent" (to invoke American choreographer and filmmaker Yvonne Rainer's words).[11]

Notes on Gesture

In a lecture from 1989, entitled "Revisiting the Question of Transgression," Yvonne Rainer compares the political commitment of artists in the 1960s with the late 1980s. She concludes by calling on artists to continue to engage in experimentation, research and social struggle, most importantly "to point to—and protest—existing social inequities."[12] Dumb type's approach to choreography is indebted to American postmodern dance, and especially to the Judson Church artists which included Yvonne Rainer. The collective's activities both on and off stage resonate with Rainer's call for gestures of resistance.[13]

For the purpose of this essay, I will focus specifically on the "gesturality" of dumb type's choreography and explore the critical potential of the notion of the gesture to examine this work. In this context, I propose to look at the small as well as the large gestures: from the daily gestures and pedestrian actions that form the basis of the movement vocabulary developed in individual performances, to the potential of this oeuvre as a whole to be a larger critical and political gesture.

Despite the evident centrality of dance in the company's performances and video installations, very little has been written about this aspect of their work. It is also impossible to look at dumb type's choreographic practice in isolation, independent from the multiple other strands that come together in such highly collaborative work. Below, I will investigate how gesture might provide insight into precisely how such diverse elements (from high art to activism, from the latest digital technology to Michel Foucault) are drawn together and coalesce around the specific corporeality displayed in the group's work. I also introduce gesture as a lens to locate the sense of urgency dumb type's work embodies, and examine their experiments with dance as a political gesture.

In "Notes on Gesture," Giorgio Agamben uses virtually the same words to define gesture and politics. He describes gesture as "the exhibition of a mediality ... the process of making a means visible as such,"[14] while in "Notes on Politics" the author defines politics as "the exhibition of a mediality ... the act of making a means visible as such."[15] Agamben continues to define one in terms of the other, as he locates gesture "in the realm of ethics and politics,"[16] for instance, and writes that politics is "the sphere of pure means, that is, of the absolute and complete gesturality of human beings."[17] Agamben's ideas on gesture are my starting point to probe the tension between gesture and politics as I see it manifested throughout dumb type's oeuvre.

In the context of 1980s and 1990s Japan, dumb type is a rare example of a collective of artists explicitly concerned with the social and political impact of their artistic practice. The company set itself apart by the way in which it put pressure on the limits of the theatre, not only by integrating a large variety of media but also by broadening its practice to include exhibitions and publications, direct action and activism, outreach activities and grassroots movements, AIDS and safe sex awareness campaigns, and (underground) acts/actions in nightclubs, cafes and the sex industry. Company members took on a range of alternative identities (as drag kings and queens, S&M mistresses and sex workers) and initiated spin-off groups and new performance units (including OK Girls and The Biters),[18] which were/are (internationally) active across diverse platforms and contexts.

The performances I will discuss below are consequently one node in a network, and part of a movement which operates in and across different layers of Japanese society. The work is defined largely by what happens off the stage. Individual performances always gesture towards such other activities. This is but one example of how choreography in the context of dumb type's work operates as a critical practice, an intervention, and as an extended social and political gesture. I focus specifically on the performances *S/N* (1994) and *OR* (1998). The two performances are separated by the untimely death of Furuhashi Teiji in 1995, and are both, in their own way, significant gestures towards this catastrophic event.

On 11 October 1992, Furuhashi sent a letter to each one of his closest friends, disclosing that he was living with AIDS.[19] *S/N* was the company's collective response to this shocking revelation: a moving gesture of friendship, love and mourning. The performance explicitly takes up the issues raised by Furuhashi in this letter: the role and meaning of (making) art in the face of severe illness and death; the contrast between the violence of the disease and the romantic way in which it tends to be portrayed in theatre and film; the personal, social, economic and political consequences of AIDS, and its devastating effects on love, friendship and relationships.

OR was made a few years after Furuhashi's passing and addresses the borderline between life and death, and the impact of medical and other technology on this threshold, as well as on the limits of the body itself.

S/N (1994)

In his introduction to the first publication in English of the text of *S/N*, Japanese theatre scholar Nishidō Kōjin writes:

> In this piece there are no actors who (as in conventional drama) are meant to give flesh to the words, not even an "author" who attempts to convey to the audience some plan for the performance. One could call this script a post-Foucauldian "death-of-the-author," deconstructed text, accumulated out of fragments, citations from various writers, philosophers and opinion-makers.[20]

Similarly, the choreography of *S/N* draws on an eclectic range of sources, from American postmodern dance to body art and New York-style solo performance, to drag queen shows and cabaret. From the scarce information available on the genesis of the dance material, we learn that Furuhashi Teiji, who choreographed *S/N*, found inspiration in "people dancing disco" and in "cheap-looking materials and movements from daily life,"[21] and that seeing Robert Wilson and Philip Glass's *Einstein on the Beach* while living in New York City in the 1980s influenced his approach to choreography in an important way.[22]

While Nishidō characterises the script as "a record of a performance"[23] and as "the traces left by the performance, the tracks of their actions,"[24] the dance is, in turn, to a large extent developed from words, and from the citations that make up this performance text. The most important source for the dancers was Furuhashi Teiji's letter to his friends, which not only determined the content of *S/N* and its form—which is based, as we will see later, on the gesture of coming out, also performed by the letter—but it was also the concrete starting point for its dance vocabulary. During rehearsals, company members came up with and fleshed out a series of images derived from Furuhashi's writing and ideas on the meaning of life, death and love, and subsequently explored these images from multiple perspectives through movement.[25]

Other movement material resonates with an interview with Michel Foucault, first published in France in 1981 and entitled *Friendship as a Way of Life*, from which fragments are projected during the show. In this text, Foucault calls on the gay community to ask itself "what relations, through homosexuality, can be established, invented, multiplied, and modulated?" The performance takes up this challenge as it showcases a "multiplicity of relationships" (manifested "in words and gestures") as a strategy to open up alternative identities, modes of communication and expressions of love, and to call into question and subvert established patterns and conventions.[26] Indeed, the choreography provocatively evokes Foucault's words, when he states that: "Institutional codes can't validate these relations with multiple intensities, variable colours, imperceptible movements and changing forms. These relations short-circuit it and introduce love where there's supposed to be only law, rule, or habit."[27]

As in all of dumb type's performances, the dance vocabulary of *S/N* consists mainly of everyday movements. Familiar actions and simple gestures are submitted to choreographic procedures, repeated and executed in different formations and combinations and at varying speeds. The choreography of the very explosive dance section in the beginning of

S/N, for instance, shows performers quoting and transforming a range of concrete gestures expressing friendship and love. They greet each other and hug, shake hands or push each other away; they establish or break off relationships (with co-workers, superiors, lovers or friends); they walk and run (towards or away from one another), and jump and fall down, in different variations.[28] In this particular segment, such daily gestures are interspersed with such involuntary gestures as might be exhibited during an epileptic or "hysterical" fit.[29] Other scenes are developed as short theatrical vignettes and include more concrete, dramatic or theatrical gestures, including applying make-up, showing one's passport at immigration control, or cutting one's wrist to exchange blood. The choreography plays on the combination of, and the friction between, concrete and abstract movements.[30] It also makes ample use of camp, humour, irony and parody to deconstruct and refigure familiar gestures. Throughout *S/N,* such gestures are isolated and amplified, embellished, theatricalised and queered.

Dumb type dancer Sunayama Norico cites conversations with activists as another major source of inspiration for the dance in *S/N*.[31] The performance was a somewhat delayed response to Furuhashi's coming out, but it was preceded by grassroots activism, including interventions in night clubs, the start of the AIDS Poster Project (inspired by Visual AIDS and ACT UP in the United States), and the "seminar show" for *S/N,* in which the issues addressed in the stage performance had already been examined (in panel sessions) from diverse points of view in artistic and academic fields and disciplines. *S/N* retains many of the topics and ideas introduced during these more informal exchanges. In this sense, the production clearly gestures towards what came before. It is informed and marked by the layers of traces of previous actions, as well as by what the show aspires to achieve outside of the theatre. It aims to be a political and transformational gesture, as well as a social gesture of support, extended towards people infected with HIV and towards other sexual and racial minorities who are discriminated against or without a voice, and consequently oscillates between art and action/activism.

On different levels, dumb type plays out the "in-between" status of the gesture, as it straddles the borderline between dance and everyday life, movement and language, communication and representation. Gesture is both dance and not dance. It writes the everyday into dance. Dance in turn puts the everyday gesture in relief, makes it larger, more visible, and puts it on display. It recontextualises daily gestures, and creates distance, a space for reflection and critique. Repeated, "multiplied and modulated," a gesture cited is simultaneously familiar and strange, continuously shifting and transforming—in motion. While corporeal and concrete, the gesture remains ephemeral and unclear, unfinished somehow, imperfect, open-ended. Dumb type's gestural choreography plays incessantly on this fluidity of form, meaning and perspective.

Company members frequently refer to the notion of the boundary as a recurring theme in dumb type's work.[32] Performances challenge binaries, seek out limit situations and speak to moments of transition or transgression. The dancers' bodies hover in the twilight zone between appearance and disappearance, presence and absence, subject and object. Oftentimes the performer's body is presented as the site of such a boundary, as an interface, or a limit space—at times in control, at times restrained, infected, rebellious, out of control.

From the very first scene in *S/N*, it is not only the boundaries between art and activism, art and life, reality and representation, communication and representation, self and other, public and private, life and death that are at stake, but also the tension between de Certeau's operations of "incarnation" and "intextuation"—or between flesh (corporeality) and text (language, writing, words).

Flesh/Text

Nishidō Kōjin's point, quoted above, that the performers in *S/N* refuse to "give flesh to the words" of the text, and thus in a sense resist assimilation of this writing, or "intextuation," is provocative in the context of the ways in which the gesture operates in this performance. The choice of the name "dumb type" already hints at an ambivalent relationship to the (written and spoken) word. Furuhashi Teiji mentions that the term refers to a dummy used in the printing process in order to open up a space in-between words. The emphasis in dumb type's theatre shifts from the words of the conventional dramatic text to the unspoken, to the non-verbal aspects of communication, to punctuation, rhythm, timing and movement. In addition, it opens up a space for reflection, for interrogation.

The titles of all of the collective's early works echo this idea. Always made up of two letters, which may or may not be separated by punctuation marks, they gesture simultaneously towards multiple possible readings and meanings, generated and moving incessantly in the space between these letters.[33] The forward slash in *S/N*, for instance, calls attention to the relationship between the S (signal) and the N (noise), while underscoring the border between the terms they stand for. It reflects the company's broader project to break down categories. *S/N* makes numerous references to familiar binaries to be challenged: normal/abnormal, us/them, immoral/moral, self/not-self, men/women, heterosexual/homosexual.[34]

In an often-cited quote, Furuhashi further explains that the company's choice of name was informed by the realisation that Japanese society is "overstuffed with information, but cognisant of nothing."[35]

> We named it dumb type because we didn't want to use any dialogue in our performances. In Japan especially there is too much information, and most theatre groups use *lots* of words. We doubted words were the main form of interpersonal communication, and we wanted to explore deeper levels.[36]

The performance *S/N* grew out of a veritable catastrophe of language as well as of the body. In his letter, Furuhashi writes that he felt betrayed and deserted by his own body,[37] but that as an artist he feels it is his role to experience the world as well as to communicate directly through the body, as *tōjisha* (the person concerned, or affected, as subject as well as object), and that addressing the issue of AIDS demands doing so in actual reality as opposed to in virtual reality.[38] *S/N* explores multiple forms of communication, both between the performers and between performers and audience. This approach is informed by the fact that AIDS, as Furuhashi points out in a conversation with Nishidō, "initially lead[s] to a destruction of communication" but ended up giving rise to alternative forms of exchange (which "entail risks"), and new kinds of relationships, love and pleasure.[39]

In *S/N*, Furuhashi sets out to shatter the "conspiracy of silence" concerning HIV, sex and sexual identity, topics persistently covered up in Japanese society, medicine and popular media, and aims to foreground theatre as a mode of communication that is direct, open, and has the capacity to "wound." In an interview broadcast on Japanese television shortly after his death, the artist argues for the kind of "real" conversation that affects all parties involved, and may hurt others or leave oneself hurt.[40]

According to Agamben, gesture (as well as politics) concerns the "exhibition" of a means itself, and operates in the "sphere of pure and endless mediality."[41] Agamben describes gesture as a kind of suspension, a process, a movement rather than a fixed form. Returning to Nishidō's characterisation of the text of *S/N* as a collection of fragments, we could say that the performance also does not come together to form a whole or to reach a specific conclusion. Ideas are conveyed in the process of forming and remain open to contestation and reformulation all throughout the piece. In "Notes on Gesture," Agamben defines the gesture as the "communication of a communicability," and writes:

> It has precisely nothing to say because what it shows is the being-in-language of human beings as pure mediality. However, because being-in-language is not something that could be said in a sentence, the gesture is essentially always a gesture of not being able to figure something out in language; it is always a *gag* in the proper meaning of the term, indicating first of all something that could be put in your mouth to hinder speech, as well as in the sense of the actor's improvisation meant to compensate a loss of memory or an inability to speak.[42]

S/N in particular was the result of "an inability to speak." Furuhashi was able to write the above-mentioned letter to his friends only many years after he first received the verdict about his HIV status. As mentioned above, the performance—the answer to this unspeakable revelation—again came with a delay. In the letter, the artist addresses the inadequacy of words when faced with AIDS. Also, elsewhere, he elaborates on the painful repercussions of opening up about one's HIV status. It makes the one who comes out vulnerable and exposes others, alters relationships and demands an urgent response. In the above-mentioned interview with Nishidō Kōjin, Furuhashi recounts how in the 1980s, when he was first confronted with the disease while living in New York, merely mentioning AIDS felt like a death sentence. Faced with this traumatic experience, members of the communities the artist belonged to resort to gesture rather than words.[43]

While there is a lot of talk in *S/N*, the piece also questions the meaning and the power of words. Language here is presented not only as a tool for communication but also as a source of oppression, and is bound up with the laws, rules and habits of a society that is sexist, racist, intolerant of homosexuality and difference, and ignorant of AIDS.

In *S/N*, Furuhashi asks whether it is "possible to protect ourselves against words" and calls for "the wisdom of silence."[44] He claims the space of gesture, and turns to dance at the moment when his body is fragile, and both acutely present[45] and threatened by disappearance.[46] In the opening scene, Furuhashi Teiji translates for Alex (Ishibashi Kenjirō) between English, Japanese and the language Alex, who is hearing-impaired, has invented for himself—a language which, he remarks, is "not normal." "Because he can't hear very well," Furuhashi continues, "he's had to watch other people speak, copy their gestures, create his own way of speaking."[47] Alex's isolation from the "normal world" is represented through the gesture of dancing the tango alone. We see him moving across the stage on all fours, while humming an unidentifiable tune, and wearing a pair of women's shoes on his hands. Later on in the show, Alex repeatedly utters the phrase: "Here's my discipline to fit the codes of the world. The violence of signals so plain to my eyes."[48] The performance addresses the effect words and images have, not only on how we see AIDS ("The image of AIDS moves on its own")[49] but also on how we perceive ourselves and establish our identity. It aims to expose how people are "trying to pattern themselves after images ... actually created by the media."[50]

Dumb type performers talk about questioning this mechanism in relation to their own behaviour, and express the intent to also confront themselves with the stereotypes about others that they might themselves be perpetuating. In this way, *S/N* aims to visualise our tendency to interiorise certain binaries and categories. Kawaguchi Takao explains, for instance, that the above-mentioned first dance section of the show, in which the performers continue to fall backwards off a raised platform, depicts not only a stage dive "into the people" but also a "dive into the self."[51] Consequently, this segment may be read as a translation into a concrete gesture, into dance, of this confrontation with how people see themselves as well as others.

Exposure/Erasure

> "I have a mission to explore ways to give visual form to AIDS."
> "I wanted to counter stereotypes in AIDS art."[52]
>
> *Furuhashi Teiji*

While, in the first scene of *S/N*, Alex continues to dance with himself, Furuhashi and African-American actor Peter Golightly strike up a casual conversation about the labels attached to their suits—which read "Japanese"/"homosexual"/"HIV+" and "American"/"homosexual," respectively. Then, in a Brechtian gesture, Golightly turns directly to the audience to state: "We are sorry to say that we are not actors. We are what we are labelled."

The entire play is structured around the gesture of coming out. It includes multiple scenes in which actors "show themselves." They expose themselves and reveal their "true" identities, asking to be seen by the audience not as actors but as who they are in real life. In the same move, they also make themselves vulnerable to being labelled, categorised, judged, marginalised or discriminated against.

This scene puts in relief "the general gest of showing, which always underlies that which is being shown,"[53] thus challenging the boundary between reality and representation, and truth and fiction in performance. This "act of showing"[54] is amplified as all three actors come out as gay and Furuhashi makes it publicly known that he has contracted HIV. Coming out in such a public manner renders extremely tangible the vulnerability in the fundamental gesture of stepping out onto a stage to be scrutinised (voyeuristically) by an (anonymous and critical) audience.

This opening sequence presents as a condensed exposition of what is at stake in *S/N*. It is, however, also troubling in its rawness and informality, and exemplary of the ambiguity of the revealing gestures that punctuate this production. On the one hand, *S/N* presents the body as the surface onto which identity is "scripted," very literally here; on the other, however, it also resists or offers a counterpoint to this process of "intextuation" by introducing gender, sexuality, nationality and race as mobile signs that can freely be attached to and detached from the body.

Throughout *S/N*, we witness various such performances of the self and examples of the fluidity and ambiguity of sex and gender. As the distancing Brechtian gesture of the above-described scene illustrates, the way in which the self is represented here opens up a space for critique, for reflection on the workings of representation itself, and for a probing of its limits and politics. Performers continue to enact and re-enact, exhibit, expose, displace and transgress what defines their identities, and question the relationship between identity, on the one hand, and the body and sexuality/sexual practices, on the other. In addition, sex and sexuality are used to reveal and challenge the "mute processes" referred to above. "Showing oneself" is linked with revealing how things work; or, to refer back to the above-mentioned interview with Foucault, to "dig deeply to show how things have been historically contingent, for such and such reason intelligible but not necessary."[55]

OR (1998)

In Giorgio Agamben's terms, both gesture and politics involve the process or the act of "making visible." When looking at *S/N,* it immediately becomes clear that it not only aims to reveal "that there is a great power in this world that we usually don't notice,"[56] but that it is also, quite literally, concerned with vision and visibility.

The dance is constructed around the dynamic between gestures of exposure (confession, disclosure, revelation, appearance), on the one hand, and gestures of concealment (cover up, conspiracy, erasure, disappearance) on the other. Many of the concrete gestures that define the movement vocabulary play on acts of unveiling or revealing: dressing and undressing, lifting up skirts, applying make-up, performing in drag, striptease. The fragments of text, projected or spoken, refer to disappearing rights, possessions, blood, nationalities and genders,[57] and to conspiracies of silence or science. In addition, the multimedial aspects of the performance create layers upon layers of frames, lenses and grids, manipulating vision and visibility/readability: from peepholes and surveillance cameras, to medical and pornographic imagery, shooting targets and viewfinders.

In the performance *OR* (1998), we can see that this investigation into the politics of vision is pushed to the extreme. *OR* was made a few years after Furuhashi's passing (in 1995) and further pursues a track initiated by the company's charismatic leader of probing the borderline between life and death. The work takes apart the gestures of looking and seeing, and exposes the limits of perception and of what can be achieved technically in this context. It epitomises the tension characteristic of dumb type's performances, between the choreography, on the one hand, and the scenography, on the other—and between corporeality, the materiality of the human body and its image, its mediated, disembodied forms, or its immateriality.

In *OR,* the company's main concern was to find a way to move forward after Furuhashi Teiji's death. While in *S/N,* Furuhashi took on the role of the director, in *OR* dumb type's members all share this function (as they had before). The collective was founded when video, film and personal computers were beginning to become more readily available. The work foregrounds the individual artistic research of its members, including

Takatani Shiro, Fujimoto Takayuki and Ikeda Ryoji, into the latest innovations in sound and vision. Dance and cutting-edge technology come together throughout dumb type's history, and, as noted above, experiments with bringing together these two domains in innovative ways determine the aesthetic of the collective's work.

The choreography for *OR* is, to a large extent, shaped by Ikeda's musical score, resulting in a much more linear performance structure than that of *S/N*. In addition, *OR* was created during an extended artists' residency in France, and new computer technology offered the possibility of perfectly synching all elements of the scenography in a live setting. The result is an overwhelming and disorienting sound and light scape that also physically draws in the audience, erasing the boundary between performer and viewer.

OR makes maximum use of light effects, speed and repetition to arrive at a kind of vision not normally available to the naked eye, and not previously used in a theatrical setting. By making sound and video images tangible/tactile, and by playing on the appearance and disappearance of bodies and objects, the performance plays out the duality of gesture, as simultaneously physical/concrete and ephemeral/incomplete/abstract.

The show draws heavily on the aesthetic of photography and film. In *S/N*, dance sections were already presented as a kind of moving images, or movement images. Dancers are squeezed into a frame, as it were, as they perform—assaulted by unrelenting strobe flashes and deafening sound—on a treacherously elevated platform, in an elongated space evocative of a movie screen. This space is itself delimited by two other gigantic screens onto which images of bare upper bodies, tumbling pills and text fragments are projected. Similarly, in *OR* the dancers are incessantly attacked by a barrage of strobe flashes, evoking the flash of a camera. Their bodies are, as it were, immobilised in virtual photographs, transformed into shadows, unidentifiable appearances.

The dance vocabulary of *OR* draws on the multiple possible readings of the letters that make up its title, from (either) "or," and Operation Room, to "o r," the imperceptible centre of a circle. As mentioned above, the work is concerned with the boundary between life and death, in medical and other terms, and pursues the collapse of time and space into one single point, a vanishing point in which both realms merge and everything virtually disappears. In the scenography, this effect is obtained by a disorienting soundscape and by the blinding whiteouts, used excessively throughout the piece, which efface the boundaries of the space. All demarcation lines between the back wall and the floor, foreground and background, the space and the people and objects in it are erased.

Continuing another trajectory that also began with *S/N*, *OR* explores the path of life, foregrounding the notion of the journey, an important theme in subsequent dumb type productions (including *Voyage*, 2002). Consider the scene, for instance, in which one of the dancers stands in front of the screen onto which the driver's view during a road trip is projected. She becomes part of the image, disappearing into the screen.

While *S/N* investigates how the use of the body in representation is complicated by AIDS, *OR* examines the effects of the increasing invasiveness of computers, media, virtual reality and medical technology (on the body). The performers' movements are determined by the effects on the body of the engulfing music and the light, as well as by the enormous curved scrim that spans the entire width of the stage. Dancers are over-exposed to noise and light, and at the mercy of this hazardous environment. Kawaguchi Takao recounts how the dancers are severely disoriented by the strobe effects, lose control and inadvertently slam up against the back wall or end up in the wings.[58] They are merely a part of the total choreography of the performance space. Light, sound and set design are so imposing that they end up drowning out the dance. The set becomes the principal dancer. The performers' bodies become mere figures or silhouettes, automatons deplete of individual characteristics, just appearances and surfaces; they literally dissolve into the background. The environment is in control and the performers are engulfed by it, submit to it, they are moved about by it. Blackouts and whiteouts cut up and distort their movements and make their gestures difficult to discern.

Even though the performance includes short theatrical sketches and gestures that put the performers' bodies in relief, as does *S/N*, the dancers mostly appear isolated, alone, alienated in the barren landscape that is created on the stage. The over-exposure—to technology, and light—in *OR* results in a blurring of their movements and the outlines of their bodies, which all but evaporate. The show exploits the body-in-motion to underscore its limits. How much pressure can the body resist? What are the risks? Where does the body begin and where does it end? Is technology an extension of the body? Do we experience through technology or through the body? Who is in control of our bodies; what limits their movements, their mobility? How can the body be recovered?

In *S/N* the performers' bodies are equally over-exposed, albeit in a very different sense. Here, they often appear obscenely present and vulnerable. Indeed, *S/N* introduces a panoply of overly determined or marked bodies: pornographic, sexualised, fetishised, infectious, hysteric, foreign, disabled, objectified, fallen and falling bodies. Throughout the piece, actors exhibit themselves as they engage in a series of confessional monologues. During the dance scenes, performers wear revealing see-through dresses or underwear. And in the finale, in a scene reminiscent of Carolee Schneemann's *Interior Scroll* (or an Annie Sprinkle show),[59] visual artist, activist and sex worker BuBu de la Madeleine is pulled across the stage on a moving platform, lying on her back, pulling a long string of colourful national flags out of her vagina.

S/N addresses the desire, on the part of the actor and the dancer, as well as of the stripper or the lover, for instance, to be noticed or watched, to be looked at in a certain way, or to be seen differently. Yet both the dance and the theatrical sections put the performers on display; they are exposed as the objects of violence, fantasy and desire. BuBu's spectacular scene with the flags is an example of how the show literally pierces the boundary of the skin. It tests the limits of what may be divulged or shown in a theatre production. It makes the audience uncomfortable and shifts the (location of the) borderline between viewer and performer, whose relationship, too, is transformed and modulated throughout the piece. This begins with the above-mentioned Brechtian gesture at the beginning of the play, during which the audience is interpolated in a very direct way, is placed at a distance and urged to call into question what is being looked at and how it relates to what it is being seen, continuing on to BuBu's personal revelations and her flag scene, which place the viewer squarely in the position of the voyeur.

By variously exposing how images (and the popular media, and medical and other discourses) determine our perception of who we are and showing how such images operate and are read, *S/N* addresses the politics behind what can and cannot be represented. While the show exposes much about the private lives of its performers, it is, in the same move, also preoccupied with how such revelations are perceived and what it means to be looking at someone in the act of exposing him or herself. The result is often ambiguous, especially when considering the status of the women in dumb type's work, who often remain anonymous in these productions and whose gestures, while they are undoubtedly the most radical and transgressive, are hardly straightforward.

We can read the strategies proposed by the female dancers in *S/N* as part of what Amelia Jones, in her analysis of the body art performances by artists such as Carolee Schneemann, Yayoi Kusama and Annie Sprinkle, describes as playing out and displacing the way in which the female body is commonly represented, objectified and sexualised, and by questioning the relationship between the body and the self. "Body art," she writes, "through its very performativity and its unveiling of the body of the artist, surfaces the insufficiency and incoherence of the body-as-subject and its inability to deliver itself fully."[60] A performance such as *S/N,* as the examples elaborated above illustrate, similarly underscores the absence of one body or one fixed or easily defined gender, identity or subjectivity.

In the company's productions, and most explicitly in their artistic practice outside of dumb type, BuBu de la Madeleine, Sunayama Norico and the other female performers, whose vital contributions to the collective's oeuvre are undervalued and deserve a much more extensive discussion than I can provide here, appropriate and reiterate (often overtly sexual) gestures, words and imagery, and adopt a variety of stage names and roles—from drag kings, strippers, pimps or S&M mistresses—to call into question conventional ideas surrounding identity and sexuality. BuBu, who in *S/N* outs herself as a sex worker and as a victim of sexual abuse, is also an activist engaged in AIDS prevention and safe sex campaigns, and in her artistic practice integrates these activities and identities.

In her impressive body of work, Sunayama Norico similarly plays on subtle shifts of agency (especially in sexual relationships and the sex industry, in which she is also employed) in order to take control of her own sexuality, intimacy and body; to set and protect her own personal boundaries, and to (subtly) recode the structures and relationships of power in a culture that continues to be macho and repressive.[61] Sunayama's performances and installations address the violence inherent in the objectification of women experienced on a day-to-day basis in present-day Japan. They do, however, also painfully highlight the resilience of such established attitudes and patterns.[62] As a result, her provocative "gestures of refusal and dissent"[63] are not always so clear-cut. They trace the borderline between effectively claiming the power to act or intervene and merely making visible an inescapable sense of powerlessness in the face of such experiences by reiterating or re-enacting them, a borderline perhaps inherent to dumb type's performances as well, and to the notion of the gesture.

Endurance/Resistance

> "My body remains the enduring reality."[64]
>
> *Yvonne Rainer*

> "The laws of motion of a society are not to be demonstrated by 'perfect examples', for 'imperfection' (inconsistency) is an essential part of motion and of the thing moved."[65]
>
> *Bertolt Brecht*

> "If dance is gesture, it is so, rather, because it is nothing more than the endurance and the exhibition of the media character of corporeal movements. The gesture is the exhibition of a mediality: it is the process of making a means visible as such."[66]
>
> *Giorgio Agamben*

In "Notes on Gesture," Agamben locates gesture "in the realm of ethics and politics" and writes that "what characterizes gesture is that in it nothing is being produced or acted, but rather something is being endured and supported. The gesture, in other words, opens the sphere of ethos as the more proper sphere of that which is human."[67]

I began by mapping the role corporeality plays in dumb type's oeuvre. Examining two of the collective's major works reveals that dumb type's gestural choreography aims to make visible the ways in which the body, its movements, actions and behaviour are shaped, coded, perceived and interpreted. In this scheme, the dancer's body operates as a screen and as an interface between different realms: the individual, social, cultural and political. *S/N* and *OR* expose and put on display, or, by contrast, erase the body, and investigate how it is acted upon by its environment. The performers are shown enduring and resisting the situations they are put in. In performances such as *pH* and *OR*, their actions are chiefly re-actions against the forces (literally) coming at them. In *OR*, space is revealed/reconfigured as oppressive and the relentless passage of time made tangible through the sound of ticking clocks and the beating of the heart. The performers, as well as the viewer, are too busy enduring this reality to offer resistance. There is arguably no space for friction, no critical distance left.

In *S/N*, too, the performers' bodies are bombarded with quotations and images, and incessantly framed and reframed by cameras, scanners and viewfinders. They are literally exposed to violence and made to endure abuse, voyeurism, medical examinations, moving platforms and treacherous heights, but they continue to run, fall, get back up, recover and repeat. Dancers are captured inside various contraptions, caught in cutting-edge machinery. Their gestures and actions result from the situations in which they find themselves and by which they are formed and marked. These settings effectively demonstrate the influence of what Agamben calls "apparatuses" (like de Certeau, above, referring to Foucault's notion of the *dispositif*).

In "What is an Apparatus?" Agamben proposes to divide beings into three classes: living beings, the apparatuses "in which human beings are incessantly captured,"[68] and the subject. He calls "an apparatus literally anything that has in some way the capacity to capture, orient, determine, intercept, model, control or secure the gestures, behaviours, opinions or discourses of human beings." His long list of apparatuses, he points out, includes not only the categories addressed by Foucault, but also writing, computers and language itself, for instance. The subject, he writes, is "that which results from the relation and, so to speak, from the relentless fight between living beings and apparatuses":

> The boundless growth of apparatuses in our time corresponds to the equally extreme proliferation in processes of subjectification. This may produce the impression that in our time, the category of subjectivity is wavering and losing its consistency; but what is at stake, to be precise, is not an erasure or an overcoming but a dissemination that pushes to the extreme the masquerade that has always accompanied every personal identity.[69]

"Today," Agamben goes on to argue, "there is not even a single instant in which the life of individuals is not modeled, contaminated, or controlled by some apparatus."[70]

His words speak to the worldview represented by dumb type starting out in the mid-1980s. Sunayama Norico notes about the choreography of *OR* that it is about resisting the world created on stage, as well as about people generally not being able to resist the powers that be. As noted above, the dance vocabulary in this particular work is structured precisely around the "relentless fight" between the performers and the elaborate light and sound scapes developed in *OR*. "We were performing the difficulty for a tiny body, for a human being, to resist such mighty sound pressure,"

Sunayama recounts, "while really experiencing it on the stage."[71] Her words echo Yvonne Rainer's remark, "My body remains the enduring reality."[72]

This brings us back to the central role of corporeality in this oeuvre, and of dance. Agamben characterises dance as gesture, not only as "exhibition" or "making a means visible as such" but also as "endurance." We might further look into the politics of dumb type's choreography as a gesture (or as gestures) of endurance.

As I point out earlier in this essay, dumb type's oeuvre speaks to a perceived crisis of subjectivity, a loss of individual identity, of agency and of control over one's own body. The company draws heavily on poststructuralist and media theory to investigate specifically the effects of new technological developments on representation, communication and everyday life. It addresses identity politics specifically in relation to and through the (performer's) body at a time when experience and interpersonal communication appear to become increasingly disembodied.

The citation, repetition and modulation of familiar gestures in dumb type's dance is reminiscent of the need, the obsession even, to recuperate lost gestures, as discerned by Agamben in Charcot's images of hysterics as well as in the dance of Isadora Duncan, the writing of Rilke and Proust, and in silent film, and which he associates with an epoch (he writes about the end of the nineteenth century) in which humanity has lost "all authenticity" and "whose bodily existence has ... become sacred."[73] These examples show, he argues, how "a society that has lost its gestures tries at once to reclaim what is lost and to record its loss."[74]

A similar tension is evident in the role of the performer's corporeality in this work. The notion of the gesture brings something tactile or tangible to this oeuvre, which is concerned with the postmodern and posthistorical condition, and interrogates the boundaries between the real and the hyperreal, between real life and mediated life, and the extent to which human beings are turned into images. The gesture returns to the human being, who, confronted with this constant flow of information, has almost become virtual, and appears to have lost her/his gravity, a kind of materiality and substance, and a possibility for expression and communication, for establishing and maintaining relationships, as well as a link with what came before, with reality and with history.

Resistance/Dissent

> "I wanted to express that there is a great power in this world that we usually don't notice. We don't want to see it because it's an uncomfortable power."[75]
>
> *Furuhashi Teiji*

> "S is for signal. N is for noise. In audio terminology, the relative amount of effective versus extraneous information contained in a coded message is called the S/N ratio. It is a straightforward metaphor for the complexity of the times we live in."[76]
>
> *Furuhashi Teiji*

In his review of *S/N* in Brussels in 1995, journalist Jean-Marie Wynants notes that the performance "troubles and provokes questions" because of its unsettling combination of "the most sophisticated technology" with "acting that is naïve, bordering on amateurism."[77]

In the dance sections, in which we see performers putting up this "relentless fight" (in a direct, physical way), as well as in the theatrical scenes, which consist of drawn out monologues and casual exchanges, the performers do indeed appear slightly out of synch with dumb type's signature spectacular multimedia sets. Their bodies, in their "realness" and slowness, somehow present an eruption, an interruption, a stop in time and in the movement as they start to topple and fall backwards, and a (much needed) scratch or a glitch in the sleek surfaces of the screens. Different temporalities intersect as actors slow down the action to tell their stories or speed it up in highly energetic movement sequences. The body is introduced as a site of resistance, and both the small gesticulations part of the dance and the large theatrical ones rearticulate and represent daily gestures and put the body in relief. Gesture provides a counterpoint, a counter-force, as it were, to the spectacular beauty and glossiness of the visuals.

Furuhashi explains that making space in *S/N* for trivial chatter between friends, for instance, was a way to include a plurality of voices, and less formal forms of information and communication. The combination of a diverse range of influences and registers—from high art to popular entertainment, subculture, cabaret and striptease, from Michel Foucault to banal conversations on the phone, from everyday gestures to spectacular moves—is part of the director's search for a structure that may accommodate the complexity of the issues at hand. This heterogeneous material produces the "extraneous information" or "noise" of the title. This approach is part of the Brechtian gesture that is also evident in the opening sequence of *S/N*. In "A Short Organum for the Theatre," Brecht argues for bringing together different perspectives on a story (different voices) and for highlighting "inconsistencies" and "disharmony" to reveal society's "motive forces."[78]

Furuhashi further clarifies that it is also his statement against the uniformity of Japanese performing arts at the time. Underneath the glossy surface, he notes, Japanese contemporary society is in disarray. While Japanese theatre in the 1980s only shows its shiny facade, Furuhashi continues, he aimed to reveal also the less appealing aspects.[79] In these "imperfections," the performers' "real lives" come through, and "reality" finds a place inside the performance. "By general standards this would perhaps be seen as 'bad acting', but I want to really focus on that."[80]

Furuhashi also hints at the subtlety of his aesthetic interventions when he mentions that for foreign audiences the work appears futuristic, and for the average Tokyoite it merely reflects daily life, while, from his point of view, being from Kyoto and thus slightly on the edge of mainstream Japanese society, it is a critique of the direction in which Japanese society was heading at the time, a slight contortion or distortion.[81]

The use of gesture is as subtle as the critique, while blatant, is gentle. It is aimed at revealing and exposing, unravelling and recoding, repeating and exaggerating, over-exposing and blurring, queering and reinscribing familiar gestures, behaviours and identities.

S/N is an uncharacteristic performance in the sense that it displays its political character, its message, upfront, and confronts AIDS and discrimination on the basis of sex, sexual preference, gender and race in a very direct manner. Other dumb type performances do not necessarily take such an explicit stance. Even *S/N* visualises situations but does not destroy the world it portrays. Performers try to find a position, a place, but do not claim it. Consider the women's "performances of the self," for instance, which often unfold in silence, and on the level of the gesture, in the sense of "in-between": suggestive, indexical, revelatory, but not definitive, conclusive or straightforward. Furuhashi points out that the company "wanted to synthesize the visual arts to make something unique which would fit the world today"[82] and that it "has been trying to represent on stage what this world is really like."[83] However, in its attempt to visualise the current situation, does it stop short of being an effective critical gesture?

While there is a literalness, a naivety, to dumb type's gestures, the reading of these acts is not always quite so easy. While the message is direct, its delivery is nearly always mediated. Already in *S/N*'s opening sequence, the message suffers from interference. We are confronted with a plethora of languages: from Japanese and English, to English with a Japanese accent and Japanese with an English accent, to the handwriting on the labels. When later in the performance we see Furuhashi slowly transform himself into a drag queen while BuBu recounts an experience of feeling violated by her husband, we see both actors' faces projected in close-up, side by side on a split screen, literally captioned "Love Song," as if part of a variety show on TV. When female dancers are given a voice it is muffled, stories are told but are difficult to hear, voices are amplified by megaphones or drowned out by elaborate sound scores and the sheer abundance of information.

While *S/N* aims to highlight the fluidity of gender and sexual identity, it also plays on stereotypes and shows people internalising the categories they are put in by others. Furuhashi explains how this first section "makes a parody of one's own experience, one's own existence."[84] In an interview on her artistic practice outside of dumb type published in *Corpus* magazine, Sunayama refers to the same scene as a comedy that speaks to the misery of human beings, their inability to resist.[85] The same duality/tension is at play also in *OR*, as pointed out above, and in the way in which *S/N* plays on the borderline between revealing and being exposed, and so on. It concerns a subtlety or slippery slope perhaps characteristic of all of this work. Here, too, gesture is played out as a boundary, as a grey zone. The performances point to and go back and forth across various boundaries and binaries, underscoring the existence of such borders, putting them under pressure, destabilising them. These performances are themselves gestures, or acts and movements, in the process of making visible, figuring out, enduring.

In addition, the gist of dumb type's political activity happens off the stage. The art is taken back into life, life is part of art, and the art itself is incomplete in a way, a gesture, and has to be completed outside of the theatre. The social and political impact of this oeuvre depends, at least in part, on the other artistic activities and the activism members of the collective are committed to.

Gesture/Politics

> "Politics is the sphere of pure means, that is, of the absolute and complete gesturality of human beings."[86]
>
> *Giorgio Agamben*

The notion of the gesture is productive in the context of the Japanese performing arts, to which it has always been central, and has revealed itself as a site of change and radicalness, also in recent years. Since the late 1990s, so-called "Tokyo Dance" incorporates daily gestures and actions to examine everyday life in the Japanese capital. Also, the theatre saw a veritable revival of the gesture. The energetic theatre of the 1980s was characterised by the use of "lots of words," and the work of dumb type, as I pointed out above, was a reaction against this. In the 1990s, this was countered by what came to be called "Quiet Theatre." This shows situations as they progress in real time and emphasises the way in which conversations are always shaped by the context in which they take place—both in terms of the space and time in which an exchange unfolds, and in terms of its timing, or the direct impact of and on the times. Its most famous examples are Hirata Oriza's "Colloquial Theatre," which explores the relationship between the spoken dramatic text and the non-verbal aspects of communication (pauses and silences, hesitations, gesture and posture), and Okada Toshiki's gestural acting style, which is based on staggering the actors' words and movements and shows them in the process of figuring out how to communicate with each other by homing in on the awkward gestures people make while speaking and on moments of clumsiness and miscommunication.

While very different from the work of dumb type, the approaches developed by these influential artists resonate with it and provide further insights into the critical potential of gesture in dumb type's oeuvre. They similarly emphasise gesture, and locate social critique in the "in-between" space of gesture. Politics is located in the uncomfortable gaps or the friction between words and actions. It is inserted subtly in-between the lines, is gestured towards but not explicitly pronounced or explained. It resides in the space of gesticulation, and, to refer back to Agamben, of figuring something out in language.

The everyday gestures, movements and actions, as well as the grand theatrical gestures in dumb type's oeuvre, are part of a choreographic practice that is also a critical practice, a political gesture and a social act.

This inter-medial, collaborative work is concerned with what Agamben refers to as the "mediality" of gesture on various levels. Take *S/N,* which explores the process or the act of communication itself, of showing or making visible, as well as of establishing relationships—to others, to one's audience and to one's own situation and environment, and the broader socio-cultural context. In the course of this key work, relationships and identities are (to return to Foucault) "established, invented, multiplied and modulated."[87]

As we have seen, *S/N* engages with choreography as a gesture towards the viewer, as the act of opening up, of support, of sharing, and as a self-referential gesture. It aims to reveal the workings of (the means of) the theatre, of choreography and of representation, as well as to call into question the effect on "the gestures, behaviours, opinions or discourses of human beings" of "apparatuses" (Agamben) and "mute processes" (de Certeau).

The notion of the gesture draws together the diverse threads and strategies that intersect in this provocative oeuvre. It resonates with the continuous oscillation between what unfolds in the theatre and the many other activities members are engaged in outside of dumb type, between art and activism, daily life and dance. As shown above, the company employs the "in-between" status of gesture to support its explorations of a range of other borderlines. Dumb type's choreography plays on gesture, in all its variation and specificity, as "reaching across" (boundaries), and as "pointing toward," without necessarily reaching an end. It exhibits, reveals and exposes but remains open-ended, inserts question marks but does not explain. The notion of gesture (as exhibition, endurance and resistance) can consequently also accommodate for the tensions, ambiguities and frictions embodied by this provocative oeuvre.

Notes

1 The moment Teshigawara Saburō was awarded a prize at the international choreographic competition in Bagnolet, France, in 1986 for his piece *Kaze no sentan (La pointe du vent)* is commonly considered the official beginning of "contemporary dance" in Japan.

2 In my mind, it was always self-evident that dumb type's performances were dance performances—perhaps in part because of the context in which I first encountered *S/N* (1994), in Belgium as part of the Kunstenfestivaldesarts in Brussels in May of 1995, not long after *Noiject* by Teshigawara Saburō/Karas and *The Bush of Ghosts* by Pappa Tarahumara had both been presented at deSingel in Antwerp, in February and April of 1995 respectively. While these three performances are very different, together they firmly established the image of Japanese dance as visually and technologically extraordinary, a reputation that stuck and which has influenced the type of Japanese performance invited to Belgian theatres since.

3 During their studies, most of dumb type's founding members were involved with Karma, a theatre club at Kyoto University of the Arts and dumb type's predecessor. Many of the initial members of the company majored in visual arts. Among the performers who joined dumb type at a later stage were trained dancers, including Sunayama Norico and Kawaguchi Takao. In 1988, dumb type collaborated with choreographer Kurosawa Mika on her production of *The Nutcracker*. Like Furuhashi Teiji, Kurosawa had spent time in New York and was inspired by the artists of the Judson Church. Sunayama worked with Kurosawa before joining dumb type.

4 While dumb type is often omitted from the literature on Japanese contemporary dance, its influence on its development can hardly be ignored. Consider Umeda Tetsuya's experiments with lighting design and its effects on the perception of the body in motion, for instance, or the so-called "Tokyo Dance" by choreographers including Yanaihara Mikuni (Nibroll). Since the late 1990s, companies such as Nibroll have presented multimedia and cross-platform productions in which everyday movements and actions are combined with colourful computer animation, fashion trends and original music to evoke the experience and challenges of daily life in the Japanese capital.

5 Michel de Certeau, *The Practice of Everyday Life*, trans. Steven Rendall (Berkeley, Los Angeles and London: University of California Press, 1988), p. xiv.

6 Ibid., p. 139.

7 Ibid., p. 140.

8 Amelia Jones, "Presence in Absentia: Experiencing Performance as Documentation," *Art Journal*, winter 1997: 16.

9 Jonathan Crary, *Techniques of the Observer* (Cambridge, MA, and London: MIT Press, 1999), p. 2.

10 "Post-human" is an example of an alternative reading of "pH" ("potential hydrogen") projected during the performance. Others are "post-harm," "post-history," "potential heaven" and "potential hell."

11 Yvonne Rainer, *A Woman Who...: Essays, Interviews, Scripts* (Baltimore and London: The Johns Hopkins University Press, 1999), p. 105.

12 Ibid.

13 At the time of the Karma theatre club in Kyoto, Furuhashi and his fellow students found inspiration in the work of avant-garde playwright and director Terayama Shūji. Even after the name change, the collective's work remained indebted to the Japanese theatre of the 1960s and 1970s, and its politics, including its involvement with student protests and direct action. The collective also played a pioneering role in the move towards highly aestheticised, postmodern multimedia performance in the 1980s and 1990s. Thus, in a sense, a performance such as *S/N* moves (somewhat uncomfortably) between the two moments addressed in Rainer's presentation, politically as well as aesthetically.

14 Giorgio Agamben, "Notes on Gesture," in *Means without End: Notes on Politics* (Minneapolis and London: University of Minnesota Press, 2000), p. 58.

15 Ibid., p. 115.

16 Ibid., p. 56.

17 Ibid., p. 58.

18 Between 1993 and 1996, dumb type members Sunayama Norico, Yabuuchi Misako and Mami performed various acts as OK Girls, mainly at Club Metro in Kyoto and at dumb type after-parties around the world. About the collective's activities

Sunayama recounts: "I guess our concept was to get rid of all kinds of constraints. We started around the time when sexual identity became a hot topic and our group was made up of three women, so people often asked if we were lesbians. This became very annoying. Let's just say that we were aiming to create incredibly interesting and good-looking stuff" (*Montage*, no. 7, 2000, p. 5). In 1998, Sunayama (as dominatrix MIKADO or Coño Snatch Zubobinskaya), BuBu de la Madeleine and Akira the Hustler founded The Biters, described by the artists as a sex workers unit. The group originated on the occasion of the exhibition "Donai yanen! And Now! Contemporary art in Japan," held in Paris in 1999, and its performance acts and video art have since been on view at galleries in Japan and abroad.

19 The letter the artist wrote to his friends is published in its entirety in *memorandum teiji furuhashi*. Teiji Furuhashi, "Furuhashi Teiji no atarashii jinsei – LIVE WITH VIRUS. HIV kansen happyō wo iwatte," in Dumb type, *Memorandum teiji furuhashi* (Tokyo: Little More, 2000), pp. 36–43.

20 Nishidō Kōjin, "Introduction," trans. Cody Poulton, in *Half a Century of Japanese Theatre II: 1990s Part 2*, ed. Japan Playwrights Association (Tokyo: Kinokuniya, 2000), p. 260.

21 "Artist Teiji Furuhashi interviewed by Carol Lutfy," in Dumb type, *memorandum teiji furuhashi*, p. 127.

22 Teiji Furuhashi, "Furuhashi Teiji interviewed by Bridget Cooper. Winter 1991," in Dumb type, *memorandum teiji furuhashi*, p. 55.

23 Nishidō, "Introduction," in *Half a Century of Japanese Theatre II*, p. 260.

24 Ibid., p. 262.

25 Sunayama Norico in an email to the author dated 13 March 2014.

26 Michel Foucault, "Friendship as a Way of Life," in *Ethics: Subjectivity and Truth: The Essential Works of Michel Foucault. Volume I: 1954–1984*, ed. Paul Rabinow (New York: The New Press, 1997), p. 135.

27 Ibid., p. 137.

28 Sunayama Norico in an email to the author dated 13 March 2014.

29 Charcot's renowned images of hysteria patients were a source of inspiration for the dance vocabulary of *S/N* (personal conversation with dancer Kawaguchi Takao [14 March 2013]). In "Notes on Gesture," Agamben refers to the focus on the gestures of the hysteric by Charcot and others as reflecting a moment in history when the gesture was perceived as lost, resulting in an urgent need to record it.

30 Dancer Sunayama Norico explains that movements were created starting from "images derived from words" and that Furuhashi, who directed *S/N*, aimed for "a mixture of concrete movements (everyday actions) and abstract movements" (email to the author dated 13 March 2014).

31 Sunayama Norico in an email to the author dated 13 March 2014.

32 Sunayama refers to *pH*, *S/N* and *OR* as "beyond the borderline" pieces. In an interview published in *Corpus* magazine, she states: "*pH* is about crossing over, either by skipping over the trusses or by laying down to let them go past. In *S/N*, we fall backwards and practice what we call 'diving into people'. And *OR* was made after Furuhashi's death and speaks to finding oneself on the ambiguous borderline between life and death and how to overcome this. I myself refer to this work as the 'beyond the borderline tripartite'" (*Corpus*, no. 3, 2007: 20). In a conversation with the author, Kawaguchi Takao similarly addressed the role of the borderline in *S/N* and *OR* (14 March 2013).

33 *S/N* officially stands for signal/noise. However, in the course of the performance numerous other possible readings scroll by on the large projection screens: sense/nonsense, state/nation, society/nature, south/north, some/none... *OR* stands for o r, or the centre of a circle, as well as for Operation Room, or simply "or."

34 Dumb type, *S/N*, trans. Cody Poulton, in *Half a Century of Japanese Theatre II: 1990s Part 2*, ed. Japan Playwrights Association (Tokyo: Kinokuniya, 2000), p. 279.

35 "Artist Teiji Furuhashi interviewed by Carol Lutfy," p. 123.

36 Teiji Furuhashi, "Furuhashi Teiji interviewed by Bridget Cooper. Winter 1991," in Dumb type, *memorandum teiji furuhashi*, p. 55.

37 Teiji Furuhashi, "Furuhashi

Teiji no atarashii jinsei – LIVE WITH VIRUS. HIV kansen happyô wo iwatte," p. 37.

38 Ibid., pp. 40–41.

39 Kōjin Nishidō, "1994, 12-gatsu. Nishidō Kōjin ni yoru tekisuto to intabyū," in Dumb type, *memorandum teiji furuhashi*, in *Half a Century of Japanese Theatre II: 1990s Part 2*, ed. Japan Playwrights Association (Tokyo: Kinokuniya, 2000), pp. 83–84.

40 In an interview in a *News 23* special broadcast on Japanese television when Furuhashi passed away in 1995.

41 Agamben, "Notes on Gesture," p. 59.

42 Ibid.

43 "In the 80s, AIDS, for me, was a private matter. From the second half of the 1980s, I often went to NY because my boyfriend was living there. When I was deeply involved with the gay community and the art community there, I was already aware of the existence of AIDS in those communities. But no one really talked about it. The fear that even just talking about it would erase one's self. The fear that just putting it into words would get one sued. It was that complex. I learned that when people are in the middle of a really serious situation, they can only react in very simple ways, by crying, laughing, getting angry, running, hugging or dancing together." Nishidō, "1994, 12-gatsu. Nishidō Kōjin ni yoru tekisuto to intabyū," p. 83.

44 Dumb type, *S/N*, p. 267.

45 In his letter, Furuhashi notes that he has come to rely on the new experience of hearing the sound of blood coursing through his veins to verify that he is still alive, for instance. Teiji Furuhashi, "Furuhashi Teiji no atarashii jinsei – LIVE WITH VIRUS. HIV kansen happyō wo iwatte," p. 37.

46 *S/N* was created shortly before Furuhashi's death from AIDS-related complications, and is an act of resistance not only against the physical, social, economic and political consequences of the disease but also against the charismatic artist's imminent disappearance. The piece acquired yet another layer of meaning when dumb type continued to perform *S/N* after Furuhashi's passing, evoking his presence through video projections. Furuhashi already repeated this disappearance in *Lovers* (1994), an installation based on *S/N*, in which visitors interact with virtual performers.

47 Dumb type, *S/N*, p. 263.

48 Ibid., p. 282.

49 Ibid., p. 267.

50 Ibid.

51 Dancer Kawaguchi Takao in a conversation with the author (14 March 2013).

52 "Artist Teiji Furuhashi interviewed by Carol Lutfy," p. 111.

53 Bertolt Brecht, *Brecht on Theatre: The Development of an Aesthetic* (New York: Hill and Wang, 1996), p. 203.

54 Ibid., p. 194.

55 Foucault, "Friendship as a Way of Life," p. 139

56 Teiji Furuhashi, "Furuhashi Teiji interviewed by Bridget Cooper. Winter 1991," p. 63.

57 "I dream my gender will disappear," "I dream my nationality will disappear," "I dream my blood will disappear," "I dream my race will disappear," "I dream my rights will disappear," "I dream my property will disappear," "I dream my power will disappear," and so on.

58 In a personal conversation with the author.

59 In *Interior Scroll* (1975), Carolee Schneemann pulls a coil of paper from her vagina. In porn actress, sex worker and activist Annie Sprinkle's *Public Cervix Announcements*, the audience is allowed to inspect her cervix using a speculum.

60 Jones, "Presence in Absentia," p. 13.

61 Sunayama Norico creates dance performances and performance art that is presented in art galleries, theatres and nightclubs, under her own name, which she spells as "Norico," as well as alter egos, including dominatrix MIKADO, Coño Snatch Zubobinskaya, and her drag king persona Snacky.

62 In an article in *Montage*, Sunayama elaborates on the transgressive behaviour of visitors to her installation *A Sultry World*, in which she invites visitors to enter the enormous skirt she is wearing. *Montage*, no. 7 ("Gura-Gura Glamour Inferno"), 2000.

63 Rainer, *A Woman Who...*, p. 105.

64 Ibid., p. 41.

65 Brecht, *Brecht on Theatre*, p. 195.

66 Agamben, "Notes on Gesture," p. 58.

67 Ibid., p. 56.

68 Giorgio Agamben, "What is an Apparatus?," in *What is an Apparatus and Other Essays*, trans. David Kishik and Stefan

Pedatella (Stanford, CA: Stanford University Press, 2009), p. 13.

69 Ibid., pp. 14–15.

70 Ibid., p. 15.

71 Sunayama Norico, in an email to the author dated 13 March 2014.

72 About a statement included in the programme of *A Mind is a Muscle*, 1968, on the conditions in which the performance was made, Yvonne Rainer writes that "it is a reflection of a state of mind that reacts with horror and disbelief upon seeing a Vietnamese shot dead on TV – not at the sight of death, however, but at the fact that the TV can be shut off afterwards as after a bad Western. My body remains the enduring reality." Rainer, *A Woman Who...*, p. 41.

73 Giorgio Agamben, "Kommerell, or On Gesture," in *Potentialities: Collected Essays in Philosophy*, ed. and trans. Daniel Heller-Roazen (Sanford, CA: Stanford University Press, 2000), pp. 77–85.

74 Agamben, "Notes on Gesture," p. 53.

75 Furuhashi, "Furuhashi Teiji interviewed by Bridget Cooper," p. 63.

76 Furuhashi, "Artist Teiji Furuhashi interviewed by Carol Lutfy," pp. 111–13.

77 "Rencontre entre les technologies les plus sophistiquées et un jeu naïf proche de l'amateurisme, «S/N» déroute et pose question." Jean-Marie Wynants, "Les parfums déroutants de l'Extrême-Orient," *Le Soir*, 3 May 1995.

78 Brecht, *Brecht on Theatre*, p. 195.

79 Nishidō, "1994, 12-gatsu. Nishidō Kōjin ni yoru tekisuto to intabyū," pp. 84–85.

80 Ibid., p. 85.

81 Furuhashi, "Furuhashi Teiji interviewed by Bridget Cooper," pp. 57–59; and in an interview in a *News 23* special, broadcast on Japanese television when Furuhashi passed away in 1995.

82 Ibid., p. 55.

83 Ibid., p. 61.

84 Nishidō, "1994, 12-gatsu. Nishidō Kōjin ni yoru tekisuto to intabyū," p. 79.

85 Sunayama, "Han-bōryoku no messeeji," *Corpus* 3, 2007.

86 Agamben, "Notes on Gesture," p. 58.

87 See note 26.

The Historical Position of Dumb Type in Japanese Theatre

The Birth and the End of the Politics of New Media Dramaturgy

ŌTORI Hidenaga

Dumb type lies at a very peculiar point in the modern history of Japanese theatre. At the risk of giving the impression of being a contradiction, it nevertheless seems to me that, given dumb type's self-avowed disconnection from theatre, they were the theatre troupe that gave concrete form to a singular aspect of modern Japanese theatre, or *shingeki*. Singularity is a term borrowed from physics or mathematics, but here it relates to how dumb type take up a place that is totally unrelated to its surroundings, a place where the standards applied to those surroundings are becoming invalid. In other words, discussing the works of dumb type, and especially *S/N*, in the context of Japanese theatre does not make any sense. Yet despite this, I believe that dumb type have put a certain singularity of the Japanese theatre into concrete form. So what is the meaning of this suggestion? I think that analysing this very distinct issue, the singular nature of dumb type, will provide us with the key to explaining the position of dumb type in theatre history.

I cannot say for sure when the planning for *S/N* started, but it is clear that, for Furuhashi Teiji, the questions that the piece raised were already important at the end of the 1980s. The *S/N* project began in 1992, when Furuhashi revealed to the members of dumb type that he was HIV positive. The "seminar show" for *S/N* took place at the Kyoto venue Mumonkan from 17 to 21 March 1993, with a combined performance and talk. This was followed by something similar at the Fujisawa Shōnandai Culture Centre near Tokyo, where, by coincidence, I was in the audience.

Instead of speaking about a "performance and talk," it may be more accurate to refer to these events as a "talk with a performance." As the audience was waiting for the performance to begin, Furuhashi came onto the stage, joined by Onitsuka Tetsurō, a scholar of Spanish literature. Onitsuka was introduced as an academic who knew a great deal about gay culture, and after introducing themselves to the audience the two men began something that resembled a *zandankai*, or roundtable discussion, on the stage. At the outset, Furuhashi informed the audience that he was gay and that he had been infected by the HIV virus. This was not a surprise to me personally, but I was shocked, however, by what Furuhashi said immediately after that:

> I think that all of you will have heard of gay people or AIDS patients in the past, but I cannot imagine that you have ever seen with your own two eyes a gay AIDS patient … so I thought I should tell you these things about myself at the beginning.

I vividly remember how Furuhashi supported his head with his hands while speaking these words. It was the first time I had heard such rebellious words in a legitimate (mainstream) performance space.

Today, however, I am more aware of several such theatrical actions, some of which were also performed in illegal, or illegitimate and non-mainstream, spaces. Examples that come to my mind include Kara Jūrō's *Jōkyō Gekijō* (*Situation Theatre*) that was performed in a tent, often occupying public land, and *Nokku* (*Knock*, 1975, 2013) by Terayama Shūji, who developed urban street theatre.

Well into their conversation, acoustic signals could be heard and something was projected onto the white wall behind Furuhashi and Onitsuka. Actors appeared on a kind of passageway above the wall who began to perform a kind of dance, peaceful and quiet, but which seemed to be aimed at interrupting the conversation that had been progressing like a meditation. It was almost like an intervention that represented the bodily realisation of the ideas being expressed in the discussion. What I saw there that day was to become *S/N*, which was performed for the first time in March 1994 at the Adelaide Festival in Australia.

Why have I recalled this episode? Because I wanted to point out an important aspect of this event: how the process of turning a theatrical space into a political vehicle was representative of transforming the system of contemporary theatre in Japan. As I noted above, such techniques arose in the work of Terayama, one of the representative artists of the Japanese avant-garde theatre in the 1960s and 1970s. Commenting on, or intervening with, the order of reality by artistic action had never had any big effect on Japanese culture, but here we witness people giving it a try once again. Theatre as critical action pointing at contemporary culture, and theatre as criticism pointing at the system from the outside, became the distinct features of modern and contemporary Japanese performances. Important within this concept is the notion of "from the outside"; the theatrical avant-garde of the 1960s once more raised the question of whether an individual's position as an outcast represents a special characteristic of the Japanese theatre.

Kara Jūrō first drew attention to the fact that actors are more than just beggars from the banks of the Kamo River.[1] Kara Jūrō liked the term *ningaimono,* meaning someone existing outside of the system. He employed this term within his work to explore the concept of an actor as a person who exists outside of the system. Kara started holding performances in places like the Ginza district (known for high-class shopping); he also used the empty lots of housing complexes. He continued to perform even after his tent was surrounded by police, whereupon the wall of the tent behind the stage would be lifted up and the surrounding space illuminated for the audience to see. This paradox of the fighting power of a "poor theatre" troupe is now evaluated as an important innovation that blurs the distinction between theatre and the everyday world.[2]

In another example, Terayama purposely developed the urban theatre in a manner that ruptured the appearance of order in the everyday. In *Knock*, his performers visited ordinary homes and deliberately tried to disturb the families living there.[3] The company sought to stage an intervention against these people who were "obedient" to the system. The performers knocked at doors in areas throughout the town and asked the people living there all kinds of philosophical questions, quizzing them as to why they did not think about such questions more profoundly.

Are we allowed to be lazy in our everyday lives? Is raising questions like this not the mission of theatre? Actions like these were, of course, against the law and they caused problems. Even so, Terayama showed how the act of standing outside the system was one of the peculiar traits of Japanese theatre. In considering why dumb type holds a special position within Japanese theatre, it is this perspective of showing life at the margins in concrete form that is important. Dumb type created singularly unique works that firmly brought issues of gender and sexuality into question. Such works had not existed in Japan before. Through making visible the existence of people abandoned or neglected by society, dumb type hoped to disturb the social order and in this way they followed in the tradition of people in the Japanese theatre world of seeing themselves as outcasts and a minority.

The first section of *S/N* is one of the most impressive, a variation of the scene from their live seminar. It is not really a theatrical scene; rather, it confronts the audience with the problem of what it is that is being put into question and why. The scene begins with a man (Ishibashi Kenjirō) crawling on the floor with his hands in his shoes, moving in a certain rhythm. Furuhashi approaches him and asks him what he is doing. We are not able to catch the man's words clearly. He cannot pronounce words normally, as he himself is deaf. But since Furuhashi is talking to this man, we grasp that he is able to understand him, and Furuhashi, like an interpreter, informs the audience what the man is saying. When we look carefully, we can see that the word "homosexual" is written on a piece of paper attached to the man's costume. Another man appears (Peter Golightly) and intervenes in the conversation between the two men. He points out that the words "homosexual" and "HIV+" are written on Furuhashi's costume, and he says that he himself is gay and a black American.

The questions that are addressed here concern what it means to be gay. What kind of problem does AIDS represent for us and how are we supposed to confront it? Walter Benjamin referred to the general tenor of such questions as "material critical inspection," and theatre is truly about this form of material criticism.[4] Therefore, this opening scene informs the audience about what kind of things we should reflect on. We are urged to critically inspect what we are about to see. In other words, we are openly presented with the shift from the aesthetic domain to the political domain.

Some people think that informing the audience about a performance's theme before it starts is not theatrical. But in *S/N* we are told through this untheatrical opening that the piece is going to be about homosexuality and AIDS. This device of telling the audience about the theme at the beginning of a performance is one that *S/N* shares with the rebellious theatre groups of the 1960s (*angura gekijō*). In works such as Suzuki Tadashi's *On Dramatic Passions* (*Gekiteki naru mono o megutte*, 1969), for example, this aspect is even reflected in the title.[5]

It might be thought that noting how the theme of a play is represented in its title is hardly worth mentioning. But consider, for example, Chekhov's *The Seagull* or *The Cherry Orchard*, plays that give very little information about the subject matter of the performance in their title alone. It is the same for *S/N*. A question about the materiality of theatre (as in Suzuki's implicit question in his play, above), the title itself of *S/N* highlights the performance's main questions. This is seen in the opening and its announcements of the themes of sexuality and AIDS, and which strikingly persuades the audience to become engaged as viewers in an act of material critical inspection. This is then followed by the presentation of many more materials deserving of the audience's further examination. According to the ways in which these are presented, the main theme of the performance is reinforced, and within their further development, we, the audience, while enjoying ourselves and going through a series of emotions, begin to think about the problems that ought to be considered in relation to the reality that the work depicts.

We need to remember that Japanese culture of the 1980s, including theatre, began to exhibit anti-intellectual tendencies and to avoid political issues, a tendency that is still present today. The idea of theatre as entertainment became more important, and the view that one should stop asking questions about political matters was promoted. There was also the idea that the world had already entered an endtime, and that our everyday lives were taking place in the time after this ending.[6] Sociologist Miyadai Shinji encouraged people to "live the never-ending everyday."[7] People spoke about life experienced as surface and without depth. Once you stop gliding over the thin surface of the ice, you will inevitably fall—the question being: how can you pass over this surface and not fall? Without using your thoughts, just easy running, is how some people seemed to think. After the political era of the 1960s, Japanese culture was full of such beliefs, and the theatre reflected this tendency. Many people believed that a theatre that did not adorn itself would not be able to survive. Direct critical expression against the system was avoided. Modern theatre in Japan did, in some instances, begin to support this system and be sustained by it.

I said initially that Japanese theatre always came from a sense of being outside: it was created by *ningaimono* with a critical stance towards the everyday world. During the 1930s, proletarian theatre was very strong, and the fact that the authorities suppressed it immediately is an indication of the power it wielded.[8] If we compare this idea to classical Greek theatre, we see how insider-outsider perspectives are made clearer. Greek tragedy presents a critical look on reality from the inside, while Greek comedy analyses conflicts while laughing about them. The tragedy existed as a place where members of the *polis* could give shape to their hope for a better life. Here, they could identify their own problems and shortcomings and work out plans for an ideal form of the *polis*. Meanwhile, comedic theatre was where the organisers from the inside (the playwrights) revealed life's shortcomings in a biting manner. It was a place where they could share ideas with each other about their vision for new beginnings of the *polis*.

There is a difference in whether problems are identified or criticised from insider or outsider perspectives, and both *shingeki* and classical Greek theatre did not neglect such important critical functions. However, many examples of the contemporary theatre in the 1980s were different. Japanese theatre of that era shared its bed with society. It continued to show what kind of life we were living but without the possibility for positive critical analysis. In other words, it reinforced the mantra: "Don't think that there is a way to survive!" It should also be said that much Japanese theatre in the present decade is overshadowed by a similar atmosphere and sense of fatalism.[9]

At the same time, *S/N* was not the only work created at that time which expressed a new way of thinking about the political in performance. From around 1993, new plays by Noda Hideki, the director of NODA MAP and of Gekidan Kaitaisha (Theatre of Deconstruction), led by director Shimizu Shinjin, suddenly started to become political. Their theatre did not only develop through addressing contemporary issues but also by finding a form to influence the thinking of the audience.[10]

Noda's *Aka Oni* (Red Demon) from 1996 was a play about why a woman committed suicide. She is referred to disrespectfully only as “a woman” in an announcement in the first scene of the play, and her lack of identity is a problem for the audience to consider. In other words, a form of material critical inspection is performed as we watch this work. The piece has four main characters: the woman, her elder brother Tonbi who is said to be intellectually disabled, a man called Mizukane who harbours secret intentions towards the woman, and a foreigner called the “red demon” who appears to drift in from the outside world. The first three characters have been evicted from their village and are, thus, outsiders, while the red demon, also an outsider, is from another place and is especially marginalised. In the play, the outcast minorities overcome their differences and establish friendships. However, the villagers see this as dangerous and they work together to hunt down the foreigner called the red demon and imprison him. Meanwhile, the other three outsiders set him free and plan to escape from the village on a boat. Their small boat is tossed by the waves, they have nothing to eat and they seem to be destined to die of starvation. The red demon dies and this is the beginning of their tragedy. When a storm brings them back to the village, only the original three remain. This story of resistance and escape from a narrow-minded society, and the eventual failure of their efforts, encourages the audience to reflect on the play as a critical statement. We are informed that there are people who live with discrimination and try to escape from under its yoke. But the performance represents more than just moving the audience to feelings of compassion towards those who die in the act of trying to overcome discrimination; it becomes clear that Noda has a powerful sensitivity towards people who are discriminated against. The reason why this play evokes feelings of sublimity is due to the fact that although the characters are placed in a hopeless situation, they remain determined and exhibit courage in attempting to transform their world.

This work is even more complicated, as illustrated in the play’s first scene, a prologue that shows an old woman carrying soup approaching a woman who has been thrown onto a beach. The shipwrecked woman is hungry and drinks the soup greedily. When she is told that the soup is made of shark fin, she is astonished, insisting that the soup does not have such a taste. It transpires that she kills herself the next day by jumping off the cliffs, an event that we do not become aware of until after quite some time has passed. When she was on the beach, in a confused state of mind because of her hunger, she was told: “eat, and live!” She ate, without knowing what it was she was consuming. And so she survived. But then she committed suicide. How is one supposed to react to this? How should her character be treated now? There are many difficult questions that arise here. The scene is returned to at the conclusion of the play. The villagers castigate her: "And we even tried to help her!" "She was an ungrateful person until the very end!" There is a sense of moral ambiguity and confusion, even if we are inclined to pray for her soul.

But what is the purpose of discussing Noda's play here? I view *Aka Oni* and *S/N* as resembling each other closely. When seen through the lens of material critical inspection, both works can be seen as tales of discriminated people and the resistance, love and courage of a minority. I consider that the intention of the artists of dumb type was to create theatre in the sense of Benjamin's material critical inspection, as is shown here.

Angura also told similar stories, but their form of resistance was different to the examples given above. Resistance in theatre of the 1960s took the form of rebellion, often presented through extreme plots of revolution and overthrow. Agitation, when expressed on the stage, was directly linked to political demonstrations. These plans of revolt were executed as illegal actions by a group of people who were different from the norm. But after their defeat and failure in the political domain, theatre makers in Japan were not sure what to do for the next decade or more.

We can see hints that show how the idea of material critical inspection and its use as a method of resistance was borrowed from abroad. Moreover, Noda and Furuhashi are both important figures in introducing these ideas to Japan: Noda from his work with Simon McBurney and Complicite in London, and Furuhashi from his exposure to contemporary performance and the queer club scene in New York.[11] This theatre did not develop from within the Japanese theatre of the 1980s but from direct contact with foreign performances and contemporary culture. We can say that these artists were also making work critical of *angura* theatre (and of the post-*angura* malaise described here). For these reasons, I believe that dumb type shouldered the responsibility of developing a new theatre in the 1990s.

In 1992, the year when the plans for *S/N* were underway, I saw a number of performances in New York that dealt with issues of sexuality, homosexuality and AIDS. For example, the performance *Roy Cohn Jack Smith* by the actor Ron Vawter of the Wooster group told the story of two men who had died of AIDS: Roy Cohn was a "gay bashing, closet homosexual" and Jack Smith was a gay experimental filmmaker.[12] I subsequently learnt that performances of this kind were held frequently in New York at that time. Such theatre dealing with issues of sexuality started in 1986 with performances such as Karen Finley's memorable *Constant State of Desire* at The Kitchen. According to performance scholar Ikeuchi Yasuko, it is possible to trace the final scene of *S/N*, in which BuBu pulls national flags out of her crotch, to Carolee Schneemann's famous performance *Interior Scroll* of 1975.[13] This was the kind of culture Furuhashi was surrounded by in New York, and from around 1986 onwards he became a member of the gay and lesbian community that created works of this kind. Admitting one's desires and becoming aware of the dangers linked to those desires was at the heart of Furuhashi's concept. Furuhashi himself became infected with AIDS as a result of one single act of sexual intercourse. This is why *S/N* also turned into an appeal for safe sex.

I have avoided mentioning the topic of New Media Dramaturgy. This is because, in my opinion, the importance of dumb type is not related to the theatrical use of new media. Other opinions have praised dumb type's usage of new media technology in many areas of their work and regard this as typical of dumb type. However, Takatani Shirō, one of the founding members of dumb type, proposed an opposing opinion, saying that if a play was without depth and just relied on the use of media technology—something he described as often being thought of as typical of dumb type—then those creating the play should deserve our criticism. In other words, members of dumb type were already continually telling us that the content, and not the media, was the important aspect of their plays. This is why the importance of dumb type, who took up speaking their mind about minorities, cannot be over-exaggerated.

This is not to deny that images from their work are presented to the audience with exquisite timing. The scene following the prologue in *S/N*, with its sound effects that mimic the heartbeat combined with the sound of a life-support machine, is remarkable. It is combined with projected images of naked torsos floating by, and I doubt that there is any viewer who does not feel a sense of shock at this moment. The upper part of the wall then seems to turn into a stage along which people run and dance. They also fall backwards off the wall into an abyss. Under the sharp flickering lights we are aware of something strong, something unified by aesthetics. But the importance of this work is not only a matter of its aesthetic strength. This brings the issues addressed in this work into a prominent and special position, but of more importance is how we then connect to the images, what we experience in terms of critical reflection.

I have written about these issues several times and have used expressions such as "collapsing skin," "medicalised space," "the neglected and exposed body" and "the fragrance of death" to describe the state of the body in these works.[14] For example, the upper parts of the headless naked bodies displayed in the round images (of the first mediatised sequence in *S/N*) look as if they are framed through a viewfinder like that used by a sniper. The same kind of device is used in an X-ray machine to target the parts of the body to be exposed to radiation. To me, these naked bodies look like the bodies of people who are about to be killed. I wonder what the performers were thinking in this scene as they disappeared, falling off the platform? As they fell, their words were projected on the wall in front of them: "I dream ... my gender will disappear!" or "I dream ... my nationality will disappear!" We, the audience, are determined to fight, even while we are stunned by the overwhelming power of the images of those people falling. This prompted me to reflect on the fact that the performance was not only about those suffering with AIDS, but also about the wider issues that affect us in our lives and about death. I have called these bodies "bodies of impossibility." In their forensic condition, they are polar opposites to the grotesque bodies (*igyō na mono*) typical of 1960s theatre.[15]

I do not know if we can see an increase in interest in politics in Japanese theatre at the present time. It seems that in Japan since 1995 such experiments have disappeared from the mainstream of theatre history. No matter what kind of death or vanishing we have experienced, we must now think of a new strategy and start again. To expect that dumb type can fill such a role, and that the answer lies in the question of how dumb type is positioned in the history of Japanese theatre, is, in my opinion, the mission that needs to be spoken about.

Notes

* This is an edited and translated transcript of Ōtori's keynote presentation at the dumb type symposium. The text was translated by Till Weingärtner and edited by Peter Eckersall.

1 Kara called members of his company *kawara kojiki*, or "river beggars," in reference to the popular and profane roots of Kabuki theatre that first began as performances on temporary stages in the dry Kamo riverbed. *Kawara kojiki* were of low status and lived precarious lives outside the rigid hierarchies of mainstream society.

2 Kara's tent performance at the west exit of Shinjuku Station (*nishi-guchi koen jiken*) was undertaken without a permit and was intended as a provocation to the Tokyo Government. It ended with the tent being surrounded by the police and some of the actors (including Kara) being arrested and taken to prison. See Peter Eckersall, *Performativity and Event in 1960s Japan: Body, City, Memory* (Basingstoke: Palgrave Macmillan, 2013), pp. 95–100.

3 Terayama's play *Nokku* (*Knock*, 1975) took place over a 48-hour period in the environs of the city of Tokyo with scenes performed in places such as parks, suburban streets and a bath house. See Shûji Terayama, *Nokku* (Tokyo: Watarium, 2013).

4 Ōtori is referring to Benjamin's concept of historical materialism. In Benjamin's essay "On the Concept of History" (1940), he writes about how material aspects of the historical past are still in play and explode the continuum of history. The consequential sense of the past existing as fragments was, for Benjamin, a revolutionary stance.

5 Suzuki's piece featured a montage of dramatic scenes chosen from diverse sources, including classical Greek theatre, Shakespeare and Kabuki, and were performed using his highly physical and stylised method of acting.

6 A helpful companion to this idea might be Francis Fukuyama's influential essay "The End of History," published in *National Interest* (1989) and developed into his 1992 book *The End of History and the Last Man* (New York: Free Press).

7 Shinji Miyadai, *Owarinaki nichijō o ikiro* (Live the Never-Ending Everyday) (Tokyo: Chikuma shobō, 1995).

8 For an overview of pre-war modern theatre in Japan, see Peter Eckersall, "From Liminality to Ideology: The Politics of Embodiment in Prewar Avant-garde Theater in Japan," in *Not the Other Avant-Garde: The Transnational Foundations of Avant-Garde Performance*, ed. James Harding and John Rouse (Michigan: The University of Michigan Press, 2006), pp. 225–49.

9 For further discussion on Japanese theatre in the 1980s, see *Alternative Japanese Drama: Ten Plays*, ed. Robert Rolf and John Gillespie (Honolulu: University of Hawaii Press, 1992). Ōtori's suggestion of a sense of fatalism pervading contemporary Japanese theatre is particularly acute in plays written since the 3/11 disaster in Japan.

10 See Peter Eckersall, *Theorizing the Angura Space: Avant-garde Performance and Politics in Japan, 1960–2000* (Leiden: Brill, 2006) for a discussion on the re-engagement of theatre with politics in Japan in the 1990s.

11 Ōtori also mentions Gekidan Kaitaisha's Shimizu Shinjin and feminist performance artist Ito Tari as important figures in this regard.

12 Roy Cohn is described in a *New York Times* review of the film release of *Roy Cohn Jack Smith* as "a gay-bashing right-wing lawyer and a steadfast protector of the 'American Family.' He was also a closet homosexual." *The New York Times*, 4 August 4 1995, http://www.nytimes.com/movie/review?res=990CE4DF1130F937A3575BC0A963958260 (accessed 26 March 2015). He was also fictionalised in Tony Kushner's *Angels in America, Part One: Millennium Approaches* (1993).

13 Ikeuchi Yasuko, *Joyu no Tanjo to Shuen—Pafomansu to Jendaa* (The Birth and Demise of the Actress-Performance and Gender) (Tokyo: Heibonsha, 2008). For further information on *Interior Scroll*, see Carolee Schneemann's website: "Schneemann ritualistically stood naked on a table, painted her body with mud until she slowly extracted a paper scroll from her vagina while reading from it," http://www.caroleeschneemann.com/interiorscroll.html (accessed 26 March 2015).

14 See Ōtori Hidenaga, "90-nendai engeki ni okeru nikutai no hyōshō – moshikuha eizuteki shintai he mukete"

(Symbols of the Body in the 1990s – Towards a Body of AIDS) in *Shintai no Mirai* (The Future Shape of the Body), ed. Takayuki Tatsumi (Tokyo: Treville, 1998); Ōtori Hidenaga, "Igyō kara isō he – sarasareta shintai no hen-yō" (From Odd shape to Odd Form – Transfiguration of the Exposed Body), in *Onna? Nihon? bi? - Aratana jendaa hihyō ni mukete* (Woman? Japan? Beauty? Directions in New Gender Criticism), ed. Takaaki Kumakura and Kaori Senno (Tokyo: Keio University Press, 1998).

15 Ōtori notes that some of these ideas were also being explored in performance internationally and cites William Forsythe's *The Loss of Small Detail* (Ballet Frankfurt, 1991) as a work that has similar themes to those discussed. This piece premiered in 1991 and was a collaboration with the composer Thom Willems and designer Issey Miyake.

Dumb Type Women

Where Corporeal Precarity Meets Media Terror

Katherine Mezur

Throughout dumb type's *pH,* three women in white slips dive and flatten themselves to the ground beneath the continuous horizontal swiping of the arm of a giant copy machine. In *S/N,* a woman is bound into her own dress with her skirt pulled up and over her head; she walks blindly on the edge of a platform until she loses her balance and falls in a strobe flash into the darkness. In *OR,* a woman stands still in a narrow shaft of light against the white cyclorama, disappearing and reappearing through a projected highway that streams forward as if we are driving madly on a twisting mountainous road over her body. In *memorandum,* a woman dances frenetically in silhouette against three screens churning with urban images of cars, streets and buildings and neon lights flashing by; she dances faster and faster against the rush of images that swallow her like a black *tsunami.* In *Voyage,* a woman lies crumpled and frozen on an AstroTurf island with projections of glaciers and mountains rising up out of her body. In *OR* again, three women on transparent hospital gurneys move methodically in slow motion, preparing themselves for the death of their projected heartbeat.

These action images are among the iconic body and media acts of the dumb type collective's works from the early 1990s to the 2000s. Women members of the group created and performed these action images, in which bodies meet media full on, communicating visually and kinaesthetically the precarious co-existence of technologies and the human body. While some of the performances by the women in dumb type are triumphant, such as BuBu de la Madeleine pulling the string of national flags from between her legs in *S/N*, most action sequences are performed under duress as media and bodies endlessly repeat cycles of actions with no escape. These acts are produced by a particular interaction of live bodies with media, where bodies move between layers of media. What are these interactive material and virtual conditions? How did these women create these sequences that resonated in and beyond Japan and illuminated some of the darker questions concerning new media and the living? What if we probe and reimagine dumb type women's experiments from within their movement and media interface? What links their perception of physical precarity to media terror? While I will only begin to approach these questions here, this initial examination should stake a claim for these artists' investigations into corporeal and media empathic interaction and affect.

For this theorisation, I draw primarily on Thomas Lamarre's work on the animetic interval in limited animation and the perception processes created by animation machinery that links directly to how bodies and projections interface. For a background on contemporary precarious conditions in Japan and a culture-based theory of precarity, I turn to Anne Allison's *Precarious Japan* (2013), and her extensive research on gender performance in twentieth- and twentieth-first century Japan through its popular cultures and practices. I also draw on performance studies and social science research from other voices.

Men in dumb type have taken on major roles in devising the themes and designs as well as dramaturgy and directing of performances. However, within the collective's collaborative performance strategies, women stand out for their acts of corporeal precarity in dumb type's landscape of new media performance. Through identifying and theorising dumb type women's creative (and precarious) bodily and media acts, I hope here to suggest a different and more detailed reading of dumb type's new media performance art works. I will also examine how these actions illuminate a world of precarious experience that is driven by the women performers in their corporeal encounters with media.

To begin, their actions are not illusions. Whether disappearing into bright white light or darkness or being propelled or frozen by projections, dumb type women performers perform "at risk" in a world of moving and still projections, strobes, sounds and objects. By "at risk," I mean that the dumb type women themselves devised these performance sequences fully aware of the possibility of accidents and injury. I suggest that they developed an aesthetic of corporeal media terror in order to gain the attention and kinaesthetic participation of the audience. It is the possible and fantastic situations of moving their live bodies in intervals of media that characterise the dumb type women's creative, manipulative and destructive live and media acts. The group's live and media acts stand out as dumb type's signature acts of corporeal precarity and media terror. In order to set the context for such creative and disturbing performance strategies, I outline some of the disastrous events in Japan through the 1990s and into the 2000s, particularly in terms of the new social conditions for women that were created by the ongoing economic downturn. I suggest that when the women combined technologies of gender and media in these downwardly spiralling and volatile economic conditions, they set themselves up for a risk-taking practice that had a brilliant political edge in a Japan that was failing as a nation state and sinking into economic and social stagnation.

Who are the dumb type women? They are the main female performers who collaborated in devising dumb type's major performances from the late 1980s through the early 2000s. They created and performed acts of corporeal and media transformation and disappearance. Among them were Takatani Yoko, Fujiwara Manna, Tanaka Mayumi, Yabuuchi Misako, Ouchi Seiko, Hirai Yuko, Sunayama Norico and Kagita Izumi (BuBu de la Madeleine).[1] Theirs was a choreography of animated bodies that moved into and out of what I examine here as the intervals between live and media spaces. Their live/media acts were central to the impact of dumb type's social, political and aesthetic aims in their mix of performance, projections, texts and sound. I argue that the women performers pushed dumb type's combinations of visual and physical acts to new levels of intensified kinaesthetic interaction between the performers, spectators and the production crew. Their physical, media and conceptual risk-taking innovations set the stakes for their corporeal "precarity," which they created through their encounters with various analogue and digital media. Their precarity, which I will explain, in their live/media acts reflects the layered precarity of being women artists on stage/screen, and as women in Japanese society.

It is important to briefly outline some of the immediate context to dumb type's media terror and corporeal precarity. In the spring of 1995, the Aum Shinrikyo religious cult released sarin nerve gas into several trains of the downtown Tokyo subway system. There were thirteen fatalities, but over 5000 were injured and the group's plans for further attacks, with more lethal substances, were extensive and global. This attack in the mid-1990s alerted the Japanese populace to the deep divisions in society. According to the Japanese drama critic Yasumi Akihito, and others writing during the Aum cult infiltration of the 1990s and the devastating 1995 Kobe earthquake, the 1980s had been a time of display and "euphoric nothingness, in which traditional value systems were declared dead..."[2] Yasumi felt that the apocalyptic theatre boom of the 1980s gave way to the next wave of media and "quiet theatre" artists. Deeply concerned with social issues, dumb type leader, HIV positive Furuhashi Teiji, focused the group on a deeper political engagement with HIV AIDS issues.

According to BuBu and Sunayama Norico, in conversations and interviews in the 1990s through 2003,[3] they wanted it made clear that they did not earn their living through dumb type but through several different jobs. They worked as dancers in bars and developed many of their acts within the freedoms and restrictions of that milieu. Performing seductive acts and striptease in close contact with audiences made them both very aware of the expectations for the stereotyped heterosexual female gender patterns of gesture and the gaze. BuBu was an advocate for sex workers' rights, and both Bubu and Norico worked on AIDS awareness projects. They also commented on being the educators of the public on openness to sensual physical expression. BuBu and Norico were the main negotiators for creative and leading roles for women performers in dumb type; and they were also, at the same time, a part of the "female precariat" of the Japanese workforce of part-time labourers with no security.

In what ways are women especially precarious in Japan? Anne Allison's analysis of precarity in the last two decades in Japan begins with an important overview: "Precarity is the word of our times. ... At its base, precarity refers to conditions of work that are precarious ... Precarity references a particular notion of, and social contract around, work. Work that is secure;

work that secures not only income and job but identity and lifestyle ... Precarity marks the loss of this...” And she reminds us that workers are, for the most part, always already insecure.[4] Japan may be quite similar to some other nations in its job insecurity, but from WWII to the mid-1990s there had been unmitigated growth in consumption and stability in the work place, home and sociality. “When the bubble burst in 1991, triggering a recession that lingered on (and on),”[5] the job and social stability of the home went into meltdown. Japan’s stable work and social culture became “‘*muen shakai*’—the relationless society. Social precarity. Liquefied Japan.”[6] While *muen shakai* can also mean a society of neglect, Allison presses on the *muen* where situations have separated individuals, who used to rely on family relations for their stability.

How does “precarity” work in dumb type’s acts, and how do dumb type women “work” with the sense of risk in their daily lives in their performances? In being depicted alone, isolated, in pain and insecure they show a material precarity of their bodies meeting the virtual precarity of their visual form within their mediated performances. It also arises from the deep precarity of contemporary Japan’s economic decline and social disorder over the last twenty-five years. The lifetime of dumb type aligns with a period of slow burgeoning societal displacements and radical labour shifts due to the economic bubble collapsing and continuing to remain flat. Furthermore, “natural” disasters such as the 1995 Great Hanshin earthquake, and the Great East Japan earthquake, tsunami and the Fukushima nuclear disaster of 2011 (known as “3/11”) have exacerbated these conditions of precarity.

When I use the terms “precarious” or “precarity” in association with dumb type women, I am thinking of combinations of what Allison calls “multiple precarities—of work, of sociality, of life (and death).”[7] Allison also reminds us that women workers in Japan were always among the precariat, “even during the boom period of the bubble economy women were overly representative in the peripheral workforce as part-time workers (which they remain today with seventy percent of female workers employed in irregular jobs and eighty percent of temp workers being female).”[8] And today, in the aftermath of 3/11, perhaps we can see dumb type women’s acts “straddle the precarity of life in a particular dance with death.”[9] And we, the spectators, kinaesthetically participate in their corporeal precarity and media terror.

For example, in most of these works, women performers are solo figures;

or they are look-alike and move-alike pairs or trios of female figures. They perform like a puppet-doll chorus in a threatening physical situation. There are also challenging duets where women perform heightened combative moves, in dangerous pulsing total blackouts and blinding strobes. They are isolated and insecure in how and when they should move to avoid collisions, falling or pain. Instead of being daily scenes of women in precarious situations that are driven by various visual and aural media, repeating cycles of projections, strobes and blackouts propel their actions while images stream over and through their bodies.

How do terror, precarity and animetic intervals work in dumb type women acts? To better understand their precarity in their acts of movement in media, I draw on Rustom Bharucha's explanation of "terror" and Thomas Lamarre's study of the animetic interval in Japanese animation (*anime*). In *Performance and Terror,* Rustom Bharucha writes that "terror can be felt, experienced, embodied, but it can also be inflicted and imposed.... To pin terror down to any particular discipline, within the strictures of any one vocabulary or institutional framing, is to miss out on its deadly elusiveness."[10] In every performance, dumb type women create and perform experiences of terror which share a "deadly elusiveness" that keeps returning. The embodied experience of terror combined with the use of media in dumb type's work leads me to an understanding that these works convey "media terror" that is gendered and expressly shown by the women in their performances.

"Media terror" is already ubiquitous. The media theorists Donna Haraway, Katherine Hayles and Rosi Braidotti have all turned to new technologies and machines in relation to humans in the rapid infiltration of new media in the contexts of the 1990s and early 2000s.[11] But "terror" has become its own discourse, when media, in the various Gulf Wars, 9/11, the Arab Spring, 3/11, and ISIS hostage executions have brought the corporeality of our bodies-on-screen smashing into our previously well-kept distances. Our increased sense of visuality through mobile media has finely tuned and subdued our physical receptors to constant overwhelming states of shock through an overload of images of anguish or terror, whether live and/or virtual.

In the performances by the women, images, actions, kinaesthetic practices, sensuality and terror meet at the interface of body and media. Acts of volatility, such as falling or disappearing that are produced between the body and media, are in this sense acts of terror. The choreography of the body and media produces these acts of material or visceral instability. Such acts wrench our perceptions in radically different directions, shifting our consciousness out of our usual safety zones. I believe the conditions and outcomes of these body/media sequences speak to the dissolution of human security as we now know it. I consider several sequences from *OR* and *memorandum* (and *Voyage*, as well as referencing *pH* and *S/N*) where performers and media meet, entangle and change each other.

This essay foregrounds the interaction of two apparatuses: gender and media. For dumb type, gender and machines producing "media" have always been interacting.[12] The dumb type artists were an urban Japanese collective led by fellow artist Furuhashi Teiji's social and political agenda on AIDS awareness, queer cultures and disability rights. They were all encountering, to some degree, a particular moment in media and performance, between 1985 and 1999. Dumb type's use of media, from analogue slide projectors to digital computer-timed multi-screens, was entangled in the struggles in Japan of issues of power, racial homogeneity, gender and sexuality, and the deeply toxic state of capitalist consumer culture and ecological ignorance. It is within this political context that I wish to base my analysis of dumb type women's action images.

In contemporary media such as *anime* and computer games, humans, animals and objects morph from one form into another in fantastic visual displays. These processes take the senses by surprise, jolting the spectator's sense of safety and wholeness. In live media performance, live bodies are added to the digital mix; there is nothing that is not in motion, nothing that is not precarious. Dumb type women worked with these moments of visionary collision where bodies crashed into pre-digital media and the analogue tools of light slide projectors, strobes, screens and the architecture of the spectators' viewpoint of the performing bodies and screens.

Dumb type works were cellular compositions and this modular structure allowed for collective creativity and openness to spectator interpretation. In the examples drawn from dumb type, I examine how corporeal repetition and stillness meet projected cyclical movement and stillness, creating a counterforce of sense-tension within the performers as they play with and against light, images and texts. They may or may not see themselves but they do see the other performers appearing and disappearing. They must imagine their bodies screened and what this means for the spectator. Performing *between* darkness and light, image and text, risk was essential to dumb type's art. It is no longer a question of agency or identity for the performer/body; instead, a somatic transference passes from one body to another, performer to performer, and performer to spectator. As a collective work, it also means that everyone is engaged in the falling, the disappearances and the re-emergences. Bodies are media and media are corporeal. Flashing strobes, streaming projections tune our bodies and escalate our senses inside the moment of light, darkness and corporeal/image encounter. Media turns into materiality in this repeated constellation of gesture in light and darkness.

Dumb type's "Animetic Intervals"

Akira Mizuta Lippit writes:

> No signifier is more imaginary in cinema, more primordially elsewhere, perhaps, than that of the moving body. The moving, gesturing body in cinema signals its presence in the world, a presence transposed in the umbilical, photographic continuum that binds cinema to physical reality, but also its withdrawal, its status as an imaginary signifier that becomes a figure for absence: a figure of the absent figure.[13]

I suggest that dumb type's performance is comparable to Lippit's figures for absence but here the absence is on screen, and the live moving bodies create a presence in the intervals between themselves and the media projection. With this idea of the interval I turn to Lamarre's explanation of the animetic interval: dumb type's bodies are also animetic[14]—that is, they move in media between the intervals of surfaces or planes such as the projections, lights and moving bodies. I will examine how dumb type women devised performance in these animetic intervals, and how precarity and terror are built into these processes.

What is this animetic interval and how does it work here? Lamarre begins with this emphasis on how "animation techniques imply a way of thinking about technology. *Anime* thus promises to open new ways of thinking about how we inhabit a technologized world."[15] Dumb type pursued this thinking about technology with their complex themes of machines, human desires, queer identities and life/death passages through a similar emphasis on the "moving image." In fact, movement is at the centre of animetic theory. Lamarre emphasises how the force of movement that we perceive in animation arises from the shifting of the planar layers of the animation machines. These planar layers of celluloid move across each other to create a sense of movement between layers. In this movement between layers, there is an interval, which arises between the planar layers. Likewise, dumb type stages were constructed as layers of projection screens and movement corridors. The stages' movement, by necessity, moves across and between these planes, screens and body surfaces. They animated their bodies across the moving images. The effect is similar to Lamarre's understanding of animation:

> You feel the openness between the flattened planes of the image, which imparts a distinctive sense of movement. Rather than move into a landscape, you seem to move across it. ... animetism is not about movement *into depth* but movement on and between surfaces. This movement between planes of the image is what I will call the animetic interval.[16]

Lamarre also explains in great detail how this layering of planar images allowed for a distinct way "to harness or channel the force of the moving image in distinctly animetic ways. More contemporary animation actually suppressed the sense of movement between layers of the image."[17]

There are several characteristics of Lamarre's explanation of *anime* that can be directly applied to dumb type: the layering of medial planes (back screens, front projections, film rear projections, live camera projections on different surfaces), and the movement of these projections and the performers inserted on the stage between these different intersecting planes of projections. Lamarre suggests that navigating through the animetic interval offers a different way of being in the technologised world.[18] He argues further that the "animation stand" apparatus "generates a field of material orientations by channelling the force of the moving image in specific ways."[19] I consider that these intervals generated between screen, light and image planes demonstrate how dumb type performer/creators "had an animetic rather than cinematic sense of depth and movement."[20] That is, their bodies could also play differently with genders and sexualities. Dumb type women's choreography between the planar screens engages directly with this channelling force. I suggest that the worlds of dumb type do not set out to exploit or seize viewers but, instead, do what Lamarre suggests, that "this is a world that opens to us even as it remains apart from us. As it opens, you see depth, but these depths are not calculable by Cartesian geometry. This manner of viewing thus invites awe and reverence. We are witnesses not raiders."[21] Dumb type women invite us to join them in their animation of movement in media in a way that invites the revelation of a new perspective.

To put the animetic interval in the work of dumb type women, we can see that moving across planes creates a potential for disappearance and transformation. The slippage between surfaces of bodies and planes here is not animation, but disturbs the "natural" suture of live and media bodies and movement. Dumb type women chose these unnatural shifts. They took great advantage of the animetic interval and deployed it to also register their sense of precarity and terror with the technologised world.

So, the provocation here is how the dumb type women managed to recreate and animate themselves through what I call movement *in* media, a media choreography. I concentrate on how the performers in live and projected forms move in relationship to different medial machines, screens and projections. It is in these relationships of media to their moving bodies where their physical precarity increases exponentially. Moving *in* media puts bodies at risk; or, the performer is forced into that state of reincarnation where body, gender and identity/self are always disrupted through the projection surface, speed, focus, the frequency of flashes and total darkness. In dumb type, the female performers dare the restrictions of this awkward arena of precarity in media.[22]

Media also restrains their movement. For example, when performers move in front of a screen with rear projections, they become a shadow or a dark silhouette. Behind the screen, they become diffused figures or soft pastel shadows. Because of this, dumb type carefully distinguishes men from women, with women wearing skirts and dresses and men wearing pants and buttoned-down dress shirts, sometimes jackets. In shadow on the screen, these clothes distinguish who is male or female. In the white brightness of *OR*, women wear even more gendered attire with high heels, skirts, blouses, coats, all made of flowing materials. In their striking runs across the curving stage, the women charge, dodge, jump, fall and roll to standing in a darkness shot with flickering white strobe flashes. *Flash*, their skirts whip into the air; *Flash*, their legs kick and jerk; *Flash*, they strut out in T-shirts and little skirts; or a woman in a bikini walks another woman as if she is a dog on a leash, which turns into a striptease as the human walker passes the dress down the leash and the dog-woman slips into it. But this is not so simple. In the screened flashes and digital imagery, we see the slip-slide between animal and female, dog-in-a-dress, bikini-woman, naked dog. This is a slippery sliding across bodies, species and genders: moving in media.

In the following examples, I will suggest how each movement in media example demonstrates one use of media-gender, and an amplification or animation of sensorial politics and their terrors and pleasures. I observe how a performer moves in media, how they radicalise what is seen/felt in a particular way that is precarious. Each example is only one kind of trajectory for shifting between intervals and devising/creating new body and projection relationships. Each example articulates the "animetic intervals," and the performance (outcomes) of female bodies in those action images. We move between bodies and media within the intervals of screen, images and live bodies, where movement determines the degree of precarity and terror. In the examples, there are different degrees of precarity and terror directly related to the diversity of the animetic interval and the variations in the force of movement between image layers. The effort of pulling the always-moving targets of visual and corporeal forces into partial and momentary alignment is central to the dumb type women's art labour.

In the following examples, the degree of precariousness for the performer bodies, and how much the animetic interval interacts with the force of movement of the live performer and projections, is unique to each scene. Dumb type women use the interval and movement forces of the media to create the exact choreography to perform under these conditions and communicate the content of the scene's intended action images and their significance in the theme of the work. While the four examples are different, they all share Allison's characteristics of precarity in their body and media acts. A sense of insecurity, isolation, alienation and an aching or dull pain moves from example to example because of this configuration of bodies and media. Over time, dumb type women skilfully created a craft of their body/media acts. They knew the exact amount of time, momentum, repetition, tension and release necessary for burning into their gestural vocabulary to communicate their insecurity and isolation, their sense of loss and their individual fears.

Stillness and Precarity: Floating Terror

In *OR* and *memorandum* there is an accelerating pitch in the intervals of light, darkness and blended images. Everything seems to be shaking.

In the opening sequence of *memorandum,* the voice of a young girl tells us the story of a girl being terrorised by three bears from the children's story *Goldilocks and the Three Bears.* After the girl and a companion's projected images waiver, suspend and crawl up a screen of projected words, we are plunged into streaming videos running left to right on three screens that take up the entire back wall of the stage. The videos are in colour, and vary from ocean scenes to a wide-angle lens view of a Tokyo underground station, like a slightly tilted view from inside a fish bowl. People in the video seem to stretch across the screen; distorted screen-digital bodies. A performer runs in and appears as a sillouette that is "caught" between images, unable to run away, she gyrates to the explosive streaming imagery.

Projected Precarity and Dancing in the Dark[23]

In *memorandum,* the darkness is palpable. When the first sequence of the four screen digital and analogue projections flashes on, a woman gets caught in the images of waves, then a train station, light and dark flashing landscapes. She contains herself in a cantered projection corridor, an interval between the screens and between different angles and speeds of projected images. She is forced to move only on one point in space. She is isolated and alienated by projected landscapes that engulf her in their light and darkness. The moving images appear to stream across the horizontal spaces of all the screens; but, in fact, each screen streams one interval from an individual projector. The projectors are not synced together but run with a dark, whipped-up silhouetted figure in shadow in the brighter screen-scape. The woman dances, shaking herself faster than the streaming images, she moves in a field of multiple intervals, enveloped and etched by darkness and exhaustion.

Will the frozen female figure in *Voyage,* who lies alone and still on an AstroTurf island, floating in the projections of glaciers and the dark black sea, rise above or sink into those depths? A soft high-pitched voice says, "I wish I were Little Red Riding Hood and get eaten by a wolf." This is a wish-for "world" full of terror, isolation and drowning in the interval. She does not move and she is not safe.

In *Voyage,* texts often float, fly or race and stream across bodies and screens. The text projections disorient by creating an interval between the text and the moving bodies, and between the text and a projected image. Here terror begins sweetly when a soft, girl-pitched female voice speaks in English, the words rising, projected on her figure and the screens surrounding her. The rising text seems to nudge her body, which appears crumpled—yet her legs are spread out so her dress rides up exposing them. Her flesh becomes the surface for her words. She lies on an AstroTurf island in the black stage space with towering screens rising up behind her, where we see her double as a projected figure. She is both on the stage and on the screen, while rising projections of glacial mountains and dark ravines move her into their landscape. The words rise as "she" speaks from a recording, creating an interval between speech and text. Her spoken and projected poem floats across her skin and the screen surface and the mountains beyond. She is alone and isolated in a stream of images. In these intervals, she is left behind, her image hovers over her body, a ghost of the flesh body that rises up. The spoken text wishes innocently, then counters with a chilling sound action image on the screen: "I wish you would kiss me / I wish I could tie you up." These wishes are dark, fearful threats. Perhaps her body has fallen out of the sky and these are her last wishes? "I wish I could kill you / I wish I were falling through the clouds / I wish I could be loved—and lost—by you." A fragment of her speech/projection moves on the screen over her freeze-framed body: "I wish I'd drown / I wish I'd be punished / I wish I were Snow White—white as snow, lips red as blood—and then wake up."[24]

The white letters glow white on several dark surfaces. The words are enunciated separately from the body and projection. Perhaps the performances of "writing" projections on bodies re-embody the power of "text" as corporeal acts? The voice of a young girl speaks a strange English as though the words do not fit in her mouth. The parallel "dubbings" of voice and body and text are each an interval in a different medium. The dumb type woman here floats between projected words, spoken words. She lies frozen between acts, screens and sound/image texts: frozen in their movement. Perhaps the interval between spoken text and projected text creates the terror of being controlled between the intervals, but out of control where her body cannot move. The intervals remain between the dubbing of text on image and voice on body. Her silent body becomes monumental on screen, and the text burning across her screened body generates the conditions for sensing terror.

OR: Strobe Acts and Intervals of Time

OR begins with a vertical white line coursing across the rear curving cyclorama, left to right, accompanied by a loud electronic "ping." After several swipes of the blinding column of light, a figure appears: a dumb type woman in a white dress stands still, halfway across the curving expansive screens. This female figure in the background, pressed against the white screen, occurs several times throughout the entire work. Sometimes she disappears into a crevice or the light/dark fold of flashing strobe light. Then she reappears again in her statuesque motionlessness like a white moth, a specimen pinned to the screen surface. In another scene, the same woman in white will be the centre of a projected road trip and fields of sunflowers. The curving road that dives into the dark tunnel then releases us into an open road somewhere in the Alps, going south as the projection of narrative-like-text has told us earlier. According to Takatani Yoko, Tanaka Mayumi, who most often played this part, must stand still without moving because she has to stay in an exact interval of overlapping projections, where the images can split, making her appear or cross over and make her disappear. In the road trip projection, her body becomes the vortex of motion, drawing every spectator with her on the road journey.[25] She is the road, the journey, the digital meshing of light, image and movement, and possibly memory. But she is also the screen, the projected surface. I would claim that her apparatus, her body-as-screen, is the space and time of appearance and disappearance.

This entire section is in darkness with only pulsing white strobe flashes that light the entire space. The floor, the curved back screen and the ceiling are white. All the performers wear white. The sound is a throbbing electronic score with a pinging pulse, which builds in waves with the increased momentum of the performers' actions. In the first section, a woman zips herself into a body bag with her earphones and a radio. She jives and bops into her bag, a limbless white pillow. She is picked up and carried off, only to reappear on a gurney with male doctor types who carefully take her out of her body bag, a limp but pliable, naked doll-like human. They walk her like a doll-puppet around the space. Four men move her arms and legs, forcing her to walk between them and through intervals of darkness and light. Is she another technology? Has she become the perfect animetic interval between human and robot? Once we are screened in x-rays, MRIs or face prints, are we captured on screen, endlessly death-less between states? Within the animetic interval, the gestures of media mark bodies just as bodies mark and move in media.

A Dance of Death to the Intervals of a Heartbeat

The screen projection sequence seems to hit a climax with the cardiogram of a heartbeat. The screens go very dark, there is a slow pulse that begins to race and crackle when the centre screen lights up with what looks like a burning nova: the explosion and death of a star, with brilliant tiny flashes which then goes black. Then the strobe starts again, like a visual drone. We see three women, Misako Yabuuchi (left), Mayumi Tanaka (centre) and Seiko Ouchi (right), roll out their gurneys into a row with slow perfunctory gestures. The gurney beds are made of a sheet of clear Plexiglas or glass, with silver legs and rolling wheels: the gurneys reflect back the icy whiteness of the stage and screens.

After the strobe sequence, the whiteness of the light beams down onto the front section of the stage where the three women perform a dance of self-preparation for death. The entire back screen, in the darkened upstage area, is filled with the electrocardiogram of a heartbeat pulsing from left to right. Comforting at first, we hear, see and feel the heartbeat on the surrounding screens. The women in white methodically line up their gurneys facing downstage, three in a row, equally spaced. The gurneys are intervals in space. The heartbeat pulses the intervals of life in the body. The women move between these intervals of objects, space and breath. The women perform a pattern of tasks: in slow motion, the three women quietly perform the gurney movement sequence against the temporality of the continuing heartbeat. They begin by dropping one white shoe over the opposite side of the bed, and gracefully sit and roll onto the gurney bed, then almost stretch out but continue to roll their feet over to the opposite side. Then they cross underneath the gurney, spreading their legs wide over the lower railing and stand for a moment before they shift their hips onto the gurney bed again, lie down, pause, then roll over, briefly stretching out like a corpse; one foot reaches below, they slip down to move under the gurney table again. They roll over and climb under and lie still on the gurney in a looped cycle of movement in unison. The heartbeat speeds, slows, continues. They perform this act of corporeal precarity, moving towards dying, with the cardiogram and its heartbeat sound quickening, slowing and almost stopping. As a spectator, I enter their carefully repeated journey: I twist up and over the gurney, lie down, pause, roll over, stand, crawl under the gurney table and begin again. Their repeated phrase is a cycle of intervals. They keep going, perfectly in time and in unison. They become the force of movement shifting between the planes of the gurneys, the heartbeat, and the crackling white pulse running across the screens.

The third or fourth time around the women stop, they lie flat on their backs like corpses in the cold space of a morgue. They still their life force. The heartbeat stops, the cardiogram goes flat, there is no more pulsing light. The light burns brighter over the gurneys. The women's bodies float like black shadows on their clear glass rectangular islands in some deep blue space. The intervals collapse in their stillness. Dumb type women perform the ends of animation. They squeeze and flatten themselves into that last interval between the planes of time and event. Theirs is a calm, brilliant terror that hides in the light. Lights out.

Notes

* Special thanks to Takatani Yoko, Sunayama Norico, Kagita Izumi (BuBu de la Madeleine), Furuhashi Teiji and Peter Golightly, who opened up the doors of dumb type to me, and to the early Artspace Mumonkan director, Endo Fumiko, who first introduced me to their work. My gratitude also goes to all the Wonder Women of dumb type (named and unnamed), especially Takatani Yoko, Fujiwara Manna, Tanaka Mayumi, Yabuuchi Misako, Ouchi Seiko, and Hirai Yuko.

1 Throughout this essay I refer to all of the women who performed in dumb type performances from the late 1980s through the early 2000s as "dumb type women." I sometimes refer to particular women in certain scenes because I know from interviews or from Takatani Yoko the name of the performer in the visual sources that I studied. However, in keeping with dumb type's prerogative to honour the collective authorship of their works, I do not name the performers by name in every circumstance. They also swapped certain movement sequences, especially when on tour. I do not support erasing their identities but for the politics of these works and this group I have opted for their group identity, except in exceptional circumstances.

2 Tadashi Uchino, *Crucible Bodies: Postwar Japanese Performance from Brecht to the New Millennium* (London: Seagull, 2009), p. 122.

3 From the early 1990s through 2005, I met with Sunayama Norico and BuBu several times during and after their involvement in dumb type. Sunayama and I were both dancers so we met at performances in Tokyo and Kyoto. Sunayama was also dancing with KyupiKyupi, a techno-music and performance group based in Kyoto, with whom she created cyborg-like characters for music videos. She choreographed her own bar dance performances and performance art/installations (see "Sex with Nation: The OK (Bad) Girls Cabaret," in *Bad Girls of Japan*, ed. Laura Miller and Jan Bardsley [New York: Palgrave, 2005]). BuBu and I met sporadically before and after Furuhashi's death from HIV/AIDS complications. In all their interviews, they emphasised how much the labour of women artists needed to be acknowledged, especially in the dumb type works, where (they felt) they had contributed a great deal of the character design and choreography for the female solos and ensemble works, which involved intense, repetitive and sometimes dangerous movement sequences. During one conversation, while having coffee at Spiral Hall, where BuBu had performed in *S/N*, BuBu and I were asked to leave the café because of our raucous behaviour, which I was also videotaping.

4 Anne Allison, *Precarious Japan* (Durham: Duke University Press, 2013), pp. 6–9.

5 Ibid., p. 6.

6 Ibid., p. 8.

7 Ibid., p. 9. The conditions of Anne Allison's reading of precarity in Japan—insecurity, alienation, and the daily pain that arises from isolation from society—match the underlying conditions that resonate from the precarious actions by dumb type women in their performances.

8 Heidi Gottfried, "Japan: The Reproductive Bargain and the making of Precarious Employment," in *Gender and the Contours of Precarious Employment*, ed. Leah F. Vosko, Martha MacDonald and Iain Campbell (London: Routledge, 2009), 76–91. Quoted in Allison, *Precarious Japan*, p. 9.

9 Allison, *Precarious Japan*, p. 9.

10 Rustom Bharucha, *Performance and Terror* (London: Routledge, 2014), p. 9.

11 See Donna Haraway, *Simians, Cyborgs, and Women* (London and New York: Routledge, 2013); Katherine Hayles, *How We Became Posthuman* (Chicago: University of Chicago Press, 1999); and Rosi Braidotti, *The Posthuman* (London: Polity Press, 2013).

12 This interaction is present but often unmarked in much live and media performance scholarship. In order to open up this area of analysis, it is my view that we need to not only reflect on how we are creating and perceiving gender and media relationships, but possibly recommit to more diverse analyses of live/media performance.

13 Akira Mizuta Lippit, "Digesture: Gesture and Inscription in Experimental Cinema," in *Migrations of Gesture*, ed. Sally Ann Ness and Carrie

Nolan (Minneapolis: University of Minnesota Press, 2008), pp. 113–31, p. 116.

14 Thomas Lamarre, *The Anime Machine: A Media Theory of Animation* (Minneapolis: University of Minnesota Press, 2009), p. 25.

15 Ibid., p. 11.

16 Ibid., p. 7.

17 Ibid., p. 9.

18 Ibid., p. 25.

19 Ibid., p. 25.

20 Ibid., p. 38.

21 Ibid., pp. 38–39

22 Yasumi Akihito quoted in Tadashi, *Crucible Bodies,* pp. 56–57, http://en.wikipedia.org/wiki/Aum_Shinrikyo (accessed 12 December 2014). Randy Martin writes, in an article on precarity, dance and finance: "Precarity bears its own undoing ... surely moving through disequilibrium and divining ways through spaces made for infinite possibility are what dance does best. ... Performances are, after all, derived from many other times ... of rehearsal, of training, of touring; they gather together movements from myriad locales, experiences, and sources to recalibrate and recompose them for a given intervention. Seen from this expanded field, dance is already everywhere. Rather than appearing merely fleeting and ephemeral in performance, dance is the concatenation of varying durations, of reaches near and far that nestle among the moving bodies." Randy Martin, "A Precarious Dance, a Derivative Sociality," *TDR/The Drama Review* 56 (4), 2012: 62–77, pp. 62–63.

23 Distinguishing male and female bodies in the dumb type performance conditions of darkness, shadows and strobe lighting could be difficult, but here costume choices gender the silhouettes, the shadows and the front-lit bodies. There are a few exceptions, such as Furuhashi Teiji's drag role as Dolly in *S/N*, and a line of men and women performers dressed in girl's skirts, tops and long haired wigs in *OR*. Men wear pants (trousers) and shirts, and women wear a variety of skirts, dresses, coats or playful girl fashion outfits that show that they are "female" in their shadows and backlit silhouettes. While not exaggerated as femme, butch or drag, we read the female and male bodies in media through non-mediated gender acts. I suggest that media can gender the performers differently than their bodies—but here, dumb type men and women chose the conservative and careful structures of Japanese social gender constructions. Thus, wonder women perform in dresses, bras, high heels and other accoutrements, such as Sunayama Norico's breast nipple chains, hot pants and stiletto heels, which she wears like a maid or bar hostess. Spectators recognise the women through these styles of dress. A few dumb type women perform without clothes in brief moments of strobe flashes. The women create their own precarity with their costumes: making themselves recognisable in shape, shadow and movement.

24 Fujiwara Manna spoke this text in *Voyage* in 2002. The text of the wish poem was sent to the author by Takatani Yoko in a personal email.

25 During this scene in *OR* there is spoken and visual text that streams across the cyclorama, telling us about a road trip going south.

Dumb Type Technology

Man and Machine in Japanese Art and Society

Gunhild Borggreen

The stage set for the dumb type performance *pH* (1990–93) resembles a giant photocopying machine.[1] Two horizontal bars or trusses span across the white floor area that makes up the stage, and they move back and forth lengthwise on rails set at different heights: one of them at a height of two metres, the other only forty centimetres above the ground. During most of the performance, the lower truss moves at a constant pace, and when it reaches the end of the space, it stops and turns back again at a uniform speed. White neon light tubes are mounted underneath the lower truss, and the bright light projects onto the floor as the truss moves. It is this light in a dark space, combined with the uniform rhythm of moving back and forth across the stage, that suggests the association with a photocopying machine: the repetitious and uniform movement of light back and forth, like a photocopier scanning a document in order to produce one or many copies of the original document.[2] I will allow the association of a photocopier to form the structure of my discussion in the following analyses: the issue of "scanning" may be seen in a larger societal framework of surveillance technology and visuality, while the repetition of the act of duplication refers to automation and robotic behaviour that has infiltrated many societies since industrialisation in the late nineteenth century, and increasingly does so in the current context.

The dumb type collective are praised for the experimental way in which they apply various technologies and media platforms in their performances and art installations, and through their productions they have inspired many other performance and dance companies around the world to engage in experiments with current technologies.[3] In this essay, I will provide a cultural and historical background for discussions of human–machine relations in Japanese art and society, and argue that the way in which dumb type applies machinery in *pH* and other works attests in general to a highly elaborate vision of technology, both as an aesthetic strategy as well as a context for social and cultural critique.

pH

According to dumb type's publication *pHases* (1993), the title of the performance work *pH* refers to pH, potential Hydrogen, an indicator for the level of hydrogen ion density in solutions that shows the degree of acidity or alkalinity. In the dumb type text, the scientific scale of pH levels (usually identified somewhere between 0 and 14, with 7 as neutral) is compared to another set of opposites, namely Heaven and Hell. This system of indicators is entitled "a game-theory of post History for auto-determination of global human destiny."[4] The performance is divided into thirteen scenes or phases (written as pHases), organised in contrasting pairs such as fact/fiction, public/private, production/reproduction, man/woman, external/internal, and others.[5] The movement of the truss back and forth between each end of the stage signifies a technological manifestation of such a dichotomy of extremes, but also points out how the system is never in complete balance; it will keep searching for an equilibrium that it will never attain. In addition to the white light from the lower truss, slide projectors mounted on the upper truss project various images and coloured light on to the floor, sometimes in movement, at other times still. Lights and projectors are placed along the sides of the stage space and aid the projection of various types of light as well as still and moving images onto the end walls or onto the actual performers in the space. There are five performers on stage in *pH*: Furuhashi Teiji, founder and director of dumb type from its beginning in 1984 until his untimely death in 1995;

three female dancers: Tanaka Mayumi, Sunayama Norico and Yabuuchi Misako; and the male dancer Peter Golightly.

As in all dumb type performances, there is no narrative structure, but rather a sequence of thirteen parts each representing a set of dichotomies, as sketched out above. The shift between the parts can be made out mainly through the shift of light on stage or in the soundscape. The thirteen sections form a circular structure because the performance ends with the same scene as the one with which it began, thereby suggesting an endless repetition of the sequences. The thirteen parts have different lengths, and the formats and modes of presentation are varied as well: sometime the stage is engulfed in uniform golden light and there are snippets of music from songs associated with American jazz from the 1930s. At other times, the soundscape is chaotic and intense, filled with sound bites of sirens, radio noise and electronic beeps mixed with fast, rhythmic beating taps. Visual modes of presentation include the performers on the stage as well as projections on the floor and on the end walls. These shift between recognisable images of faces, groups of human figures, currency, company logos and diagrams, to more abstract formations of light in various colours and intensity.

The dancer Peter Golightly is either dressed in a suit and tie, or stripped to a pair of white underpants. Periodically, he sings and dances to the 1930s jazz tunes. There are also a few passages in which he speaks in either English or Japanese, imitating the questions immigration officers often pose at national borders. Otherwise the performance is true to the dumb-ness of the group's name by communicating in non-verbal formats of sound, image and movement. The other male performer (Furuhashi) is present on stage also in a suit and tie, at one point placing objects on the floor, at another picking up pink mechanical toy pigs and putting them into a shopping basket, or manoeuvring around face down on the floor on what may be a skateboard or a set of small wheels under his stomach. The three female dancers move in synchronised patterns next to each other or in a line, their body stature and short hairstyles almost identical. They are all dressed in white slips and black dance shoes with a low heel in the style of the 1930s. Performance scholar Katherine Mezur calls these kinds of female groups in dumb type performances "phantom women" because they appear as "part human, part ghost/fantasy, and part machine."[6] Mezur argues further for a feminist reading of these phantom roles because they may provide women with the opportunity to critique restrictive social roles.

Surveillance

In *pH*, audiences are seated on steep risers along both sides of the 16-metre-long narrow rectangular white floor and look down upon the stage from above. This in itself provides an unconventional relationship between performers and audience, for although many conventional theatre buildings have rows of seats that ascend slightly towards the back to give the audiences in the back seats a view of the stage, the audience of *pH* are placed much more radically above the performers. The viewing position here provides an at once totalising but also a somewhat distorted view of the human bodies on stage because they are seen from above. The audience exercises control over the stage by their all-seeing power, and they may indulge in what Michel de Certeau identifies as "the pleasure of 'seeing the whole', looking down."[7] De Certeau's notion of the scopic drive that constructs the modern day urban space as a panorama-city may be echoed in fragments of video projections on the end wall of the stage that represent groups of people walking in slow motion across an urban plaza filmed from above. The video projection is superimposed by other moving images, and the pedestrians in their transparency could refer to what de Certeau calls "an *opaque and blind* mobility characteristic of the bustling city."[8] The elevation has made the audiences distant to the centre of the action and emphasises the gaze of the voyeur that the audience possesses, not only as those who have the economic means to purchase a ticket and thereby have a right to look, but also in terms of scopic power relations of visual pleasure. The three female dancers, for example, lay down flat on their backs on the floor, exposing their bodies to a full scrutinising view from above, and a surrender to gendered and eroticised scopophilia.[9] This kind of reading of the female body in *pH* is challenged, as Katherine Mezur argues, by the way in which the dehumanised and mechanical aesthetic framing provides empowerment to the phantom women.

Another media for enhancing the visual is the searchlight. The trope of the searchlight comes up several times in *pH* as a round spotlight moving across surfaces, sometimes accompanied by the sound of sirens. In one scene (pHase 13), the searchlight is accompanied by a voice from a loudspeaker posing questions such as "Do you have some form of identification?" and "Is this trip for pleasure or business?" in a forceful manner. In a short essay entitled "True Stories," Furuhashi Teiji recounts several of his personal memories of crossing national borders by plane or train that often ended in humiliating experiences. Furuhashi also recalls how the African-American performer Peter Golightly was often singled out from the other Japanese dumb type members to stand in a different line at passport control. "When we meet again at the booth exit, he is always sweating and forcing a smile like an actor."[10] In pHase 7, the framing of close-up moving images in black and white of the male performer is superimposed by a grid of small red crosses or plus signs, equivalent to those used in sighting mechanisms in weapon technologies. In the next pHase, pHase 8, an image of a gun sight in a purple colour signifies the same type of potentially violent vision technologies. The distant and voyeuristic position of the audience becomes even more pronounced through a number of image technologies installed on and above the stage: a video camera is mounted on the truss facing downwards so the camera can record activities taking place below and, in some cases, project the image onto the end wall.

Machines

In all of dumb type's performances, the use of technology such as neon lights, loud speakers, slide projectors, searchlights, video cameras and other devices is significant and fully integrated into the performance rather than being hidden away behind stage settings or "outside" the stage as in many conventional theatre performances. Instead of using standard stage systems, most of the technical stage lighting equipment is made and operated by dumb type members themselves in an attempt to challenge what dumb type director Furuhashi criticised to be a "confining" aesthetic level of standard stage light. Instead, dumb type wants to recreate the atmosphere of light in everyday urban space, such as highway lamps and tunnel lamps, or the sunset in a local park. "There is an aesthetic regard for pure light in the space around the light source," says Furuhashi, "what we try to do is transplant such space into the field of the stage."[11]

Dumb type's technical apparatus has several functions: not only does it provide technologies for transmission and amplification of sound, projection of light and images, etc., but it also carries meaning in itself and becomes a device that the human performers and the audiences interact with as part of the conceptual design. In *pH,* the main technological elements on stage are the two horizontal trusses. In most of the scenes (pHases), the lower truss rides back and forth at constant speed and appears to be moving automatically along a set of rails on each side of the stage floor, controlled by a pre-programmed setting of computerised motors. The repetitive movement of the truss back and forth provides a rhythm that adds to the general sensory experience of the performance, both auditory in the form of rhythmic beating of electronically generated music, and visually because of the bar's bright white lights that point downwards. This consistent and uniform movement appears to be totally automated, and it determines and controls the movement of the human performers on stage. In the opening scene, the male performer, who is clad only in underwear, crawls flat on the floor and therefore has his body positioned under the bar as it passes over him with only a minimum of space between his body and the moving device. In pHase 2, the three female performers lie flat on their backs as the bar passes over them, with the bright light illuminating their bodies in a moving band of visual exposure in an otherwise dark setting. In this situation, the female bodies are indeed "photocopied" by the automated movement of light: they are scanned, monitored and exposed to the gaze of the audiences as the machine performs its surveillance of the floor. In pHase 3, the male dancer walks behind the bar and approaches the three women on the floor, pulling each of them out from under the bar one at a time. Later, the three female performers walk towards the bar, but are stopped, and then lie down again, negotiating the space in front of, behind and underneath the moving bar. In other scenes, the performers crawl under or jump across the bar, or run in front of it, as if to escape the spatial confinements created by the moving bar. The moving bar exhibits a threat of violence when three folding chairs are placed on the stage, and the three women sit or stand on the chairs until the bar approaches—and then, in the last second, the women throw themselves flat on the floor and crawl away while the bar hits the chairs so they fall backwards and fold up.

In other words, it is clear how the machine in the performance is enacting a dominant influence on the behaviour of the human bodies. The truss moves in constant and predictable patterns accompanied by monotonous sound, while the humans are subject to the regulations of the mechanic movements by literally being subjugated into positions beneath the truss. In contrast to the smooth, uninterrupted motion of the automated machine, the human bodies move in the space in fluctuating, volatile and chaotic manners, displaying a state of precariousness in the presence of the dominating machine. The three female performers move in synchronised choreographed motions as if they are contaminated by the mechanic precision and encoded with computerised repetition; a repetition that is not only manifest in the iteration of certain patterns of movement but also in the clone-like similarity in their corporeal presence. According to Mezur, the way in which the three female dancers move in and out of the stage lights provides "a sense of vagueness and unease about their identities," and the mixture of ephemeral and mechanical movements of the identical bodies provide a ghost-like anonymity that she understands as potentially subversive because the figures are no longer "fugitives" in the machine space, but take ownership by appropriating the pulse and driving power of the machine.[12]

Critique of Machinic Society

The technological predominance in *pH* is often read as a critique of the automation of everyday life, and the way in which machines structure spatial surroundings and limit social interactions between humans. For example, Carlota Alvarez Basso, head of the audio department of the Museo National in Madrid, writes in a catalogue text how the staging in *pH* constricts the movement of the performers and strips them of will and initiative. Instead, the performers become robots or automatons in their extreme synchronisation. "Individuals are seen as social subjects (not social agents), constrained and co-opted into alienation by the values and conventions of the society in which they live."[13] Furthermore, many critics connect the notion of automated behaviour in *pH* with Japanese society and consumer culture in general. Media art scholar Chris Salter describes the movements of the dancers in *pH*, as well as in the earlier dumb type work *Pleasure of Life* (1988), as mechanical, "almost robotic," and finds that the audio-visual environments of synthesised ambient techno sounds and searchlights combined with fluorescent fixtures are both sterile and dystopian, yet seductive. For Salter, dumb type projects create "a critical image of current Japanese society obsessed with the new."[14] Literature and theatre critic Tetsurō Onitsuka writes about the performers in *pH* (he witnessed the performance at the 9th Granada International Theatre Festival in Spain in 1991) that "the characters at times seemed too much like robots, all-too-manipulated by the system," and he finds this to be "a result of their being patterned on Japanese society."[15]

In other words, many critics seem to read dumb type's technology as a critical sign of dystopian systems of control and manipulation in which humans become mere robots subjugated to the machine. Much of this reading of dumb type performances in general and *pH* in particular links to a notion of Japan as a nation of technology and consumption. Industrialisation and mechanical rationalisation is part of the growing impact of mass production that supply an equally growing domestic and international market for consumer goods. At the same time, the rectifying mechanisms in the machinic system are often compared with the ways in which consumption creates equally suppressing structures of the individualised subject through the mechanisms of desire for material possessions. Late nineteenth-century Japan was infused with not only industrialisation and technological innovations from Europe, but also Western humanism and Romanticist philosophy in the spirit of *bunmei kaika* ("civilization and enlightenment"), the catchphrase of the era. According to historian and media scholar Seth Jacobowitz, literature and visual culture were concerned with the notion of mechanisation, and machinery became a metaphor for degrading humanity during this time of Japan's first machinic age. Romanticist notions of the modern individual in popular print media, as well as in the literary writings by Natsume Sōseki, Tayama Katai and others, evoked a homosocial self-pity among men for enduring the alienation evoked by a technological and industrialised lifestyle. The idea of the "mechanical man" emerges from the anxieties of technology during the Meiji period, and is reflected in many cultural productions of the period.[16]

The historical perspective of the imaginary concerning relations between man and machine was a characteristic of modernism in the early twentieth century. In Japan, as well as in Europe and the United States, there was a pronounced artistic attention to the new experience of the Machine Age. In western societies this gave rise to a nature–culture divide in which the human body was understood as a natural whole in contrast to the automated machine. This divide was challenged in the arts, as when the Futurists advocated a bonding between humans and machines as a way of bringing together those separated modes of being. The Futurists created what Hal Foster calls a "double logic of the prosthesis" because technology functioned simultaneously as an *extension* and a *constriction* of the human body.[17] Specific local histories related to the reception and negotiation of modern lifestyles in Japan appear similar to the philosophical notions and visual representations expressed by European and American artists and intellectuals at the time. Different phrases in Japanese art circles signified an interest in machines and technology, such as *mekanizumu* (mechanism), *kikai bigaku* (aesthetics of the machine) or *kikai shugi* (machine-ism). In Japan, as elsewhere, there was a variety of responses to new technologies and machines spanning a spectrum of thought from the optimistic belief in a bright and optimistic future due to technological innovations, to the critique of industrialised society and mechanised modernity.[18]

Technology and Theatre

The concept of the "robot" entered Japanese culture and vocabulary when the play *R.U.R.* (*Rossumovi Univerzální Roboti*, or Rossum's Universal Robots, 1920) by the Czech author Karel Čapek was translated into Japanese and published in 1923 by Uga Itsuo with the title *Jinzō ningen* (Artificial Human Beings). The play was performed by the modern theatre company Tsukiji Shōgekijō in 1924, and unlike the first staging of the play in New York in 1922 where the characters of the robots were clearly distinct from those of humans, the Japanese version featured a visual conflation of the human and the robot on stage. According to curator Kawanishi Yūri, this indicates that the image of robots as machines made of metal did not exist in Japan at this early period.[19] In her study on the pre-war avant-garde movement of MAVO,[20] visual culture scholar Gennifer Weisenfeld notes that this and other Marxist-inspired art movements were strong during the 1920s in Japan, and that some artists and intellectuals grew tired of the Futurist surface-like fascinations with technology. They wanted to explore and reveal the back end of technology, which included considering the politics of labour and a critique of the "bourgeois" approach to art that they found the Futurists to support; they turned instead to the Russian Constructivists. This was also an attempt to change aesthetic values in art by acknowledging the socially transformative potential of innovative aesthetics.[21]

The post-war attention given to machines was explored in various types of artistic practices. One example was the artistic group Jikken Kōbō (Experimental Workshop), headed by the influential Surrealist artist, writer and critic Takiguchi Shūzō. He was one of the main figures in the art world who managed to tie together avant-garde activities from before the war with a new artistic environment after 1945 following fifteen years of censorship and suppression of the arts during wartime and military rule in Japan. Art historian Tezuka Miwako points out how the totalitarian rule of wartime nationalism and the emperor system turned people into "automatons under this supreme authority."[22] She also accounts for how

Jikken Kōbō were connected to the Bauhaus school through Takiguchi's personal ties to the Bauhaus painter and photographer László Moholy-Nagy, and how this led to a radical approach to adopting technology and mechanical mass production in art.

One of Jikken Kōbō's most significant works was the dance production entitled *The Future Eve* (*Mirai no Ivu*) that was performed at the Haiyūza Theatre in Tokyo over three days in March 1955, in which two large humanoid mechanical devices made of metal tubes, sheet metal and wires were moved around the stage on wheels and challenged the spatial dynamics of the dancers. In a review by Takiguchi, he comments on these large metal mobiles on stage, and notes how "the bodies of the dancers were completely ruled by these objects."[23] Tezuka argues that Takiguchi's own approach to the use of technology was more in line with Moholy-Nagy's radical take on art and technology in everyday life as a means for Takiguchi to reject lyrical romanticism and other emotional forms of expression. Tezuka also argues that *The Future of Eve* was Jikken Kōbō's commentary on the materialism and commercialism of post-war mass production, and that humanity and social unity would be lost in a mechanised world. But it also appears as if Jikken Kōbō used the advancement of new technology to explore new modes of artistic expression in their work, and that the dominance of the machine on stage provided a new set of aesthetics that could challenge the conventions of romanticism and human-centred emotions in theatre productions at this time.

Techno-nationalism

During the late 1950s and through the 1960s, the Japanese government supported industries that had developed high levels of innovation and skill, such as car manufacturing and electronics. As exports to USA and Europe developed and Japanese electronics and other high-technology products became increasingly praised for their quality, the catch phrase "Made in Japan" evoked pride among many Japanese people. Sociologist Yoshimi Shunya points out how the notion of "techno-nationalism" signifies the way in which advanced technology was often linked to traditional culture—for example, through references to excellent craftsmanship or the inclusion of "native" Japanese culture in naming the new electronic products.[24] The first world exposition outside the West was held in Osaka in 1970, and this event, known as Expo '70, provided the opportunity for Japan to focus on new technological developments such as robots, electronic equipment and new types of communication and transportation systems. Expo '70 became a major showcase for Japan to demonstrate that the nation not only had "caught up" with the advancements in science and technology elsewhere but, in some areas, even surpassed them. The myth of the Japanese as the most machine-loving people in the world can be traced to Expo '70 at a time when the entry of Japanese industrial and consumer products to the international market gave rise to equal amounts of fear and admiration.

During the 1980s, Japanese technological development shifted from large-scale industry related to shipbuilding and car manufacturing towards electronic appliances, as well as computer software and gaming. David Morley and Kevin Robins discuss how new technologies have become associated with the sense of Japanese identity and ethnicity, and describe the concept of "techno-orientalism" in gendered terms as they suggest that technology has been central to the "potency" of Western modernity. The significance of technology has been crucial for Western identity and, therefore, Japan's advancement in the area of new technology during the 1960s became a challenge for the West. Morley and Robins argue that the West fears that "the loss of its technological hegemony may be associated with its cultural 'emasculation'."[25] This techno-orientalist perspective on technology from Japan became even more pronounced in the West during the 1980s when ideological and economic interests between the US and Japan clashed in a series of "Japan bashing" incidents, triggered by not only the global dominance of Japanese hi-tech electronic devices, such as the Sony Walkman, video cameras, computer software and the like, but also by a number of spectacular Japanese corporate purchases of American entertainment industries as a way of controlling the technological hardware and media products to cater for a growing entertainment and content industry.[26] Such events were often seen in the West as an outcome of a Japanese mentality associated with a rationalised, robotic system driven by consumption paradigms with economic gain as the sole purpose, and with no respect for cultural, historical or emotional factors.

pH = post Human?

Many readings of dumb type's integrated use of machinery and technology in their performances relate to the ambiguities of human–technology–machine relationships of modern society that have unfolded in various modes and media throughout the modern era. Many critics see dumb type performances as a critical comment on how machines impose restrictions and control upon the human body, forcing it to adapt to automated and repetitive movements that are alien to human nature. While some find the exploration of the human condition in dumb type performances bleak and pessimistic, other approaches argue for a more nuanced understanding of their depiction of human–machine relationships. Art historian Jane Blocker, for example, writes about memory, body and technology in the dumb type performance *memorandum* (1999–2002) and challenges the notion of the victimisation of humans. She suggests that dumb type do not present humans and machines as mutually exclusive or hierarchically ordered, but, rather, that their work explores the limitations of the machine itself.[27]

The dichotomy of human versus machine is also challenged in more recent philosophical approaches of posthumanism and transhumanism, in which future biotechnological advancements point towards a radical integration between human bodies and technological devices. This may lead to the next step in human evolution, in which there is no longer a contrast between man and machine because the two will merge together into new types of entities. Transhumanism regards the biotechnological future as optimistic because humans will no longer depend on the vulnerable "container" of the human body. The somewhat broader concept of posthumanism also includes more sceptical and critical approaches, some of which acknowledge a possible merger between human and machine, but at the same time fear that unique human qualities may be lost if, or when, human bodies and technology are united.[28]

The concept of posthumanism was not yet formulated clearly at the time when dumb type performed *pH* in the early 1990s. There seems to be more of a distinct line back to the aesthetics of the avant-garde experimental theatre such as Jikken Kōbō and the use of advanced technology on stage as a way of challenging the prevalent romanticist inclination. In a poetic statement in the book on *pH*, Furuhashi Teiji himself suggests that the use of technology in dumb type's performances is a means to overcome the narrative structures and artistic content by replacing "emotion" with "motion." The first part of the poetic statement reads: "Emotion – the Wings of Imagining enlisted / to seek out artistic content / Motion – the motors of Technology cutting across / that so-called content."[29] This seems to suggest that *content*—the "meaning" of the performance that critics are eager to interpret and transmit in reviews and academic papers—is challenged by *form*, for which technology provides a perfect frame. The content of *pH* seems to emphasise the way in which human bodies are subjugated to the automated movements of the truss, while the truss, at the same time, is also an aesthetic formality that leads possible perceptions away from *what* this means to *how* it means. The dominance of the structure or the system in the performance diminishes the elements of human emotion and mental reflection, and hereby places emphasis on the body in a phenomenological state before feelings and reflections intrude. As Furuhashi states in the final lines of his poetic statement: "Mechanical Motion without human mind which technology provides saves 'me' from overflowing Emotion."[30] This is indicated in the extreme preciseness of the choreography and the interaction the human dancers have with the technology. The human bodies negotiate the restricted space created by the moving truss and become part of that space by physically adapting to distance, rhythm and movement. The machine becomes not just a representation or a symbol of the automated and regulated conditions of society, but is an aesthetic tool that provides the performance itself with the conditions for its own creation.

Notes

1 I refer in my descriptions of the work to the video release entitled *pH*, produced by Wowow in 1993.

2 This allusion to a photocopying machine is not original; the reference is mentioned in Judy Annear, "Museum of Contemporary Art, Sydney/Australia," in *pHases*, ed. dumb type (Tokyo: Wacoal Art Center, 1993), p. 53; as well as in Chris Salter, *Entangled: Technology and the Transformation of Performance* (Cambridge, MA: MIT Press, 2010), p. 74. Katharine Mezur references Furuhashi for the comparison with a copy machine in Katherine Mezur, "Fleeting Moments: The Vanishing Acts of Phantom Women in the Performances of dumb type," *Women & Performance: A Journal of Feminist Theory* 12 (1), 2001: 191–206, p. 195.

3 For example, the Danish theatre company Hotel Pro Forma, under the artistic leadership of Kirsten Dehlholm, collaborated with dumb type in the performance *Money Business Class* (1996). "Hotel Pro Forma Projects," http://www.hotelproforma.dk/projects/.

4 *pHases*, p. 14.

5 Carlota Alvares Basso, "The Performance pH," in *pHases*, p. 13.

6 Mezur, "Fleeting Moments," p. 192.

7 Michel de Certeau, *The Practice of Everyday Life*, trans. Steven Rendall (Berkeley: University of California Press, 1988), p. 92.

8 Ibid., p. 93.

9 See Laura Mulvey, "Visual Pleasure and Narrative Cinema," in *Film Theory and Criticism: Introductory Readings*, ed. Leo Braudy and Marshall Cohen (New York: Oxford University Press, 1999), pp. 833–44.

10 Furuhashi Teiji, "True Stories," in *pHases*, p. 50.

11 Oda Hiroko and Furuhashi Teiji, "Dialogue," in *pHases*, p. 9.

12 Mezur, "Fleeting Moments," p. 195.

13 Alvares Basso, "The Performance pH," p. 13.

14 Salter, *Entangled*, p. 74.

15 Onitsuka Tetsurō, "Dumb type in Granada," in *pHases*, p. 29.

16 See Seth Jacobowitz, "Between Men, Androids, and Robots: Assaying Mechanical Man in Meiji Literature and Visual Culture," *Mechademia* 9, 2014: 45.

17 Hal Foster, "Prosthetic Gods," *Modernism/Modernity* 4 (2), 1997: 8.

18 Wu Chinghsin, "Transcending the Boundaries of the 'Isms': Pursuing Modernity Through the Machine in 1920s and 1930s Japanese Avant-Garde Art," in *Rethinking Japanese Modernism*, ed. Roy Starrs (Leiden: Global Oriental, 2012), p. 339.

19 *Robotto to bijutsu – kikai vs shintai no bijuaru imeeji / Robots and the Arts – Visual Images in 20th Century Japan*, ed. Hibari Takayama et al. (Tokyo: Kōdansha, 2010), p. 29. See also Gunhild Borggreen, "Robot Bodies: Visual Transfer of the Technological Uncanny," in *TransVisuality: The Cultural Dimension of Visuality: Volume 2: Visual Organisations*, ed. Toke Kristensen, Anders Michelsen and Frauke Wiegand (Liverpool: Liverpool University Press, 2015, pp. 175–88).

20 MAVO was an avant-garde art movement active between 1923 and 1929, and many MAVO artists created disjunctive and pessimistic visualisations of industrialised societies.

21 See Gennifer Weisenfeld, *Mavo: Japanese Artists and the Avant-Garde 1905–1931* (Berkeley: University of California Press), 2002, p. 3.

22 Tezuka Miwako, "Jikken Kōbō and Takuguchi Shūzō. The New Deal Collectivism of 1950s Japan," *positions* 21 (2), 2013: 355.

23 Cited in Tezuka, "Jikken Kōbō and Takaguchi Shūzō," p. 369.

24 Yoshimi Shunya, "'Made in Japan': The Cultural Politics of 'Home Electrification' in Postwar Japan," *Media, Culture and Society* 21 (2), 1999: 162.

25 David Morley and Kevin Robins, *Spaces of Identity: Global Media, Electronic Landscapes and Cultural Boundaries* (London: Routledge, 1995), p. 167.

26 Ibid., p. 150.

27 Jane Blocker, *Seeing Witness: Visuality and the Ethics of Testimony* (Minneapolis: University of Minnesota Press, 2009), p. 84.

28 See N. Katherine Hayles, *How We Became Posthuman: Virtual Bodies in Cybernetics, Literature, and Informatics* (Chicago: University of Chicago Press, 1999).

29 Furuhashi Teiji, "pHase 3," in *pHases*, pp. 22–23. The English translation of the poetic statement by Furuhashi Teiji reads:

"Emotion – the Wings of Imagining enlisted / to seek out artistic content / Motion – the motors of Technology cutting across / that so-called content / If only that, the sole contribution – / the blow Technology can deal to Art / If only that, our one means of escape from the jail / Then Technology's good for something

Technology – doesn't pander Art / Technology – betrays Arts / Technology – rescue it from the Factory! / Technology – rescue it from Art! / And yes, Technology saves Art from History

Technology adores Art.

Mechanical Motion without human mind which / technology provides saves 'me' from overflowing Emotion."

30 Ibid.

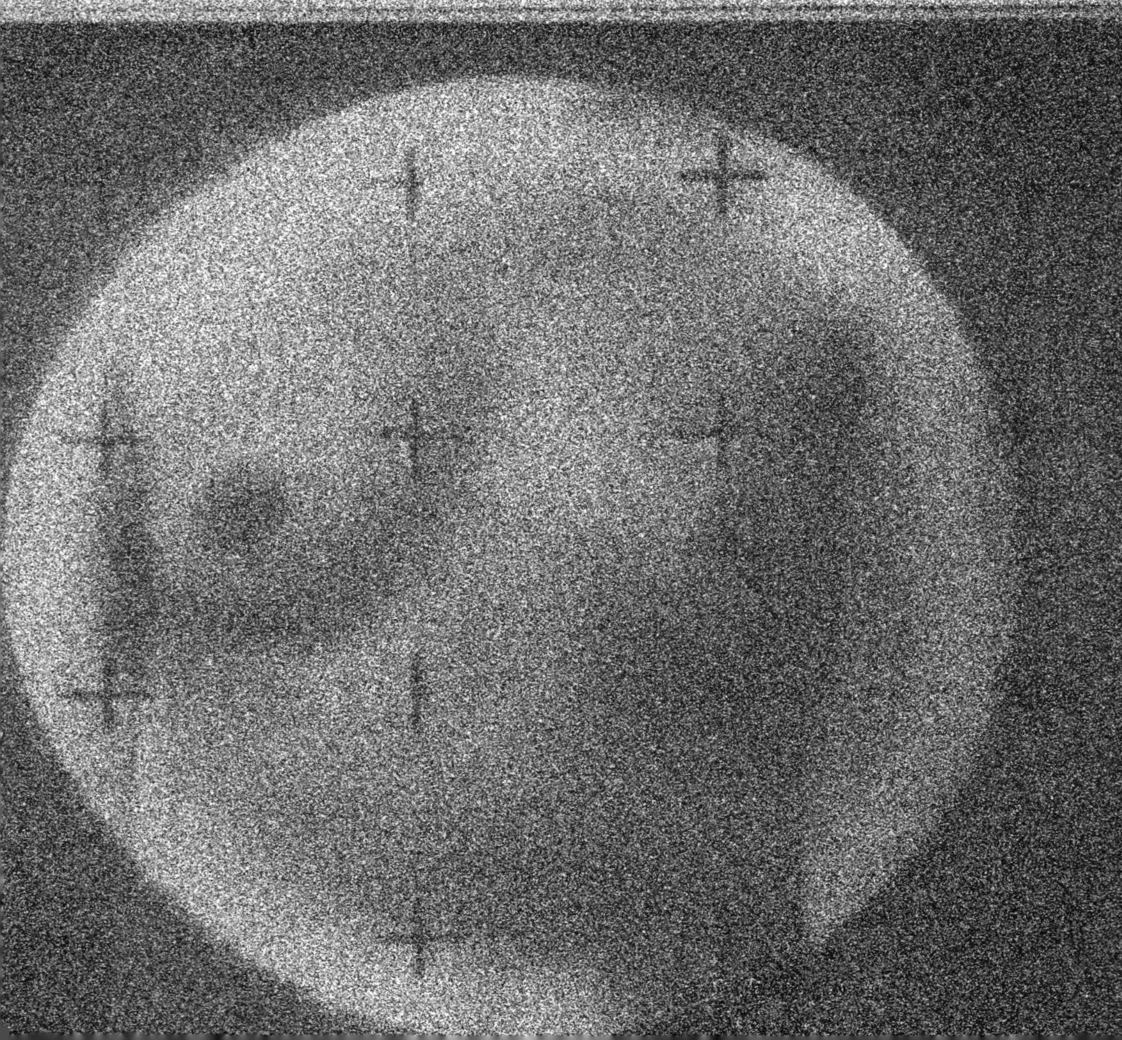

S/N

The Creation of *S/N* and the Debate about Sexuality in 1990s Japan

Wim Lunsing

While conducting fieldwork on sexuality and gender in Japan, I became acquainted with dumb type in the beginning of 1992. At the time, Japan was experiencing a period of lively debate on sexuality, and male homosexuality in particular was being discussed in virtually all media and in many groups and organisations. In October 1992, Furuhashi Teiji sent around his famous letter to his friends, stating that he was gay and had AIDS. I failed initially to note the enormous impact this had, as so many people were investigating their sexuality and already openly talking about it. His request that dumb type members help him create *S/N* under his direction immediately led to many meetings in which people investigated sexuality and AIDS.

Already in March 1993, the "seminar show" for *S/N* was staged, in which parts of the later performance *S/N* were shown, interspersed with serious panel discussions of the issues. Most dumb type members themselves had never given these issues much consideration and underwent a process of development towards better understanding them. Ever increasing numbers of people from the art scene, students of all sorts, lesbian, gay and transgender people, and so forth, engaged in the discussions, which were further promoted when *S/N* was being staged. Through these discussions, communities were established which have endured. Based on my continuing fieldwork since 1992, redeveloped after taking into account oral histories carried out in 2010, I investigate here how *S/N* impacted on many people's lives.

Exclusion

In Japan, people are taught, in many ways, not to be different from others. Traditionally, children are kept in line by placing them outside the home when they misbehave,[1] and when children do so in public contexts and do not follow their parents' wishes, it is common for the parents to threaten to leave them. At school, beginning in kindergarten, teachers often enlist the support of the rest of the class in ridiculing and jeering at children who are naughty. This practice may even continue at university level, where professors may invite other students to ridicule a student who makes a mistake. Adults are also constantly aware and reminded through gossip how strong the forces are that keep everyone in line. Most will do all they can to give the impression of the normality and decency required by society, as exclusion is a major organising principle of Japanese society (and, I believe, of most societies, although this is ignored in many as it does not fit anti-discriminatory ideals).

The much discussed concepts of *uchi* (home/inside) and *soto* (outside), where inside is safe and outside is dangerous, shows the importance of belonging to and being on the inside. The concepts of *omote* (front) and *ura* (back) indicate what people are expected to show in public contexts (*omote*) and what should be kept in private contexts (*ura*). This may, for instance, entail not kissing a close friend in front of one's house for fear of neighbourhood gossip. The very prevalent use of the concepts of *tatemae* (socially moderated behaviour) and *honne* (actual feelings) shows that people are used to making clear distinctions in what to say in which context. Thus, people are keenly aware of the fact that it is often preferable not to show how they really feel (*honne*) about something. In this context, homosexuality belongs outside the *uchi*, where there is no place for it, while at the same time being part of the *ura* subculture, in which people can explore their *honne* or true desires.[2]

Recently, the rigidities of this cultural value system has led to young people being unable to follow social standards, experiencing anxiety and, in many cases, becoming tired of social contacts all together. This may lead them to withdraw from social life. This form of self-exclusion was initially problematised in the case of schoolchildren, but increasingly also in that of older people as a personal rather than a societal issue, with the term *hikikomori*. A similar category is that of NEET (Not in Education, Employment or Training), which concerns people of a slightly older age (in Japanese statistics the bracket of up to 35 years of age is commonly used), who similarly avoid social contacts by staying in their private bedrooms.[3] The most extreme form of self-exclusion that can be related to these phenomena of social withdrawal is, of course, suicide.

Boom in a Bubble

In 1989 the women's magazine *CREA* published a special issue on male homosexuality, which was very popular among its readership. Following this example, many other women's magazines also published about gay men, gay cultures and gay politics, and by 1992 this trend had spread further to the most serious general (or should I say men's) magazines and the major national newspapers. In the same period, Fushimi Noriaki published his *Puraibēto gei raifu* (My Private Gay Life, 1991), which for many gay men and others in Japan was the first serious publication on homosexuality. This book was followed by numerous other books on male homosexuality, and eventually also female homosexuality, pioneered by Kakefuda Hiroko's *'Rezubian' de aru, to iu koto* (On Being "Lesbian," 1992).

Many gay-themed films followed, and on television, documentaries on gay culture, gay people and gay politics became part of the programming on many networks. Gay men started to come out at work and in their homes in larger numbers than ever seen before. It was a very active and lively period. I was, for instance, invited by one of the gay organisations I was doing research with to have a group discussion with volunteers helping mentally disabled people in Nara, and with a local fire brigade, and also with another organisation to discuss with the Osaka city and prefecture authorities how to deal with AIDS in the case of male homosexuality. As part of this, I was reported in some Japanese national media as being in a gay relationship with Onitsuka Tetsurō.

Homosexuality was widely discussed in a positive manner in the media as well as in many local contexts. Japanese society seemed to be making an effort to overcome its exclusionism and to grant space to a larger range of lifestyles. Yet members of parliament were still heard saying such things as "they hated gays" in, for instance, the discussions on a law to make it possible for people to keep their respective family names when marrying, which to date remains impossible. A struggle seemed to be going on to change common sense ideas that was highly revolutionary and would have meant that people not only change their *tatemae* attitudes towards homosexuality but also their *honne* feelings. Homosexuality as a topic was dealt with in the *omote* context. Perhaps, the economic wealth of the period provided some leeway for people to step out of line and place themselves on the spot as different from normative society.

Dumb type and Diamond Nights

While investigating these issues, I became acquainted with the academic Onitsuka Tetsurō who was also engaged in gay activities, in particular in OGC (the Osaka Gay Community). Onitsuka took me to the Diamond Nights at Club Metro in Osaka, where a number of dumb type members performed together with other drag artists. Here, I first saw people like Furuhashi Teiji, Peter Golightly, Mabuuchi Misako, Tanaka Mayumi, and a number of drag performers who were not members of dumb type—such as, for instance, Simone Fukayuki, a close friend of Teiji and famous throughout Japan as a drag performer and singer. Not long after this, Onitsuka also took me to the dumb type office where I met more of its members and for the first time briefly spoke with Teiji, now not in drag. Next door to their office in Seiwa Tennant House was Voice Gallery, which was (and still is) run by Matsuo Megumi, who also came to play a major role in the making of *S/N* and its aftermath.

These initial contacts were gradually strengthened by going to the Diamond Nights and other club parties. I also visited Voice Gallery openings, and went to parties Onitsuka hosted where dumb type members, Diamond Night performers and a variety of other people such as students and people we knew from gay networks were invited, and, in turn, also going to social gatherings hosted by the guests at these parties. The atmosphere at all these events was very open. People brought food, drinks and friends. Sexuality and personal relationships were much discussed; so, apart from being a pleasant way to spend my time, it was also very valuable for my research as I was meeting people I could interview in depth for my research project.

Undressing

In October 1992, when most of the dumb type members were away in Copenhagen, Onitsuka showed me the letter Teiji had sent to his colleagues and friends, Onitsuka included. Onitsuka was sad to learn about Teiji having developed AIDS but also said that he had been suspecting this for some time. I took the news in a kind of matter-of-fact way. Of course it was sad to learn that Teiji was not going to live very long, but, for me, people dying of AIDS had been a fact of life for some time already. I had known that he was gay before this, and it was a surprise to discover later that some dumb type members had not been aware of this fact at all, as the oral histories showed.

From then on, the parties became more frequent. As soon as the dumb type members were back in Japan, Onitsuka and I visited their office, where the first of many study meetings concerning AIDS and sexuality were held. On receiving Teiji's letter, none of dumb type's members had felt they could refuse to cooperate with Teiji's plans for *S/N*—which was still to be developed but now with Teiji as the central director. Sound and music maker Yamanaka Tōru had even been playing with the idea of quitting dumb type, but now felt that he should give Teiji and dumb type his unwavering support.

The next month, dumb type went on a European tour to perform *pH*. After this tour, things really took a turn. Meetings were held incessantly. I was present at some of the many nights in the dumb type office that were devoted to talking about creating *S/N*. Night-time was the best time for meetings, as those with day jobs could attend. We would, for instance, talk from midnight until five a.m. As dumb type members were predominantly straight, much explanation was needed to help them understand homosexuality, which was one of the reasons that Teiji asked Onitsuka and me to participate when we could. Later, he also brought in the character Alex (Ishibashi Kenjirō), who, being deaf *and* a gay person, would broaden the scope of the performance.

According to dancer/performer Peter Golightly, dumb type was ideally

> a collective and … everything was run by consensus, so there's always several levels happening at once. Being a collective, you have visual artists and lighting artists, video, the actors, the texts, and, of course, the social comment of that time. So all of this is happening, and then there is decision-making about who is going to do what and who is going to present what. And so

> working with dumb type, at one level, was endless meetings, some totally about technology. It just went way over my head.[4]

It was clear that much of the discussion about sexuality and AIDS/HIV similarly went over the heads of some of the other participants. I believe that rather than finding a general consensus about the performance, the consensus focused on agreeing to let Teiji lead.

At some point the discussion considered transcending the borderlines between the performers and the technical staff, and the desirability that everyone show themselves on stage. This also aimed at overcoming one means of exclusion. Later, this could be seen most evidently in the acts of Teiji, Peter Golightly, Alex (Kenjirō) and BuBu de la Madeleine talking about their own lives and moments in them. It can also be seen in an even more direct manner in the performers being naked on stage, as well as somewhat more abstractly in many of the acts where performers publicly investigate their feelings and what movements and sounds these feelings make them perform.

When the discussion focused more on Teiji, Alex/Kenjiro and Peter's own stories—and on their saying on stage that they were gay and HIV-positive, gay and deaf, gay and black American, respectively—was when I offered, as far as I can remember, my only input during the discussions. I felt that when talking about these personal issues to an audience, the question as to what or who the individuals in the audience were should be raised. For us, this was also a manner of overcoming exclusion, whether it be the exclusion of the audience or the exclusion of the actors by the audience. Peter resisted this idea. He thought that it would be too confrontational for most audiences and definitely for a Japanese audience. However, when, years later, I first saw the final product in 1995 in Maubeuge, France, it was Peter who said "How are you?" at the end of the first talk between Teiji, Alex and himself, after which the stage went dark and silent.

Some dumb type members remained apprehensive about the idea of undressing and baring themselves to the audience. Lighting specialist Fujimoto Takayuki said:

> In the beginning, when we started creating *S/N*, I felt, like, is it all right to make this kind of work, this way of presentation? We did the "seminar show" and took one step at a time, but can this sort of work be held up as a performance? Is this possible in Japan?[5]

It was, but the question remains whether this is still possible today and with the same amount of approval, or whether *S/N* was a product made possible in a period when Japan was relatively open and tolerant. Even at the time, the openness did not necessarily extend to the families of the performers. Teiji's own brother, for example, did not learn about *S/N* and its contents before Teiji was on his deathbed.

Inclusion

It took only four months for the performance to reach the stage in the preliminary form of the "seminar show" for *S/N*, which was staged in March 1993 in Mumonkan in Kyoto, and in Fujisawa near Tokyo. With hindsight, this was a very short period of time indeed, showing how ardently everybody had been working. The "seminar show" for *S/N* was a combination of acts that made it into *S/N*, acts that were later dropped or altered, and panel discussions by varying groups of people, discussing sexuality, AIDS and gender. I participated in the panel of two performances but I did not feel very much a part of the project. At one point, however, I did intervene when another panel member made a generalising remark about lesbian women and I began to explain how varied they also can be. The audience very rightly criticised the fact that a completely male panel was speaking on behalf of women. It was the last time I was on the panel. Instead, Japanese women were sought out to speak, as women's voices were by now seen to be lacking, and including them was another way to counter exclusion.

By this time, ongoing discussions were also held in the newly established space called Artscape, which became a community centre for people involved in the arts as well as those involved in sexual politics in an ever increasing scope. Teiji must have realised from the outset that a performance focusing on AIDS and homosexuality should not centre too much on himself only. He involved Alex, and, after ample discussion, BuBu was also given a major role. Peter had been there all along, but was now more explicit about his homosexuality.

BuBu was asked to talk about herself as a woman, whether it be in her capacity as a divorcee who had experienced marriage or in her capacity as a sex worker. As we can see, she managed to combine both. Although the sex work issue clearly takes precedence, she does not fail to relate it to her experience of being a monogamous housewife whose husband (and husband's family) expected all sorts of things from her, including sex when she did not feel like it. So, her performance in *Love Song* not only counters the exclusion of sex workers but also the position of housewives who are made to abandon their individuality in marriage in order to escape exclusion. Her act with the flags was first performed at a party called Kantsubaki (Withered Camellia) hosted by Simone Fukayuki in what was a gay pub in Osaka in December 1993, at which only invited people were present, mostly dumb type and Diamond members but also a few other friends, such as Onitsuka, Sakamoto Ryūichi and myself. At the party, all performers showed their own striptease acts created for the occasion, but after seeing BuBu's act with the flags Teiji pressed her to use it in *S/N*.

This was not the only act which transgressed the lines between the highbrow performance we were used to seeing from dumb type and that of the entirely different drag queen scene. Here, we see an example of something that belongs to *ura* (or perhaps even *angura* = underground) culture,[6] which is overlooked by "decent" people, entering the stage of *omote* (to be read here as socially accepted and arrived) culture. Drag performances themselves were quite new to Japan at the time. Beginning with the combination of Teiji Furuhashi and Simone Fukayuki in Osaka and Kyoto, it developed during the 1990s to involve hundreds of drag queens in clubs throughout the country. In *S/N*, this development was foregrounded by Teiji's drag performance.

In the final version of *S/N*, we witness a number of acts that deal with exclusion in their own manner and which are all taken from real life contexts inside and outside Japan. Yabuuchi Misako tears up her passport in desperation over all the questions she is asked by customs (exclusion based on nationality). Sunayama Norico becomes the victim of bullying by boys tying her dress above her head and leaving her standing with her pantyhose exposed (as happened at high schools in Japan at the time). And we see the homeless man living in a box, and Alex (Ishibashi Kenjirō) saying his lines: "Do not make me into a being that fits your eyes. Do not think that you understand what I am really trying to say. Do not entwine everything in your code." He then throws off his hearing aid to find some peace. These words point at the tendency of most, if not all, people to try and make sense of things they do not readily understand by fitting them to their preconceived ideas, rather than investigating them in order to understand them thoroughly in their own right. This obviously requires much less effort than trying to understand what people are actually like, but it inevitably leads to exclusion. Alex's words are an appeal for real inclusion. Throwing his hearing aid off, however, suggests that he is giving up.

Communities

After returning to Japan in December 1993, I was again invited to meetings, which by then had taken on an entirely different character, with many younger people participating in undirected discussions about AIDS/HIV, homosexuality, sex work, deaf people and people with other disabilities, transgender issues, and so forth. These talks not only took place in Artscape but also at other locations which kept being created—like Chienryō, an old student dormitory at Kyoto University where mainly people gathered to enjoy cheap drinks; and Bazar Café, a house near Doshisha University, which was more of an afternoon affair, with food sharing playing an important role. Kyoto was brimming with activity and discussions about various issues, and remained so during most of the 1990s. One of the major qualities of all this talking was that people were volunteering their most personal stories and relating them to the broader themes at hand.

This was also the case with a number of dumb type members, although not all of them participated to the same extent. When they were touring with *S/N*, they could not easily find the time to do so, and afterwards some of them lost interest. Nevertheless, activities that can be traced back to the time of the creation of *S/N* continued well after *S/N* ceased to be performed, and some continue to this day.

The most important organisations that can be related to these meetings are the AIDS-prevention organisations called DISTA, based in Osaka, and later ACTA, which was based in Tokyo. Led by friends of Furuhashi and supported by the Department of Health as well as the respective cities, they worked to provide gay people in particular with knowledge concerning HIV/AIDS and made great strides in getting people to undergo testing. Unfortunately, efforts to create a similar organisation for sex workers were less successful due to a lack of interest on the part of the authorities to provide them with funding. Already in 1996, club parties began to be organised to inform young people about sexuality and AIDS, starting with ClubLuv+ at Club Metro in Kyoto, where the Diamond Nights were also held, and later in Tokyo where they continue to this day, although they are now more focused on living together, whether with or without HIV.

The scope of these activities spread beyond Japan. In October 1998, a number of related Kyoto artists were invited to the École Supérieure des Beaux-Arts in Paris for a special exhibition of Kyoto artists called "Dounai-yannen," and in May 2004 a group of drag queens and related performers, centring around Chō Yukio and other people from ClubLuv+, as well as people engaging in AIDS activism at club parties in Tokyo, were invited to stage a number of parties in Lille, then the cultural capital of Europe. Much more research is needed to unveil the richness of the influence the creation of *S/N*, and of the many people involved in the surrounding discussions, is having on Japanese club culture, youth culture, community activity and art.

Conclusion

The performance *S/N* is a prime example of the influence art can exert on civil society and community building. A performance group that, apart from Teiji, was dominated by straight men made one of the queerest performances Japan ever gave the world. However, afterwards, it can be seen to have unqueered itself, first by members who were "different" quitting, as BuBu did, and later also by excluding members who were too "different," such as Peter Golightly and Ishibashi Kenjirō. Of course, the performances after *S/N* have important merits in their own right and are of a very high technical and theatrical quality, but it seems that dumb type, rather than continuing to address its audience with issues concerning society and people, has returned to a more distant position of contemplating issues in a highbrow manner that relates only vaguely to societies and their people. I believe artists and others who have been participating in the activities and events rooted in the discussions surrounding *S/N* are the true heirs of the work of Furuhashi Teiji and his quest for the celebration of variety and inclusion.

Notes

1 See Joy Hendry, *Becoming Japanese: The World of the Pre-School Child* (Honolulu: University of Hawaii Press, 1986).

2 These binary systems have been extensively described by many anthropologists doing work on Japan. See, for instance, Wim Lunsing, *Beyond Common Sense: Sexuality and Gender in Contemporary Japan* (London: Kegan Paul, 2001).

3 See Wim Lunsing, "Review: The Creation of the Social Category of NEET (Not in Education, Employment or Training): Do NEET Need This?," *Social Science Japan Journal* 10 (1), 2007: 105–10; and Tuukka Toivonen, '"Don't Let Your Child Become a NEET!": The Strategic Foundations of a Japanese Youth Scare," *Japan Forum* 23 (3), 2012: 407–29.

4 Conversation with the author, no date.

5 Conversation with the author, no date.

6 Underground (*angura*) culture in Japan refers predominantly to the underground art movement in the 1960s and 1970s, which had links to more politically-motivated movements such as the anti-Vietnam war movement and the anti-AMPO movement, although it remained quite independent in its artistic expression.

Teiji Furuhashi: On "Coming Out" in *S/N* (1994)

Keiko TAKEDA

S/N premiered in 1994 at the Adelaide Festival in Australia and was created after Teiji Furuhashi (1960–1995) informed his close friends about his HIV-positive status in October 1992. Much attention has been paid to this performance piece and some critics have indicated a political orientation or social criticism in *S/N*.[1] It has also been said that a non-hierarchical system operated in dumb type.

The objective of this essay is twofold: firstly, I will present how *S/N* problematised the issues of "coming out" and functioned as a medium to present the performers' "coming out" through a performance piece and in the context of the creative process. Secondly, I aim to present new evidence on how Furuhashi and *S/N* are related. Although Furuhashi has always been central in creating and producing this work, it was also a collaboration by all of the artists in the group through their flexible roles.[2] The essay is based on an analysis of the recorded performance footage,[3] on interviews with the performers,[4] and refers to media and documents related to HIV/AIDS[5] as a context for the creation of *S/N*.

Before I elaborate on "coming out," I will give a brief introduction to this work of performance art. *S/N* is part of the *S/N project,* a multimedia presentation that included a CD, a "seminar show" and installations. Hybridity, or decentralisation, is the initial characteristic of *S/N.* The elements of the performance are juxtaposed on the stage, and include texts, moving bodies, synthesised music, lighting, dialogue from the performers, and the projection of moving images. It contains at least eleven citations from other artists or researchers' earlier works or books.[6] Sometimes used as a screen, the stage set is a big white wall topped by a catwalk on which performers can move or fall down from the stage set as a choreographic effect. I will explore initially the social context in which *S/N* was created, and then discuss the issue of coming out in 1990s Japan and the risks associated with this. Finally, I relate this to the performance of *S/N.*

Japanese HIV/AIDS Discourse in the 1990s

The acronym AIDS (Acquired Immunodeficiency Syndrome) first appeared in the Japanese press in 1982. Reports talked about the spread of a "strange disease" among gay men and intravenous drug users in the United States. The first Japanese case of AIDS confirmed officially by the Japanese Ministry of Health and Welfare was a gay artist residing in New York. The mainstream discourse differentiated those "guiltlessly" infected by blood products from those infected by sexual transmission, including female sex workers and "male homosexuals." By 1993, only two other Japanese males, besides Furuhashi, who identified as homosexual had disclosed in public that they had HIV.[7] Gay magazines reported that "male homosexuals" thought they could never reveal their homosexuality, and certainly not that they were HIV positive or had AIDS. They tried to pass as "normal" (i.e. straight and HIV negative) in general society. "I want to die when I have the symptoms of AIDS" said the voice of an HIV-infected bank clerk, as reported in the gay magazine *Barazoku.*[8] *S/N* was created as a response to extreme discrimination in Japanese society. After Furuhashi revealed his HIV-positive status through a letter he wrote in 1992 to his close friends in Kyoto, the group embarked on various activities related to HIV/AIDS, art, sexuality and gender. Working from an office called Artscape in the Sakyo Ward in Kyoto, the participants in this movement, who included members of dumb type, collected AIDS posters from other countries, designed a new one, and created a special women's diary project. They planned a symposium at the International AIDS/STD Conference in Yokohama in 1994, and opened a café called the "weekend café" in order to offer a communal space where people could drop in and exchange information.[9] In his letter, Furuhashi said, "Art can be a valid means of healing the afflicted spirit of we human beings who live in contemporary society."[10] The phrase "afflicted spirit of we human beings who live in contemporary society" suggests the discrimination in the Japanese media discourse. *S/N* was created through interaction with these wider AIDS and sexuality-related activities taking place at Artscape, as well as the need to respond to the negative and misinformed reporting on the topic.

"Coming Out" as Social Change and its Risks

Furuhashi's letter relates to the idea of coming out, and indeed *S/N* and its wider arts activities spoke to the need to make AIDS-related experiences more visible and "out." In order to see how this notion was understood in Japan, I would like to review some previous arguments on coming out. Coming out can change a person's sense of identity and their relationships to others, as well as to social institutions and general culture. In Japan, coming out could mean to stand out, and this visibility and difference in a nominally group-orientated or consensus-based society has associated risks.

The sociologist J. I. Kitsuse observed that in the 1960s and 1970s, people from different minority groups began to come out—that is, declare their minority sexual and cultural identities as positive ones. Kitsuse pointed out that minorities "came out of the closet" and thereby changed the social meaning of their identity:

> They have come out to challenge conventional conceptions and judgments of their conduct, to question "expert" assessments of their disabilities, "handicaps," and devaluation of their capabilities, to reject the diagnosis of their various conditions and the attendant prescriptions for corrective treatment, and to publicly demand their rights to equal access to institutional resources.[11]

The political scientist Shane Phelan writes that coming out with a lesbian identity is "partially a process of revealing something kept hidden, but it is more than that. It is a process of fashioning a self—a lesbian or gay self—that did not exist before coming out began."[12] She names it "(be) coming out." Mark Blasius also argues that coming out is part of a process of becoming lesbian or gay, and this process is a "lifelong learning of how to become and of inventing the meaning of being a lesbian or a gay man in this historical moment."[13] Japanese gay activist Kazuya Kawaguchi agrees with these perspectives when he says, "I think the act of 'coming out' is a process of noticing 'being gay' and 'becoming gay'."[14] Critics of the idea of coming out have also suggested that becoming lesbian or gay as a goal entails being attached to a fixity of identity that forecloses the possibility of future change. Sociologist Tomoyuki Kaneta claims, "After all, the singular focus on identity (as a category) alienates the individual and risks reification of the 'I' in respect of identity politics."[15] As someone who lives within an idea of multiple identities, Kaneta argues that these cannot be reduced to a singular focus on an "I."

"Coming out" was an effective strategy for social change because by insisting on their presence in society minorities altered the meaning of the category to which they had been assigned. Nevertheless, this disclosure entails some risk because it inevitably forces the attachment of identity into a fixed category. In this sense, the arguments about coming out somewhat resemble Michel Foucault's concept of human subjection (see below).

In an interview in 1995, Furuhashi talked about his concerns about being treated only as an individual who was HIV positive:

> I don't have a primary identity. I'm just saying that being HIV-positive is not it. I want to stress this because people who get to know me let the fact that I am HIV-positive dominate our interaction. This has a particularly strong impact on people who don't have a lot of HIV-positive friends; it immediately becomes my first identity in their eyes. The point is that I don't want this to be the only criterion for how people respond to me.[16] Being an Individual Subject / Being Subjected

S/N contains quotations from an interview with Michel Foucault that was published as "De l'amitié comme mode de vie" (Friendship as a Way of Life) in 1981.[17] Foucault's work refers to new concepts of power that are not administered by a single authority, but, rather, power that is internalised and omnipresent. Accordingly, people are willing to obey without being visibly coerced by external forces. According to Foucault, we are not individual, autonomous subjects. Instead, our subjectivity is constructed by our subjugation to power. In *The History of Sexuality,* Foucault describes how one of the main institutional forces governing subjugation is the notion of confession: "The confession became one of the West's most highly valued techniques for producing truth... [noting how] truthful confession itself was inscribed at the heart of the procedures of individualization by power."[18] As an instrument of subjectivity, the power of confession spread in the nineteenth century. According to Foucault, the truthful confession "plays a part in justice, medicine, education, family relationships, and love relations."[19] *S/N* includes actions that resemble the performers' truthful confessions. These moments in the performance show the rich complexity of "telling the truth" or confessional identities.

However, when one "comes out," one must be within an existing discursive formation in order to be recognised. Hence, truthful confession can be a kind of subjection. We cannot help subjugating our diverse aspects into narrower categories, and, ironically, the strategy of coming out with one's true identity entails the risk of becoming fixed—that is, subjugated to this identity. If viewed from this perspective, *S/N* can be seen as a political process of subjection in Foucault's terms, and yet the very issue of subjection is also explored in ways that might avoid a narrowing of the discursive options.

Invention of Their Ways of Life: Analysis

By altering the expected performer–audience relationship, *S/N* problematises the act of coming out in relation to the question of subjection. It develops this through corrupting theatricality and not presenting the performers in terms of limited categories of identity. Hence, during the piece's opening scene, the performers reveal their identities to the audiences, using terms such as "HIV positive," "homosexual," "Japanese," "American" and "deaf." These labels are attached to the suits the performers are wearing. Peter Golightly, who is African-American, says, in English, that each identification is true and then asks the audience to think about their own sense of identity. The scene enacts an idea of coming out because, in the social context, people infected with HIV rarely reveal this fact. The audience, which may have expected a fictional story, might feel anxious because they are confronted with the truth of the performers' existence. Confession, or revealing oneself, needs a receiver just as a confessor needs a priest. Thus, the audience must acknowledge the confession in this case. The mode of direct address works to break down the barrier between audience and performer. Viewers must acknowledge the performers and in so doing they begin to think reflexively about themselves.

As Golightly says in the scene, "I'm sorry to tell you but we are not actors. We are this" (pointing to the labels on each of the suits). Tei-chan (Furuhashi) says with a cynical tone, "Probably no one's sure what's real here or not anyway. Or, perhaps you all came here to escape from that kind of reality?" The act of showing themselves as "real" homosexuals, as HIV positive or deaf is important in relation to the question of subjection. The performers insist these are their "true" identities. However, as they are also on the stage, the confession of truth can be read as a fiction. This sense of passing back and forth between moments of truth and untruth is at the heart of the idea of confession because the truth being confessed has *become* the truth by the very act of confession. In other words, the truth is constructed.

In this scene, the performers corrupt *S/N's* theatricality and change the expected performer–spectator relationship, therefore differentiating the performer's actions from the truthful confession. Moreover, by displaying multiple identity labels on the costumes and then drawing attention to the fluid reality of this situation (we are this, but we are also that), this scene avoids the risks associated with an essentialist view of coming out.

This theme is also prominently addressed in Scene 5 of *S/N* that is actually titled "Coming Out." In this scene, Alex (Kenjiro Ishibashi), who is hearing- and speaking-impaired, declares: "Here's my discipline to fit the codes of the world. The violence of signals so plain to my eyes. I do not depend on your love/sex/death/life, I invent my own death/life." This declaration reveals that Alex does not want a limited, categorised identity, but instead wants to invent his own life by avoiding acts of categorisation. His pronunciation is difficult to understand, which raises the related questions of language and communication. Moreover, in terms of Alex's action and movement, he does not use sign language, and the way he opens his mouth is not typical of a deaf person who has undertaken training at a school for the hearing- and speech-impaired. Alex, as Ishibashi, has invented his way to communicate with others.[20] I have mentioned that coming out carries the risk of confession, and is a form of subjection to power. Alex's movements and pronunciation lead the spectator to think about the invention of subjectivity and identity. Alex's action and voice embodies the being that is not withdrawn by the stereotypic form of representation of deaf people.

Judith Butler notes, on the issue of censorship and hate speech, that

"The declaration that is 'coming out' is certainly a kind of act, but it does not fully constitute the referent to which it refers."[21] She claims:

> Though that referent cannot be finally named, it must be kept separate from what is nameable, if only to guarantee that no name claims finally to exhaust the meaning of what we are and what we do, an event that would foreclose the possibility of becoming more and different than what we have already become, in short, foreclose the future of our life within language, a future in which the signifier remains a site of contest, available to democratic rearticulation.[22]

Butler emphasises the importance of the possibility of our becoming a different being within language. Because Alex does not use the specific categories, he can avoid having his identities fixed further, although Butler does not dismiss categorisation.[23]

In *Gender Trouble* (1990), Butler says that "identity" itself is constructed performatively as an effect that results from action. Furthermore, the citation and the reiteration of its act inevitably generate a "version" of identity, and that means subversion of existing discursive formation and identity itself. The reiteration of the act does not need "will" or "subject" as a precondition.[24] Butler's argument resembles the problematisation of "subjection" in *S/N*. It opens up Alex's identities to changeability.

S/N suggests no state is completely free from the power of subjection or categorisation. In Scene 1, figures in underwear on top of the white wall cry out, "I dream my gender will disappear. I dream my nationality will disappear. I dream my blood will disappear. I dream my race will disappear. I dream my style will disappear." This text is also projected on the wall. In Scene 6, the same text is projected on the wall. In this scene, the performers remove their underwear and dive off the top of the wall. The text and divested underwear symbolise the freedom from categorisation and autonomous subjectivity; the falling bodies, pulled downward by gravity, suggest that power is ever present.

The difficulty in erasing identities is also evident in Scene 3. A Japanese woman speaking strangely accented English is stopped at a passport control because she cannot prove her identity, which neither can be proven by the parts of her body. She shows the audience her eyes, ears and the inside of her skirt with the micro-camera. Finally, she tears up her passport and asks, "Can I quit? Asian female?"[25] Her question shows the difficulty of abandoning or removing identities that already exist and are fixed with the body.

It could be said that the subjection issue dealt with in *S/N* not only pertains to minorities, such as homosexuals or people with AIDS, but to "ordinary" people as well. In Scene 4 and at the beginning of Scene 5, a quotation from the interview with Foucault (*Friendship as a Way of Life*, 1981) is projected on the wall: "We should do our best to become gay, there is no need to insist on seeing ourselves as homosexual beings." Although Foucault explicitly refers to homosexuality, this text can be applied to almost everyone. In the same interview, Foucault states, "To be 'gay,' I think, is not to identify psychological traits and visible masks of the homosexuals but to try to define and develop a way of life." For Foucault, being gay is not being part of a homogeneous tribe, "gay" means people who try to create their being. Even a heterosexual can be "gay" if he/she defines and develops a way of life. The message of *S/N* is about all of our daily lives, and is not applied only to minorities.

The scenes described here illustrate that, like Alex, although we cannot run away from the power of subjection and categorisation,[26] we do have chances to change in the future.

Teiji Furuhashi as "Adjuster"

Finally, this essay examines the relationship between *S/N* and Furuhashi using new evidence of how Furuhashi functioned in *S/N*, and how *S/N* functioned as a medium to present performers' coming out through a performance work. Following the discussion above of the issue of coming out and identity in Scene 5, how, I ask, does Furuhashi function in *S/N* in order to accommodate flexibility of identity, which makes the coming out effective?

I previously suggested that *S/N* problematises some effects of coming out and celebrates the undecidability or flexibility of one's identity. However, if Alex's distorted voice isn't perfectly understood, then, as it is in the pre-linguistic domain, *S/N* cannot convey the meaning of the utterance. Furthermore, if identity itself becomes too unstable, then one will have other problems. Some criticisms of Judith Butler's "performativity" of identity note that subversion of identity cannot have a goal, as it may demerit the very person who acts subversively because one cannot estimate orientation by oneself.[27] Such arguments indicate that the fluidity or flexibility of identity as represented in *S/N* also have another problem. I suggest a solution to this, which Teiji Furuhashi himself embodies.

In scene 5, Alex does not present his identity with fixed categories or obvious pronunciation, but spectators understand what he is saying by reading captions projected onto the stage setting (a white wall). Based on some new evidence, it became obvious that Furuhashi chose and combined multiple citations of existing works or scenes that were created by other members, as all of dumb type's members contributed to the creation of *S/N*.[28] Furuhashi did, however, retain some control over the creation of the piece; he also created the text that Alex utters in Scene 5, and because Furuhashi's words are actually projected, the meaning is conveyed to the spectators. Moreover, the performer's lines or acts are almost decided; that is to say, the aim of the performance can be anticipated to a certain extent, but the probability is low that S/N became the cause of censure of a subversive act. I would also like to avoid acknowledging that Alex was exploited as a tool by Furuhashi, because Furuhashi, and even Alex himself, cannot completely control the actions of Alex. As Shoshana Felman indicates, bodily actions can say more and may speak differently than they mean to.[29] Alex's utterances themselves are based on bodily actions, such as the movements of his throat, tongue, jaw, and so on. His performance is constructed by bodily actions. Thus, the performance itself can subvert the will or intention of performer or director.

To some extent, Furuhashi "pins down" meanings of words and Alex's identity. It is my view that adjustment is important in order to "come out" effectively. Furuhashi makes identities flexible, while at the same time "pinning down," or fixing, identity. When one "comes out," identity should not be either too fixed or too flexible.

To summarise, I have examined how *S/N* functioned as a medium of coming out, and the role of Teiji Furuhashi both in and through the performance piece. Furuhashi acted as a mediator on coming out (in enabling the sense of adjustment, above) and because of that, coming out in a work of performance was effective as a form of social reform. Firstly, as a medium of coming out, *S/N* problematises the power of "subjection" and celebrates the flexibility or undecidability of identity. Secondly, *S/N* can convey meaning to the spectators, and reveal the presence of a new kind of "way of life" and does not become a cause of demerit for the performer who acts subversively. *S/N* opened up a new possibility of coming out and social reform, and suggested a changeable future both practically and concretely.

Notes

1 See, for example, Hidenaga Ōtori, "Igyou kara isou he" (From Freak to Transvestite), in *Onna? Nihon? Bi?* (Woman? Japan? Beauty?), ed. Takaaki Kumakura and Kaori Chino (Tokyo: Keio Daigaku Shuppankai, 1999), pp. 221–38; Takaaki Kumakura, "Damutaipu: ai = koutuu to shit-eno shintai he" (Dumb type – to the body as love=traffic). *Datu-geishutu/datu-shihonshugiron: kitarubeki "koufukugaku" no tameni* (Post Art/Post Capitalism: For the Coming "Study of Well-Being") (Tokyo: Keio Art Center, 2000), pp. 100–18; Yasuko Ikeuchi, *Jyoyu no tanjyo to shuuen* (The Birth and End of an Actress) (Tokyo: Heibonsha, 2008); and Sohei Yamada, "Shimin shakai to hyougen no kanousei-dumb type niyoru S/N" (The Possibility of Expression in Civil Society: *S/N* Created by *Dumb type*), in *Jyendaa to Jiyuu* (Gender and Liberty), ed. Miura Reiichi and Hayasaka Shizuka (Tokyo: Sairyusha, 2013), pp. 269–92.

2 My doctoral dissertation indicates ways various authors' contributions, including Furuhashi's, are manifested in *S/N,* and examines Furuhashi's contribution to the performance as a specific "author" rendering Foucault's "four functions of author." This essay focuses on a part of that work.

3 The recording of the performance is edited by Shiro Takatani (1995). Dumb type Ltd. and WOWOW share the copyright. I refer to it as "performance/text #1" in *Theater Arts* 1 (Dumb type, "Performance/ Text #1," *Theatre Arts* 1, 1994: 176–91).

4 I would like to express my appreciation to all the people interviewed.

5 The material I have used includes articles, printed magazines, newspapers and the historical documents related to HIV/AIDS held at the Japanese Ministry of Health, Labour and Welfare.

6 Keiko Takeda, "S/N (1994) ni okeru Furuhashi Teiji" (Teiji Furuhashi on S/N [1994]), unpublished PhD dissertation, Ochanomizu University, 2013.

7 See Keiko Takeda, "1990 nendai nihon ni okeru HIV/eizu wo meguru taikou-kureimu no retorikku-bunseki" (The Analysis of the Rhetoric and Counterclaim on HIV/AIDS in 1990s Japan), *Nenpoh shakaigaku-ronshu* (The Annual Review of Sociology) 24, 2011: 121–32.

8 Takeshi Sayama, "Anotoki yamete ireba" (If I Stopped Then), *Barazoku,* 1993, p. 241; translation by the author.

9 Takeda, "S/N (1994) ni okeru Furuhashi Teiji."

10 Teiji Furuhashi, "Furuhashi Teiji no atarashi jinnsei-HIV kannsenn happyo wo iwatte [For Celebration of Teiji Furuhashi's infection with HIV]," *Memorandum teiji furuhashi,* ed. Dumb type (Tokyo: Little More, 2000), pp. 36–43, p. 42.

11 J. I. Kitsuse, "Coming out all over," *Social Problems* 28 (1), 1980: 1–13, p. 3.

12 Shane Phelan, "(Be)Coming Out: Lesbian Identity and Politics," *Signs: Journal of Women in Culture and Society* 18 (4), 1993: 765–90, p. 774.

13 Mark Blasius, "An Ethos of Lesbian and Gay Existence," *Political Theory* 20 (4), 1992: 642–71, p. 665.

14 Kazuya Kawaguchi, 'Kenmei ni gei ni narukoto-shutai, teikou, sei no yousiki" (Becoming Gay with Efforts: Subject, Resistance, and Way of Sexuality), *Gendai shisou* 25 (3), 1997: 186–94, p. 190.

15 Tomoyuki Kaneta, "Sexuality kenkyu no konnann" (The Difficulty of Sexuality Studies), in *Cyouhatu suru sekushuarithi: hou shakai sisou heno apuroti* (Provocative Sexuality), ed. Osamu Seki and Tetsuyuki Shida (Tokyo: Shinsensha, 2009), pp. 223–58, p. 240.

16 Carol Lufty, "Interview with Teiji Furuhashi," *Assembly International,* 1995, http://www.assembly-international.net/Interviews/html/teiji%20furuhashi.html. (accessed 2 February 2017).

17 Michel Foucault, "De l'amitié comme mode de vie," *Le Gai Pied* 25, April 1981: 38–39.

18 Michel Foucault, *The History of Sexuality: The Will to Power* [1976] (London: Penguin Books, 2006), pp. 58–59.

19 Ibid., p. 59.

20 Kenjiro Ishibashi, personal communication, 2013.

21 Judith Butler, *Excitable Speech: A Politics of the Performative* (London and New York: Routledge, 1997), p. 125.

22 Ibid.

23 The identity labels attached to the surface of the outfits in the "Opening talk" scene also indicate the unessentialised identities indicated in Butler's argument.

24 See Judith Butler, *Gender Trouble* (London and New

York: Routledge, 1990). J. L. Austin actually coined the term "performativity" and Butler developed the use of the term in her work on performing gender. Here I use "performativity" after Erika Fischer-Lichte, who writes in *The Transformative Power of Performance:* "The aesthetics of the performative ... concerns itself with the appearance of people and things, not with illusion; it concerns itself with the ephemerality of their appearance and not with life's transience. It identifies performances not as allegory and image of human life but both as human life in itself and simultaneously as its model" (*The Transformative Power of Performance*, trans. Saskya Jain [New York: Routledge, 2008], p. 205). Peter Eckersall introduced Japanese cultural conditions from the 1960s to the present as this kind of "performative" situation in his *Performativity and Event in 1960s Japan: City, Body, Memory* (New York and Basingstoke, Hampshire: Palgrave Macmillan, 2013). For more about Butler's "performativity" argument in performance studies, see Yuichiro Takahashi, "Yakusha atogaki (Afterword)," *Pafuomansu kenkyu* (Performance Studies), trans. Yuichiro Takahashi (Kyoto: Jinbun shoin, 1998), pp. 289–306.

25 This section is not grammatically correct. I think the female performer's incorrect English pronunciation or grammar portrays "noise."

26 I also indicate the connection between inventing our way of life and relating to others. In Scene 5, Alex says, "I invent our love/sex with you." In the next scene, "Blood Exchange," two performers cut each other's arms and put their wounds together. These two examples suggest relationships. Alex intends to invent his way of life, to have an orientation to relationships with others. To put wounds together symbolises a close bond, like a pledge of brotherhood; however, it also exposes them to danger from infection, especially during the AIDS era. This suggests that making new relationships is, in fact, extremely dangerous. During Scene 5, text is projected on the set, a quotation from *Friendship as a Way of Life*, which says, "They ('gays') must invent yet undefined relations A-to-Z. Relations such as constitute friendship" (from Michel Foucault, "De l'amité comme mode de vie." See dumb type, *S/N*, Kyoto: dumb type, 1995, p. 18). We construct our identities as reflections of our relationships to others and vice versa (see Anthony Giddens *Modernity and Self-Identity: Self and Society in the Late Modern Age* [Stanford: Stanford University Press, 1991], pp. 77–78). Inventing undefined relationships leads to the invention of one's own ways of life. *S/N* invites us to unknown relations and unknown selves.

27 See, for example, Maiko Odaira, *Onna ga onna wo enjiru* (Women Perform Women) (Tokyo: Shinyosha, 2008).

28 See Keiko Takeda, "Dumbtype ni yoru performance S/N (1994) ni okeru innyou no youtai" (The Citations and the Structure of Performance S/N [1994] Created by Dumb type), *Enngekigau Ronshu* (Journal of Japanese Society for Theatre Research) 58, 2014: 73–89.

29 Shoshana Felman, *The Literary Speech Act: Don Juan with J.L. Austin in Two Languages,* trans. Catherine Porter (Ithaca: Cornell University Press, 1983).

Dumb Type's *S/N* and the Archive of Kyoto in the 1990s

Shinya YAMAKI (Archive for the Creation Project)

Dumb type was founded in 1984 by students from Kyoto City University of Arts. The members of the group came from diverse fields such as architecture, fine arts, design, music or dance. Their multimedia performances, *pH* (1990), *S/N* (1994), *OR* (1997), *memorandum* (1999), *Voyage* (2002), and their installations, have been presented all over the world. The group currently continues their activities from their base in Kyoto.

S/N is the name of a project begun by dumb type around 1990. It started life under the key terms of "signal/noise" and included an installation, but it quickly developed after dumb type's central member Teiji Furuhashi wrote about his HIV/AIDS infection in a letter to his close friends in October 1992. The first production of *S/N* was presented in March 1994 at the Adelaide Festival in Australia, and before Furuhashi's death in October 1995 it was shown in twelve other countries and sixteen cities, receiving great responses. After he died, it went on to be staged in a further five countries and six cities. In the early 1990s, the *News 23* television programme host Tetsuya Chikushi launched a special programme on "Life and Death in a Certain Performance – Perspectives after HIV." I still have a clear memory of being deeply shocked by the questions "How are you?" and "And you?" in the extracts that were shown from the stage performance. The programme was talking about Teiji Furuhashi, and it was my first encounter with him and with *S/N*.

After seeing the programme, I organised a screening of a recording of *S/N* and a lecture meeting under the title "Teiji Furuhashi, the Message of the 12th Year – How Are You?" at Kyoto Seika University's media centre in 2007. To further reflect on the questions that came up during this event, I hosted regular screenings of *S/N* once a week throughout the year 2008. In addition, *S/N*, an important work in the international history of the fine arts that expresses the tense relation between individual memory and public memory through the body, became one of the topics of a joint research project between Kingston University in London and Kyoto Seika University, from 2008 to 2010. In 2009, I held two public symposiums in the UK and Japan, "What Has Not Been Told about *S/N*," in January, and "Love Song for the Future" in November. I also organised the exhibition "LIFE with ART – Catch and Then and Over" (curated by Shinya Yamaki with participation and assistance from Tomohisa Sato, Keiko Takeda, Hiromasa Tomari, Wim Lunsing and BuBu de la Madeleine) in the Kyoto Seika University Gallery in the following year. "*S/N* and Kyoto in the 1990s" was the first of the two parts of the exhibition and presented a display of oral history interviews on video with some related materials. By searching out memories and materials related to the artistic and social conditions of this special period, materials that were about to be lost, I aimed to make the situation in these years comprehensible for those who did not experience them. I also wanted to show some evidence for the relationship of art and society at that time by turning attention to Kyoto in the 1990s and the atmosphere that gave rise to such an overwhelmingly powerful and expressive performance as *S/N*.

It is only as memories of that time that we can know what was interesting about the period. In creating an archive that focuses on oral history and documentary evidence, I have attempted to collect materials from various different angles, where one has to look for points of contact between "interest and "memory." These materials exemplify memories of the past, and preserving them is of great importance in order to pass on what is interesting about that period, and about what could be called "its heated atmosphere," to the next generation. When we think about the society of the future, it makes sense to do this. The message of *S/N* is still an effective one today, and therefore I believe that it is important to continue the work on this project.

Amateurism

Inside Dumb Type

YOSHIDA Miya

In the mid-1980s, the Kyoto-based artists' group dumb type sensationally emerged with a performative approach focusing on the aesthetics of the information age. They adopted concepts and methods in their work such as sampling, copying, shuffling and other practices used in computing, and the specific logic of computer games, such as life simulations—long before a buzzword like "gamification" was hyped. Actively using diverse media and technologies at the intersection of performance, visual and sound arts, they succeeded in developing an epistemologically charged form of reflecting the aesthetics of their time.

Prototypes of what was to become dumb type, and the character of their projects, were formulated at a very early stage. After their first two performances, *Praise of the Manner of the Health* and *Addition of Starfish* (1984), the group experimented within a work-in-progress mode between 1984 to 1988 and developed the works: *Plan for Sleep*, the installation *036 Pleasure Life* (1987) and *Pleasure Life* (1988). After three years, their work was already expressly produced for international audiences and gained worldwide recognition. Their use of media technologies—such as video, slideshows, copy machines, monitors, flash lights—and distinctive televisual aesthetics as well as the digital elements of the grid, numbers, the viewpoint of the spectacle and repetition in the combination of human bodies, led them to be widely seen as a promising artistic project. The performing bodies, both visible and invisible in their performances and the installations, were frequently used as a means of objectifying everyday experiences and of visualising the tensions brought about by information technologies. For a rapidly growing audience, they made immediate sense with their ambitiously far-reaching project that had a considerable impact not only on the performance scene but also on artistic explorations of contemporary collective production processes.

This essay considers the performance piece *S/N* (1992–96), which constituted a turning point as well as being at the end of the early activities of the first phase of the group's work from 1984 to 1996). In paying attention to a whole dimension of the project, including its production process, the eponymous installation, a series of lectures, and the performance, this essay introduces the notion of the amateur as a contemporary perspective on *S/N*.

* * *

SIGNAL/NOISE
SOME/NONE
SOMA/NOOS
SOUTH/NORTH
SOCIETY/NATURE
SIGN/NAME
STATE/NATION
SYSTEM/NETWORK
SENSE/NONSENSE
SCIENCE/NECROMANCY
SAMPLE/NARRATIVE
SELF/NEIGHBOUR
SYNAPSE/NERVE
SCENARIO/NEWS
SATELLITE/NUCLEUS
SPEED/NEWNESS
SEX/NEUTER
SAFETY/NEWNESS
SOLAR/NOCTURNAL

SURRENDER/NEUTRALISE
STRAIGHT/NARROW
SHAKESPEARE/NEWTON
STOCKING/NECKTIE
SEQUENCE/NEXT
SCRIPT/NOTATION
SORT/NUMBER
SCALE/NORM
SERVO/NANO
SLAVE/NYMPHO
STYLE/NAKED
SIMULACRUM/NOUMENON
SLOPPY/NEAT
SKYSCRAPER/NATIVE
SPUTNIK/NASA
/NOSTALGIA
SHOTGUN/NEEDLE
SIN/
SURFACE/

(From a poster used for dumb type's first installation, 1993)

* * *

Above is a long list of words taken from a poster for dumb type's first installation titled *S/N*. It coupled words starting with S and N in capital letters. The list also shows the wide range of the group's members' interests, from postmodern and poststructural theory and cybernetics to gender, technology, science and cosmology. The installation was devised as a conceptual exploration of *S/N* (signal/noise) by the group and encompassed a search for what is conceptualised as "outside" of the system and as a localisation of the idea of border. The project asked what (ab)normalism is—what has (not) been produced and (not) reproduced in the decisive moments of decay of the "bubble economy."

* * *

01: EVOLUTION/INVENTION

Sound of electronic signal beats in a regular rhythm, while a dot of light runs from left to right rapidly and repetitively on the background.

"Too much is made of learning by listening, when all this noise interferes with actual knowing. Why should we lend you our ears? We demand the wisdom of silence. It may be what everyone is saying, but who is spreading the word?"

"Pitiful senile mutterings"
"Hysterical bitchy grips"
"Naïve boyish fantasies"
"Raving idiot screams"

Rhythmical beats (in a style like that of Steve Reich) begin.

"conspiracy of silence"
"conspiracy of science"
"conspiracy of scientia"

"Silence, manipulated through learning. All too soon decay. Each words, voiced, or not, begin to stifle, pollute, and so to suffocate, to violate ourselves. Nostrils quivering against the stench. Those with open mouth are – soundly thrashed lest they utter a sound."

The light of the signal moves from left to right, flashing occasionally. A man wearing a black suit bent over and walking on his hands and feet is in the corner.

"Those possessed by the desire for knowledge lack curiosity. Nothing left they can invent.
Intellect addicts, hooked in their noble habit, remain incurable. Humans didn't always exist, nor will we exist forever … which is why we must invent."

Projections of female and male torsos appear. Images are framed as if viewing through a round lens, with a blue colour filter and overlaid with grids that appear and disappear as in a scanning movement.

A woman stands naked, wearing only a pair of white socks, her face and lower body marked black to prevent them from being seen. A man stands naked, wearing only a pair of white socks, his face and lower body are also covered. Words are projected on the screen and the naked wo/man appear in turn under the spotlight. A woman touches her body, a man touches his body.

"conspiracy of silence"

"conspiracy of science"

In the darkness, two women in white slips are dancing: one with a pair of white socks, another with bare feet. They dance like broken marionettes, showing the lower parts of their bodies in underwear. A man rolls down. A man runs back and forth. A man walks on all fours, with underwear in his mouth. Juxtaposition of projected images, words, actual bodies that move around on stage. In the chaos, men disappear, with the sound of a demonstration speech from a megaphone.

All the sounds are elevated and overlapped. A flashing light accelerates at speed to reach to a climax. All the human bodies appear only as shadows. Their movement becomes like a kinetoscopic image in black and white. The abstraction of reality turns into images where the imaginary grows.

* * *

Looking back to the 1980s and 1990s, the use of a wide variety of media may already sound like the classic line "when old technologies were new"[1] and even convey a weirdly nostalgic sense of technological progress. In the field of technology it is unavoidable that ongoing development and regular updates are required, yet the conceptual thinking behind the use of media does not age as quickly as the technological advances do. Both dumb type's performances and their media installations addressed a fundamental shift in social structures, the shift from disciplinary societies to societies of control, which Gilles Deleuze has called societies of "dividuals."[2] This idea/factor appears to be increasingly relevant to consider today. Targeting such a transformation, Deleuze pointed out that contemporary mechanisms of control are no longer based on surveillance of individuals and controlling individual choices and preferences. The signs of this form of control, such as signature and identity, have been replaced by the mechanisms of "code" and "password" in order to access information in contemporary society. Referring to the emergence of this new reality, dumb type's performances and installations employed a different relationship between subject, object and the surrounding society, and produced a new visual language.

Such a "dividualisation" in a culture of "datafication"—or, rather, in a data-producing society—was more distinctively expressed in the performance and installation pieces that were to follow under the title *pH* (1990–92). In a way, this was a (re)presentation of the aesthetics of data processing. In a society of "dividuals," performance was, and maybe still is, the most suitable medium for the juxtaposition of technologies and bodies (of performer and audience) within the same temporal space. Koyamada Toru, one of the founders and a core member of dumb type until 1997, reflected on the smooth flow of digital aesthetics:

> In the production process, the group members shared sweat, time, laughs, and many other things. When the work is digitalised and transferred into another form of media, all this shared experience in the work is processed as data. In such a datafication, in digitalisation, the sense of reality is multiplied into the one of realities which are not sharing the same sense of reality any more that I felt before.[3]

Koyamada's words express his diagnosis of a datafication of the individual by its digital multiplication, which means a transformation to "dividuals" with respect to subjecthood. In this view, all experiences and emotions, such as suffering, joy, excitement and even love, are nothing else than data, or "code" in Deleuze's sense, and pervasive throughout all social apparatuses.

* * *

06: BLOOD EXCHANGE

A heterosexual couple stand facing each other. With a piece of chalk, Alex draws a circle on the floor. A man cuts his wrist and blood spurts out. A woman does the same. They touch their wrists together.

SEX MONEY DEATH LOVE LIFE

A strong vertical line of light moves horizontally, like a scanner. It illuminates men and women who are standing and scans their bodies, they scream and run around in the dark. Taking off their clothes, they fall down, disappearing one by one.

I dream… my gender disappears
I dream… my nationality disappears
I dream… my blood disappears
I dream… my rights disappear
I dream… my worth disappears
I dream… my common sense disappears
I dream… my property disappears
I dream… my lifestyle disappears
I dream… my fear disappears
I dream… my duty disappears
I dream… my authority disappears
I dream… my power disappears

* * *

Shocked by the violent encounter with AIDS that had struck the group's leader, Furuhashi Teiji, the core issue in *S/N* became strongly focused on AIDS and related social issues. Living and working together as members of the group in a community, which included Furuhashi, to the point of sharing both work and life, dumb type quickly transcended the role of being just another performance group in the cultural scene. The shared experience did not only remain within the group, but also functioned as a catalyst to transcend the group aesthetics taking questions of identity politics into the public sphere. The group confronted this experience and began to cultivate its trajectory, accepting the facts and consequences of the illness by engaging in the situation as much as possible, and seeking the notions of its own truth, which does not necessarily follow the norms, classification or process constructed and justified by the systems of science and the social institution. Learning about the social problems surrounding AIDS, about the discrimination and the medical problems such as the side effects, the support system turned dumb type into social activists that include a theatre producer, a gallerist, professors, doctors, nurses, social activists, artists, students and others. Discussions developed that covered gender, sex, and notions of life in general. As becomes visible in journals such as *Critical Space* (published by Asada Akira and Karatani Kōjin),[4] the 1990s marked an active period of critical discourse in Japan. Dumb type perceived the emergence of such modes of social interaction and reacted accordingly, and gave them a specific form as they did in their project *S/N*. In a metaphysical perspective, *S/N* represented the notion of "subjectivity" in the sense of the term developed by Felix Guattari and Suely Rolnik, "not situated in the individual field but in every process of social and materialised production."[5]

* * *

00: OPENING TALK

A man (Alfred Birnbaum) on stage in a black suit bends his body to the ground; he wears a pair of black gentleman's shoes on his feet and a pair of high heels on his hands. He walks around on all fours like a clumsy donkey. He looks just like everybody else in the street, apart from his strange posture and the noises he makes. Another man (Teiji Furuhashi) in a green suit comes in with a microphone and asks the man what he is doing, with rather exaggerated movements of mouth and body. He answers and the second man translates his words. He was dancing the tango; it is not easy to dance tango alone, as it is a dance meant for two. Stickers are applied on his body that read "deaf," "Japanese," "male." On the back of the other man, we read "Japanese," "male," "HIV+" and "homosexual."

The second man asks: "What does 'normal' mean? Who decides what 'normal' is?"

The third man (Peter Golightly) comes in. The stickers on his jacket say "black," "American," "homosexual," "gay." He asks the audience: "How about you?"

* * *

S/N begins with the opening dialogue described above. The installation shifted in its format to become a "seminar show" for *S/N*,[6] which meant there was a series of lectures and discussions about AIDS, with guests such as medical experts, social activists, and many others. This became the open production process for what eventually developed into the *S/N* performance and facilitated a significant involvement of non-members in the group's productions. During the seminars, the idea of a dialogue between performer and audience came up as the extension of a feedback system, in order to further develop the familiar understanding of performance art as well as social activities that were outside the art world. The production process of *S/N* was to create new forms and a new space for dialogue. Such a process needed to look outside of existing systems to find a concrete practice-oriented application of conceptual thinking and doing that enacts an active rejection of biopolitical governance as outlined by Michel Foucault.[7] In this way they questioned accepted categories and norms that are bounded to a system of professionalisation, that did nothing to respond to the actual needs of the people who suffer from AIDS.

In their studies of "molecular revolution" in Brazil,[8] Guattari and Rolnik saw the individual as a terminal of co-emergent subjectivities, an idea that focused on the question of how subjectivity could be reimagined as a site of flows and intensities. *S/N* appropriated this sense of oscillation, between sender and receiver in this instance. Subsequently, they adopted a feedback system into the production process that showed how the experience of individuals could be theorised as a co-emergence of subjectivities. It was Furuhashi who brought in the issue of AIDS to the process and in this way decisively influenced the other members of the group. However, following Guattari's line of thought, the group was not just a collection of individual subjectivities. Rather, dumb type gave form to the co-emergence of subjectivities in Japanese society that could be experienced in the early 1990s. In other words, *S/N* functioned as a site of subjectification within contemporary society—and may still do so for those who see the work today—as it encourages its audiences to reconsider the modes developed in normalism and professionalism that, due to their authorised and institutional relation to economy, are bound to the structure of societies of control. *S/N* strongly presents the acquisition and cultivation of one's own path outside of such control structures, in order to gain other forms of social imaginaries.

* * *

05: COMING OUT

Alfred Birnbaum stands still in front of a microphone, saying:
"I don't know what you're saying, but I know what you mean.
I don't depend on your love (sex). I invent my own love (sex) with you.
Here's my discipline to fit the codes of the world. The violence of signals so plain to my eyes."

BuBu de la Madeleine is running, rolling on the floor, and dancing alone.

"I don't know what you're saying, but I know what you mean.
I don't depend on your life (death). I invent my own life (death) with you
Here's my discipline to fit the codes of the world. The violence of signals so plain to my eyes."

Bubu is running, rolling on the floor, dancing and jumping in Alfred Birnbaum's direction. He catches her and they dance together.

"I don't know what you're saying, but I know what you mean. Here's my discipline to fit the codes of the world. The violence of signals so plain to my eyes. Don't turn us into abstractions you'd like to see. Where is the imagination to cut across borders? Noise flowing through my body … blood, information, meanings … indecipherable noise thrust on me from all your voices up to now. Building up here inside, indecipherable. Now at least, I let them go."

Using a microphone, Alex lets out a howling sound.

SEX MONEY DEATH LOVE LIFE

* * *

In many ways, *S/N* marked a turning point in the life of dumb type; a turning point for its manner of conceptual thinking, its choice of and focus on a theme, on group structure, production processes and the lifestyles of the group members. After these changes, art and life, aesthetics and politics emerged into one as *S/N*, embracing beauty. Beauty is, in a sense, not thought and experienced as a quality of the art object, but as a matter of the bodily senses: "The bodily experience of the other. There is something inherent in this otherness: an element of surprise, perhaps but much more so a sense of opening oneself up to the experience, or sensing the invasion of self by some other, be it thought or sense experience."[9]

A number of the critical assessments of *S/N* have referred to the contrast between the strong, impressive impact dumb type made with its use of technology and new media, and the amateurish performance.[10] As Sara Jansen shows (see her essay in this volume), the focus of such a critique is based on the classical tradition of a "quality" of beauty in objects, techniques and skills, and the dichotomy of "professional" vs. "amateur" is adopted in this criticism. The prototypical expression of dumb type as media-cool-technology is professional and the elusion of the body of others was understood under the notion of the "amateur" and amateurism in the 1990s. That view could easily miss a fundamental question within the conceptual focus of their work.

In this association with a modernist dichotomy of professional vs. amateur, such a critique may certainly provoke negative connotations, i.e. when the performance is referred to as being "amateurish." Even so, such a clear distinction and presupposition between notions of professional and amateur is highly questionable. Historically, the notion of the "amateur" is defined based on such a modernist dichotomy, but the opposed notions of "amateur" and "professional" are actually like two sides of the same coin. It means that they not only oppose each other but also reaffirm a shared space created in historical modernism. Certainly, under the influence of different cultural and technological revolutions in different parts of the world, the ethos of the amateur has been socially and economically co-opted thousands of times. It is neither simply one of the dilettante, nor of devotion to a cause or practice. In recent decades, the idea of the amateur has been continually reconstructed by an all-encompassing global industry of images, objects and services as the very epitome of "creative thinking," "solution-oriented management" and "innovation." In this emphatic sense, we can now speak of "professional amateurs," while "amateurish professional" still retains a negative sense. Therefore, amateurs are no longer those cultural figures whose "pure" and selfless love for particular objects or arts set them aside from other social groups. It also cannot place them in opposition to professionals who were "only in it for the money." In the course of the twentieth century, amateurs have become representatives of a cultural ideal, standing in for everything that one was ready to accept as "independent-minded," "not corrupt," "ethically sound," "offbeat" and "innovative."

The notion of the "amateur" marks a distinctive shift in the field of modern cultural production. Formerly fixed boundaries between "professional" and "amateur" are no longer easily pinned down. *S/N* succeeds in situating itself in the centre of these entangled boundaries. The emphasis on the specific aesthetics of *S/N* lies within the permeable quality of the two. In other words, *S/N* is a performance piece that sets out to "fail beautifully to achieve professionalization, and is wide open to the LOVE of the amateur."[11] *S/N* is a work of love that includes the notion of friendship—romantic, political, narcissistic, vulnerable and caring—not only to Furuhashi specifically but also, more widely and as far as possible, to those who might be reachable. At another level, the way that dumb type tackled the issues of AIDS was a labour of love, in confronting something unknown, unforeseeable and perhaps, in the end, unsolvable. I therefore propose using the term "amateurism" in order to understand the works—both the production and the process.

* * *

02: LOVE SONG

Sounds of dissonance, Peter Golightly stands right, at the corner, beginning to talk about love and sex and asking the audience how love songs deal with "love" and "make love."

"What is a 'love song' in modern society? What will it be like in the future?"

Teiji Furuhashi, in a green suit, shows up, sits at the desk in the left upper corner. A close-up image of his face is in a large projection. He points out the fact that there is a lack of love songs, especially for gay and lesbian lovers, and says:

"Some lesbians and gays pattern their lifestyles after heterosexual love songs from the media. Heterosexual men and women do, too. Yet, the closer we get to these romantic images, the further we go from love and lifestyles today."

Furuhashi begins to put on make-up. AIDS-related quotes from the world-wide media are projected.

Golightly says: "The infectious power of words seems stronger than the virus. How to protect ourselves from words and images? Nobody can escape these images. Like 'tragedy', 'victim', 'certain death', 'plague', 'punishment', 'incurable', 'hopeless'."

Furuhashi adds: "Or 'Living with AIDS', instead of such negative images. It means frequent hospital visits, taking AZT four times a day."

An image of medicine capsules rolling around in the background.

"All very expensive medicines and who knows if they really work? Some say it's just big business for pharmaceutical science, but it is taboo to say this in hospital. It is like a maths class in primary school. That is what living with AIDS is for me."

Speaking of his personal experience of life being infected by AIDS, Furuhashi continues:

"One act of unprotected sex is more dangerous than a hundred acts of safe sex. In the balance between trust and HIV, I actually learned about these old love song imageries."

The image of medicine capsules in the background multiplies from two to eight, to sixteen, to thirty-two. Furuhashi continues: "Promiscuity isn't the problem. The problem lies in old ways of thinking, like: 'safe sex isn't real sex', or 'safe sex is sex without love or trust'. The relationship between sex and love is becoming more and more complex. 'Normal' sex… What does 'normal' mean? Who decides what normal is?"

Bubu de la Madeleine takes part in the scene and is introduced as a heterosexual sex worker. Presenting herself with her hair dyed light brown, with heavy make-up and a strong red lipstick, wearing black lace underwear and with a pink curler on the front of her head, she says in her soft and calm voice: "Once I made love with my husband against my will, while I was still in the marrage. That was the first time for me to have understood what prostitution could mean."

Emphasising the importance of the awareness of our responsibility for our own bodies, she continues: "Power relations are making even sex so sad."

Furuhashi continues putting make-up on. Peter Golightly points out: "Discrimination against AIDS is also based on old discriminations within society."

The chords of a harp are heard, and Furuhashi starts to take off his suit. He stands up, transformed into a woman with blond hair, to imitate singing a dramatic love song: "There will always be people. People who need people."

The close-up image of his face is multiplied four times in a large projection. The sticker on his back says "people."

* * *

"Amateurism" may overlap partly with the notion of the "amateur," but it should not be understood as its equivalent. Amateurism is an attitude of "invention" to develop the skills necessary to fill the gaps between contemporary realities and the system of society. Different interventions of technologies, networks, the logistics of connectivity and mobility, and encounters with disease and catastrophe consequently produce different constellations of reality. Such contemporary realities do not allow us to stay in one category, one discourse and one field as "professionals." Reflecting on the flux of transformation in society forces us to consider an amateurish approach to life. Amateurism is not about form, skill or technique; rather, it is about the spirit to move out of habitual disciplinary formations of settled knowledge and instead to consider fields of the unknown in respect of profession, place and culture, and reset ourselves again to see the world from different positions. Amateurism opens up fresh opportunities to learn different ways of thinking and knowing. Moreover, this focus will shift, in a generalised way, from the "I" to the "we." After all, without developing shared strategies, no creativity will be produced: "people [who] need people."[12]

In the age of neoliberal capitalism, developing amateur stratagems in the sense of being a "labour of love" also means confronting the tyranny of a system which deprives people of their lives and pushes them to accept the new logic of a survival game, which by its tendency aims to push them into the corners. Values assigned to labour can suddenly change, regardless of skills, experience, knowledge and networks. Different forms of capital can be disregarded for the sake of adopting the logistics and priorities of a new system. Within the global flows of the economy, everything can be capitalised, even—or especially—love, emotions and human relations. It should not be forgotten that the transformation in the professionalism of people enforced by the drastic changes in social systems also strongly evokes the counter-image contained in contemporary notions of the amateur. It means that no part of the professional sphere is as stable or "reliable" as it used to be. In relation to love within the system of cognitive capitalism, Minouk Lim, an artist who lives and works in Seoul, says, "I see professionalism as considering the human being as capital, while amateurism means reconsidering existence and time as human beings. It's like conservatism and progressivism in relation to how time and existence are considered."[13] In a way, the notion of amateurism provides us with an alternative logic of economy that is beyond the dichotomy of "professional vs. amateur." After bearing witness to a system outside the world of work and consumer culture, it is a strategy to resist the overarching control of biopolitical governance in our time.

Accordingly, *S/N* is a very condensed example that can lead us to see exactly these qualities in amateurism. It is important to mention that the amateurism visible and active in *S/N* is still being carried forth in an ongoing series of projects by Koyamada. After leaving dumb type, Koyamada has been working on projects based on the acquisition of a "common" space, the (self-)organising autonomous structures of the café, mobile communication stands for drinking and chatting, building fires to sit around, as exemplified in *Weekend Café* (1994–96), *Bazaar Café* (1996–), *Common Mobile Café* (1999), *Mobile Wagon* (2001), the *Takibi* (small fire) project and most recently the Onagawa Dialogue Community Project (2012–) that became an important field of (re)empowerment and self-organisation after the Fukushima catastrophe in 2011 and in its ongoing aftermath. While professionalisation and professionalism are popular and broadly spread today—a state of affairs that can be seen as manifesting itself in a wave of certificates, degrees, and a general tendency toward quantification in education—it is interesting that in contemporary institutions of education, words such as "amateurisation" and "amateurism" have no central emphasis. This indicates the limited way in which thinking is only conceived of in terms of material progress and growth, and clearly shows us the blind spots of our world view. *S/N*, and the subsequent projects organised by Koyamada, powerfully show us the need for another way of thinking, namely amateurism, in order that we may empower ourselves instead of narrowing us down in professionalism.

* * *

07: AMAPOLA

Multiplied images of ocean are projected on the background. Furuhashi imitates singing "Amapola," lying half-naked on a float being pulled by Alex slowly from right to left.

Amapola, lindísima Amapola,
Será siempre mi alma tuya, sola.
Yo te quiero, amada niña mía,
Igual que ama la flor la luz del día.

Amapola, lindísima Amapola,
No seas tan ingrata, mírame.
Amapola, Amapola,
¿Cómo puedes tú vivir tan sola?[14]

A man carries an oversized white flag, waving it and running around, but his mouth is gagged with a cloth.

"Let us use the word 'love'."

Bubu de la Madeleine lies naked in the upper right corner, imitating singing the song and slowly being moved from right to left. Her legs are spread out and raised. From between her legs, a string on which there is a line of international flags is being pulled out.

* * *

S/N is a work in the spirit of amateurism that aims at a contemporary invention of love, sex, duty, life and death. Devising love songs to question their function as normalisers, *S/N* warns that certain types of images of love are enforced and that in reality love tolerates its diversity and is standardised. Following on from the spirit of amateurism in aesthetic experimentations, five chapters (out of seven) that were in the 1994 performance of *S/N* are inserted into this essay. These inserts do not follow the order in which they appeared in the original performance. Their sequence is rearranged in order to change their interrelations and to invent an object of knowledge different from the original. Therefore, this essay is a translation of the surrealist and chaotic overdose of the sensory information in the performance, and an exploration of the imaginaries brought on by a performative intervention in the form of writing. Looking at dumb type's early reformulation of amateurism offers ample opportunity to see the rise of a contemporary multitude of imaginaries.

Notes

1 The phrase originates in Carolyn Marvin's *When Old Technologies Were New: Thinking About Electric Communication in the Late Nineteenth Century* (New York and Oxford: Oxford University Press, 1990).

2 Gilles Deleuze, "Postscript on the Societies of Control," *October* 59, Winter 1992: 4–5.

3 Koyamada Toru, "Acquisition of A Common Space," unpublished talk at the symposium "Rethinking dumb type and the Birth of New Media Dramaturgy," International Research Center "Interweaving Performance Cultures," Freie Universität, Berlin, April 2–4. 2013.

4 *Critical Space* (*Hihyōkūkan*) was the most influential journal dealing with postmodern themes in Japan during the 1990s. The journal introduced radical left debates and published a wide range of social, political and cultural texts. The quarterly journal contributed greatly to form and contextualise the artistic community in the cultural scene in Japan in the 1990s and ceased publishing in 2002.

5 Felix Guattari and Suely Rolnik, *Molecular Revolution in Brazil*, trans. Karel Clapshaw and Brian Holmes (Los Angeles: Semiotext(e), 2007), pp. 44–47.

6 The "seminar show" for *S/N* was held at Artspace Mumonkan in Kyoto, from 17 March to 21 March 1993.

7 See Michel Foucault, *The Birth of Biopolitics: Lectures at the Collège de France, 1978–1979* (Hampshire, UK, and New York: Palgrave Macmillan, 2008).

8 See Guattari and Rolnik, *Molecular Revolution in Brazil.*

9 Sean Cubitt, "Amateur Aesthetics," https://www.academia.edu/574424/Amateur_aesthetics, p. 5 (accessed 10 March 2009).

10 This critique was introduced by Sara Jansen during the symposium "Rethinking dumb type and the Birth of New Media Dramaturgy" (see above, note 3).

11 Cubitt, "Amateur Aesthetics," p. 4.

12 "People who need people" is a quote from "Love Song," in *S/N*, performed by Furuhashi Teiji in drag.

13 Interview with the author, Seoul, November 2009.

14 English lyrics of the song can be found at Metro Lyrics, http://www.metrolyrics.com/amapola-lyrics-gene-autry.html (accessed 15 June 2014).

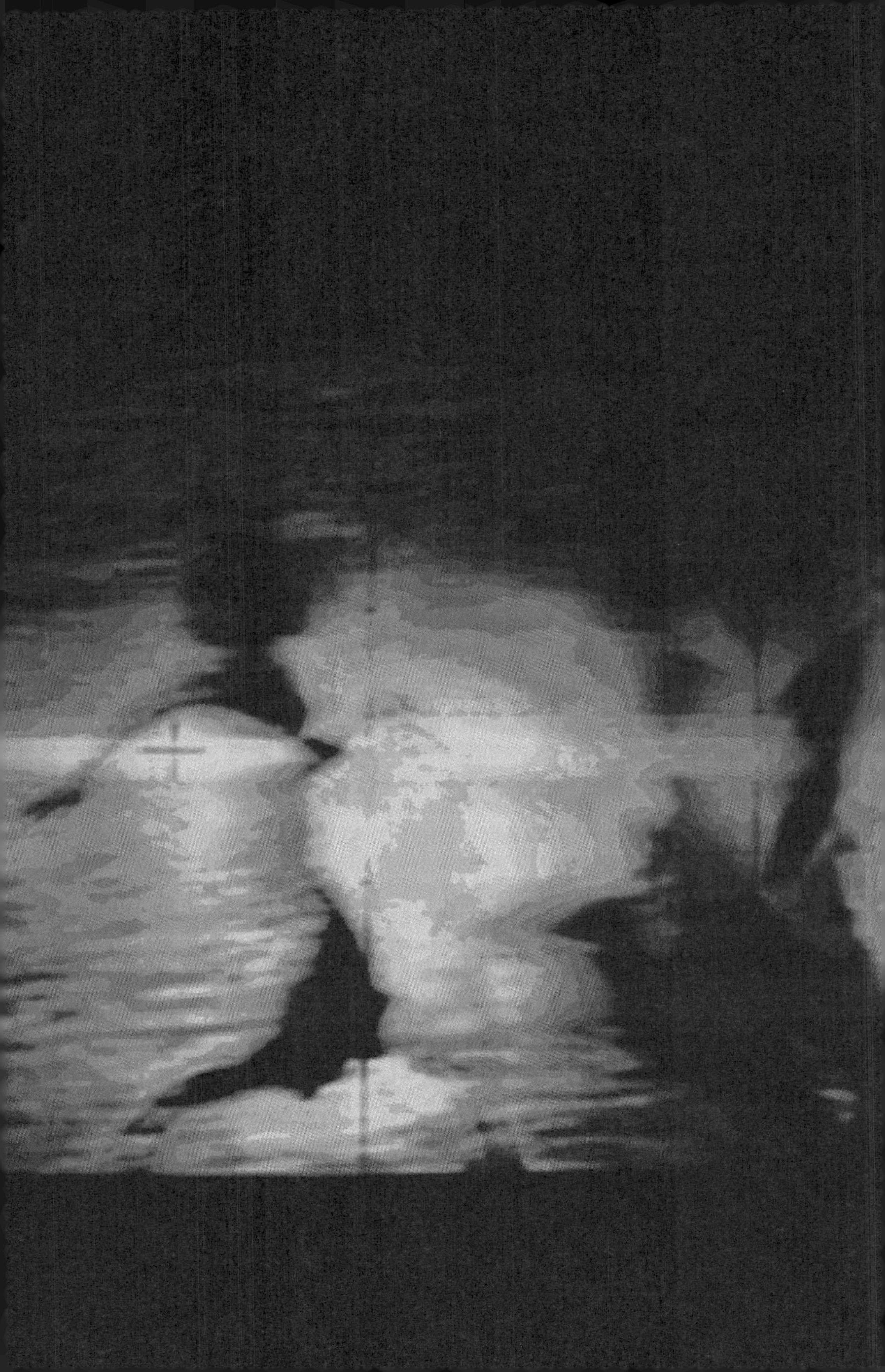

New Media Dramaturgy

Dumb Type's *XD*

A Case Study in New Media Dramaturgy

Edward Scheer

> The conception of conscious experience as a perceived relation between doing and undergoing enables us to understand the connection that art as production and perception and appreciation as enjoyment sustain to each other.[1]
>
> *John Dewey*

> As we survey the expanding and converging landscape of electronic, virtual, and immersive production, we might ask ourselves: what *material* is being worked here? Is it simply new organizations of photons, sound waves, and haptic cues? Or does the "holistic" fusion of different media and the construction of more immersive technologies actually suggest another, perhaps more fundamental material? I'd wager that the new material is indeed rather fundamental: human experience itself.[2]
>
> *Erik Davis*

John Dewey's famous 1934 essay on experience might not seem a productive or even relevant point of departure for an account of the significance of dumb type's unique new media dramaturgy (NMD) in the twenty-first century, since his scope was confined to the traditional art forms of painting and poetry. However, his insistence on both the doing and the perceiving as essential elements in the composition of the experience of art is especially pertinent to the understanding of dramaturgical labour. At its core, dramaturgy is the negotiation of ideas and actions, process and product, in the semiotic amplifier of theatre for a live audience—that is, an audience whose members' bodily sensations are responding in real time to the staged actions. These responses close the circuit from dramaturgical creation to spectatorial experience. "Art, in its form," writes Dewey in his slightly overwrought prose, "unites the very same relation of doing and undergoing, outgoing and incoming energy, that makes an experience to be an experience."[3] In what follows, I will try to describe aspects of the dumb type experience in terms of a new media dramaturgy, or NMD, in which both the doing and the undergoing are explicitly shaped by mediated social relations, stories, technical developments and life experiences. I will also discuss the notion of "experience design" or XD, a concept associated with industrial design and human computer interaction, in terms of what it reveals about dumb type's practice of NMD.

Dumb type NMD

There is a perceptible arc in the dramaturgy of dumb type's performances from 1989's *pH* through *S/N* in 1994 and *OR* in 1997, which develops in accordance with the increased accessibility of affordable lighting and data projection technologies. These three theatre works developed the company's emergent aesthetic, evident in the earlier work *036 Pleasure Life* (later restaged as *Pleasure Life*), aptly summarised by Chris Salter as "audio-visual saturation with a sterile yet seductive technological sheen."[4] This was not a purely formal concern, however, as the works were equally concerned with projecting a "future image of an urban society where political and social control, order and technology"[5] would be increasingly sources for conflict and ontological indeterminacy at the "human/system interface," as the company's own educational language emphasises. It is important to note that, while this development of the company's techno-aesthetic was enabled by technical advances, the members always maintained a critical comportment in relation to the effects of these advances on human relations and society, an attitude that is evident in all the company's output but perhaps most especially *S/N*, in terms of the balance between the forceful political messaging and seductive video design.[6] One such technical advance was the creation of the DMX512 standard for controlling automatic lighting by the United States Institute for Theatre Technology (USITT) at their conference in 1986.[7] This system massively enhanced the capacities for lighting and effects design on stage and became the global standard (after revisions were made) in 1990. This was too late for *pH*, so dumb type's lighting designer and operator, Takayuki Fujimoto, created the effects and lighting manually, a significant achievement in itself given the astonishing complexity of the scenography of *pH*. The spectators were seated around and above a six-metre-long stage area which was constantly scanned and tracked by two metal beams moving up and down the length of the area like gigantic scanners projecting texts and images onto the floor of the space. Performers had to negotiate the two heavy beams, which contained slide and film projectors as well as lights. The dramaturgy of the piece can be seen in the use of lighting and effects which functioned less to illuminate the performer's actions—dancing, striking poses ("vogueing," as described by Salter),[8] even attempting to give lectures and then running to the end of the space to avoid the scanner—and more to generate a multimedia environment for the spectators. The conceptual unity of the multimedia design of *pH* is clear as it serves at all points to reinforce the theme of the increasingly mediated nature of emergent social conditions and to focus and amplify that experience for spectators.

The genius of the work is that it imagines the then inchoate digital future of the "global info-bahn," the saturation of virtual images in social space and the changes to physical and gestural behaviour that the experience design of technologies like mobile phones would bring, while remaining an essentially analogue scenography. As Shiro Takatani, the designer and creator of the giant scanning machine, explains: "I was also interested in the idea of old technology that we're not using any more. Imagining people from the future looking back at the technology from the past."[9] Appropriately, the projectors in the giant metal beams utilised slides and 16mm film (shot on video and transferred to film). This was due to the retro-fit design principle informing the work, but also to the relatively high cost and unavailability of high-resolution video projectors at the time. This focus on design and visual effects as the key driver of the work is significant, as, while it added to the difficulty and expense of mounting *pH*, it also shows that dumb type's creation of a sophisticated virtual techno-aesthetic was developed out of a rigorous dramaturgy of machines and objects whose use-by date was imminent. As the lighting designer, Takayuki Fujimoto, says, "With *pH* we had two tonnes worth of machinery that we were dragging from one place to the next. So that was really tough. From around *S/N*, we wanted to be able to use the existing systems in the theatre rather than making our own, to make touring easier."[10]

By the time *S/N* was in development in 1992–93, the company was already working with the then brand new Mac laptops running DMX software to automate the lighting and a system to synchronise video with audio files projected with powerful high intensity lamps. Peter Eckersall, who was backstage at the Adelaide Festival in March 1994, noted that on arrival at the venue the company appeared to have little or no gear to unpack, just a number of laptops and video and slide projectors. So while *pH* is a work that anticipates digital culture in its design and theme, *S/N* was the first dumb type work to actually incorporate digital audio-visual systems into the piece alongside the analogue slide and mirror systems that were used to project text.

Three years later, the violent stroboscopic effect produced at the start of *OR,* and used throughout the work, is, in fact, video projected using HID (high-intensity discharge) lamps operating at very high intensity and an early version of Symphony software to compose different media, in particular video and audio files. In *OR,* the video flashes were triggered by sounds so the entire media scenography could be pre-composed and essentially just played back. This is, in a scenographic sense, the first entirely digital work for dumb type as it is essentially a plug-in and play, or replay, design. Shiro Takatani explains the design concept:

> there was a feeling that this piece had to be based on visuals and sound more than on text or other elements; that it was the power of the visual image and the power of the sound that would push this piece along somehow. It was an experiment in seeing how much can be done with these two elements or how they can really carry a performance, not text.[11]

The dramaturgy in *OR* is based on a more restricted palette than the previous works, reducing the textual component to a bare minimum and allowing digital sound, light and video to carry the performance.

The story of the rise and fall of different audio-visual technologies, as products of developments in electrical engineering become available on the market at different times and others become obsolete, forms a part of any understanding of dumb type's dramaturgy and contributes to a broader discussion of NMD. But the company's aesthetic was also driven by visual design principles and a strong sense of what the audience should see, hear and feel, so equal significance must be accorded to what this group of artists made with these tools as well as the existence of the technologies themselves. What dumb type made are enduring masterworks of new media dramaturgy. These three works (*ph, S/N* and *OR*) are significant not simply because of their slick surface but also in terms of the depth of their engagement with emergent social phenomena, and for the way they deliver this engagement through a revitalised theatrical vernacular infused with a new media sensibility and offering a rarely satisfying experience of the fusion of these elements to a live audience.

The design of dumb type performances is directed towards a set of intense audio-visual experiences presented alongside acute socio-political commentary. The emphasis in the dramaturgy seems to be intent on eliciting particular sensorial and perceptual responses rather than simply using a particularly exciting piece of hardware. In this way, dumb type's approach to dramaturgy shares some interesting similarities with the concept and practice of experience design.

Experience Design

In his short paper published on his blog in 2001, Erik Davis, an arts and technology writer and sometime geek spiritualist, opened the door to a dimension of design based on the entire human sensorium and not simply a mix of partial parameters: "human experience itself."[12] He proposed an understanding of design as not only engaging interactive and immersive worlds but also the flux of experience as it unfolds in time. In its broadest sense, experience design is a discourse with its roots firmly in European modernity, in Walter Benjamin's writings about cinema and technology, in the modernist culture of experiment, the "cinema of attractions," the phenomenology of theme parks and rollercoasters, and perhaps also linked to the vitalism of Henri Bergson and others. It is at once a philosophical question, how to think and design for a dynamic complex system rather than merely the components of that system, and a challenge to new media artists and designers to anticipate and activate a range of sensorial encounters between media environments and users. It is a challenge that dumb type has taken up in work that speaks in the mediated discourse of the time. As Benjamin noted, new media (he was writing of cinema) create new aesthetic possibilities as well as new sensibilities and expectations of art. They create new experiences.

Erik Davis's provocation to think about the material in time-based art, with its "fusion of different media and the construction of more immersive technologies" as "human experience," leaves open the question of what constitutes an experience and how a designer or digital artist could therefore create a new experience. For Nathan Shedroff, the guru of experience design as a marketing and design tool, there are at least six dimensions of experience for designers to negotiate: "Time/Duration, Interactivity, Intensity, Breadth/Consistency, Sensorial and Cognitive Triggers, and Significance/Meaning."[13] Shedroff's list reminds us of the reductions required to digitally encode, store and retransmit an experience. Complex combinations of these parameters offer designers huge scope for varying the environments they are creating around objects and therefore also the possible forms of user interaction with these objects in these environments. But there are obvious problems with this discourse—not the least of which is the way it has been adapted by product designers to focus on user experience, in the narrow meaning of consumer behaviour and the market advantage to be found in constructing products around stories of users to emphasise the subjective dimension of technology. This latter procedure focuses on the exchange of intimate text messages, rather than on the object that is the mobile phone. Waking to the sound of birds rather than the sound of an alarm, the XD focus is on what is done with the product rather than the thing itself. In the broader conceptual sense with which I am concerned here, it is the multi-dimensional and multi-sensorial nature of an experience that poses the ultimate challenge to the proponents of XD.

The challenges XD faces as a dimension of designing and marketing new media devices are not my focus here, but, rather, the theoretical discourse it produces and the conceptual problems it poses that are oddly reminiscent of the discourses and practical difficulties associated with performance, especially the studies of acting and actor training. XD marketers need to think about behaviours of consumers, codified to the level of Richard Schechner's idea of "strips of behaviour,"[14] which are repetitive, codifiable, storable and transmissible. An actor's gestural repertoire needs to account for a similar suite of “restored behaviour,” Schechner’s definition of performance. Each strip of behaviour contains the six dimensions of Duration, Interactivity, Intensity, Consistency, Sensorial and Cognitive Triggers, and Significance, and the human actor’s capacity for combining these is evidence of skill. For experience designers, this represents a formidable technical problematic and no doubt, as with the actor, demands an element of pure invention.

Dumb type’s NMD as XD

Erik Davis’s exploration of XD develops the proposition that art has a specific function in relation to what he calls “the production of technological experience.” He argues that

> artists are uniquely placed to interrogate … the dominant experiences which are being engineered and renormalized by massive commercial engines of subjectivity. But this critical function must be coupled with experiment, with the willingness to creatively participate in the larger cultural process of re-engineering subjectivity, of pushing the envelope of experience. This is not necessarily a matter of becoming high tech—relatively low-tech artists like Gary Hill and Bill Viola have made great strides in this direction. But it is a matter of directly engaging, not simply the new technologies, but the underlying technical “material” of subjectivity itself.[15]

To unpack this a little, XD approaches objects by imagining new behaviours for their users, new experiences “engineered and renormalized by massive commercial engines,” a process which participates in the production of subjectivity and social being through technical means.[16] Art, especially time-based art, can critically appropriate this function of XD, as XD has already appropriated visual and design techniques, but Davis argues that it should be done experimentally as opposed to being driven by a form of technological determinism. It is worth noting that at the heart of this statement is a concern with subjectivity, a concept more familiar to humanities scholarship of the 1990s than digital media theory of the twenty-first century, but which makes a welcome return in this context as a form of “technical material” itself. So, the mode of subject formation specific to digital culture is necessarily connected with the contemporary forms of “production of technological experience.” If art is to meaningfully engage with this newly technical mode of subject formation, then its critical and experimental functions need to engage with the kinds of aesthetics that are also "pushing the envelope of experience."

The case Davis makes for a critically engaged time-based art is a strong one and stands on its own terms, but I argue that it also works as a description of dumb type's dramaturgy, which is similarly engaged with the "production of technological experience" (Davis) at the "human/system interface" (dumb type). From a critique of consumer behaviours in the digital age (*pH*), to the production of the medical subject, or the object of the techno-medical gaze (*S/N*), to an explicit critique of technological determinism, especially the role of technology in determining life and death experience in *OR*, the dumb type experience is based on closely examining and representing the production of the contemporary technical subject and the critique of XD, the experience design of life in capitalist digital culture, focusing on its silences, its oppressions, its blind spots.

As Hood and Gendrich point out, "technology emerges in dumb type's world as a tangible part of our emotional, spiritual, rhythmic, physical experience; it is linked inextricably with who we have become."[17] The strength of dumb type's work is exactly in its affective power amplified by sound and image. The visual media are deployed to create an immersive multimedia scenography that doesn't neutralise the body's singularities and vulnerabilities, but interfaces with the performers in a way which suggests that the cybernetic system of the company's famous "human/machine interface" doesn't only produce clones but multiplies new differences. The cyborg in dumb type is not just anybody, it is someone very close to each of us. It is who we have become.

Scenes from dumb type's NMD

At one point in *pH* the giant scanner projects the phrase "New world order" which morphs into "New world border," suggesting that Marshall McLuhan's global village is not simply a utopian projection but contains the dystopian possibilities of a regressive nationalist politics where citizens have less mobility than commodities. As is well known, in the last years of his own life Furuhashi Teiji focused on the AIDS crisis, a disease that would consume him, and in *S/N* the company directed their energies to address the silence from parts of the scientific community and the government that marked the early appearance of the disease in Japan and elsewhere.

S/N is, at least in part, about the interaction between medical technologies and the body, slides of naked torsos with "+" marks superimposed on them, but also the power of the creative imagination to produce an independent virtual reality: "I do not depend on your death/I invent my own death." Dancers run for their lives on the floor space above the thrust screens that comprise the stage, before leaping to their deaths again and again, falling off the stage into the void space in the rear. Here the performer is the border crosser, dying and reappearing continually in the peculiar way that theatre enables but with the added sense of the action replay that media provides.

Like a number of dumb type performances, *S/N* was remediated as an installation work with the title *Lovers* (1994). This would be Furuhashi Teiji's last work before he died of AIDS and was produced as a collaboration with Tokyo's Canon Artlab. It involves timed slide projections on the walls and floor of a cubic space. Here, the bodies of the company's dancers approach the viewer with wide-open arms before falling back out of reach, the unattainable virtual body and also the ghost of loved ones lost to the epidemic.

In the performance version of *OR*, also remediated as an installation commissioned by the Tokyo ICC, the cybernetic experience is pushed and amplified into the body of the spectator. Sound designers/musicians Ryoji Ikeda and Toru Yamanaka created a pounding bass soundtrack which reverberates through the piece, which is felt as much as heard, reinforcing the sensation of an essentially mediated experience (there are no sounds like this in nature) in combination with the powerful strobing HID lights. From the opening scene entitled "Edge," *OR* establishes an emphatic experience for the audience around the liminal dramaturgy of the "whiteout" where, as the company say in their notes to the work:

> You are deprived of ability to see, where you can't recognize anything, where you don't know where you stand any more, where you may not know whether you are alive OR dead.

Hood and Gendrich describe the seats in the auditorium rattling "during the opening sequences, the vibrations slowly crawling up the audience members' bodies as adjustments are made in the tones and levels of sound."[18] Their descriptions emphasise the points I am making about the experience design of this work being of prime importance to its reception. They say that, "By the end of the production the soundtrack makes tangible Furuhashi's reflection on his mother's interaction with life-support systems: 'Observing the beat from inside her body.... I couldn't distinguish what was the border between life and death'."[19] This references the well-known anecdote Furuhashi told about visiting his mother in hospital and thinking she was dead because the cardiograph was flatlining, when it was simply that the power cable had become disconnected. For him the implications of this experience were profound and marked a new limit in human experience where at the extreme of life and death humans no longer rely on direct sense information but technological interfaces. This is the subject matter *OR* represents and reproduces.

For Hood and Gendrich, the audience in *OR*, becomes similarly "confused about what is technology and what is human."[20] But they seem to miss the essential point that this confusion is endemic to the contemporary form of subjectivity that dumb type are seeking to explore, and a product of an advanced level of cybernetic interaction at the socio-cultural level. In their discussion of the final sequence of the piece, they describe "white noise ... mixed with a pounding heartbeat that settles into the torsos of the audience" rendering them "confused as to whether the heartbeats they feel are recorded or their own," creating a cybernetic *experience* of contemporary cybernetic *subjectivity* which they interpret as the "dehumanization and disconnection that the performers have represented on stage throughout the evening," transferring across to the "bodies of their audience."[21]

The experience of the audience in *OR* is certainly as they describe it: sound that goes right through the body that resonates with the bass frequencies, while the HID light is so bright and stroboscopic that it cannot really be looked at. In designing an audio-visual experience that cannot be heard or seen in any conventional sense, dumb type is undeniably "pushing the envelope of experience" in Davis's phrase, but is it an experience of "dehumanization and disconnection"? In making sound and light that can be felt more than simply perceived as audio-visual signals, dumb type could be seen to be *rematerialising* the audio-visual experience and transferring a sense of materiality from the stage to the audience in a way that re-engages the physical experience of spectatorship through technology as a key aspect of the work.

So, rather than disconnecting humans from their environment or each other, the piece seems to enact a form of reconnection. What is occurring in the choreography and scenography of *OR* is only dehumanisation if the human is conceived as an entity removed from the sense world and devoid of possible technical interfaces. The message of *OR*, and of dumb type, is surely that technology can be humanised and that art has the capacity to re-engineer the technological experience as a human experience. As Shiro Takatani says of the effects in *OR*:

> The violence of the sound and the light that the audience can experience is for me a kind of amplification of the identification of the audience with the actor or performer on stage. In theatre, the audience identifies with the actors on stage but the technology can help by amplifying this effect, by making the audience experience these things that the body on stage also experiences, and in that way also identify with the performer in a different, additional way. ... And it wouldn't work if there were no actual bodies on stage. The bodies on stage support this whole system. Without them this circuit of experience between the audience and the performer wouldn't work and there would be no identification process and nothing to be amplified by the technology.[22]

Again, this reinforces the sense that human connection amplified through technical means is at the centre of dumb type's new media dramaturgy. But what are the bodies in *OR* doing? In terms of its choreography, a flat aesthetic seems to dominate as the movement traverses the stage in kicks, pushes and martial art moves. The gestures often resemble the movements of figures in video games, so, in a sense, the piece is again embodying a contemporary experience of technically-infused subjectivity and behaviour. This is undercut by the gesture of smoothing the blanket over the supine body of the loved one, the patient, the corpse, the gentle action of care, in stark contrast to the stagey violence of the dancers.

After this depiction of experience in extremis, the final video sequence in the piece stages a videographed journey in which the audience sees images through the windscreen of a car driving along freeways and country roads. We do not hear about a journey or have one described or mimed; we enter the sensorial world of travel accompanied by a visual text.

> **[OR] ientation 1:**
>
> Imagine yourself in a car heading South. Over the Alps, for a vacation. You do not have much time, but once you arrive you will have all the time in the world. You will be a different person when you get there. Relaxed, happy, alive. You can sit all afternoon in a sunny cafe, drinking a casual glass of wine, eyeing

> the pretty girls. The newspapers will not follow you here, not today. All that matters is that the weather is perfect, and even that does not really matter. You are already there if you want to be, and you know that is what you want.

The soundtrack reaches a crescendo as the camera takes the spectator along freeways and hurtling through tunnels. On stage, surrounded by the scenes of buildings, mountains and snow all speeding past, is the still figure of a lone woman, a recurring motif in the work and one which anchors the new media design in a human scale and sensibility. Perhaps she is the ambassador to the next life, the one standing vigil at the moment of death or the reminder, as Hood and Gendrich suggest, "that death—in all its forms—is ultimately faced alone."[23] They describe the full sequence as "akin to a roller-coaster ride or a special effects IMAX film. The peripheral vision of the audience is filled with the image of the passing scenery." What this sequence establishes is the vital and dynamic experience of motion as a counterpoint to the stasis of death. In this sense, the key material in this part of the work is the experience of a certain vitality that comes into cruel focus in the final moments of life or in extreme moments. The metaphor of the rollercoaster returns us to the question of XD. If it was only a metaphor it would not be a question of experience as an undergoing, but because the video is shot in a *pov* (point-of-view) mode and presented to the spectators as their own experience massively accelerated, it becomes more than scenography and approaches the condition of experience.

In his essay on XD, Erik Davis also turns to the example of a roller-coaster. As he points out,

> Obviously rollercoasters exist within a network of symbolic associations. But the act of subjectively submitting your bodymind to a rollercoaster ride, and undergoing the resulting thrills of adrenaline, fear, and gut-fluttering sensation, cannot be directly assimilated to the network of significations that constitute the *meaning* of rollercoasters.[24]

The distinction drawn here between meaning (thematic content) and experience (undergoing) is not only tactical but significant for this essay. In these terms, dumb type's dramaturgy is focused on experience in a way that makes meaning less a function of the chain of symbolic associations in language and more about the rollercoaster ride. It is not the same project as the North American Theatre of Images (Robert Wilson, the Wooster group and Richard Foreman), whose work actively compromised the formation of a readable account of the work in favour of an aesthetic experience. What dumb type have contributed to world theatre is not a diminution of meaning but an enhancement of the experience of live, time-based art through an engagement with social issues in the form of visually arresting and precision-engineered aesthetics. Rather than developing a purely formal technical aesthetic focused on achieving a complex interactivity or a deeply immersive experience—in other words, a kind of arts-based XD as in the Theatre of Images—dumb type designs its own kind of new media experience that works as a critique of XD. But this perception risks placing the aesthetic content and process of dumb type's NMD in opposition to XD as a consumer and market-focused process, whereas I suggest we consider them in a necessary relation. Dumb type made experiential art for an audience of first world, socially-mediated subjects whose worldview was already in the process of becoming a cybernetic product of media saturation. Rather than re-educate this audience, dumb type work to seduce us and in the process to expose the contradictions in our viewing position.

The questions that dumb type asks in all the forms taken by the company's work (performance and installation), it asks of experience. As the exhibition notes to the *OR* installation have it: "Is death unknowable? Does it transcend experience? Is it visible only to the clinical eye of medical science? Or will technology change all that...?" Death is the horizon to which their work returns again and again. The death in 1995 of Teiji, the much loved co-director, collaborator and friend, was immortalised in the final scenes in *OR*. Perhaps for the group of artists in dumb type, death was both a doing and an undergoing, a gift they received and referenced and reflected, a thing that happened to them and something they could use as material. In this way it does not "transcend experience," but through their art it survives as an experience uniquely gifted to those fortunate enough to have encountered it.[25]

Notes

* Some of the material in the present chapter has appeared in an earlier version in Peter Eckersall, Edward Scheer and Helena Grehan, *New Media Dramaturgy: Performance, Media and New-Materialism* (London: Palgrave Macmillan, 2017).

1 John Dewey, *Art as Experience* (New York: Perigee Books, 1934), p. 48.

2 Erik Davis, *Experience Design and the Design of Experience*, http://www.techgnosis.com/experience.html (accessed 9 April 2013).

3 Dewey, *Art as Experience*, p. 50.

4 Chris Salter, *Entangled: Technology and the Transformation of Performance* (Cambridge, MA: MIT Press, 2010), p. 74.

5 Ibid., p. 74.

6 As BuBu de la Madeleine says in an interview about the making of *S/N*: "While thinking about the set, the costumes for the show, the technology, music and lights, we were also thinking about HIV, what is it, what is the relationship between AIDS and sex, what is the relationship between gay and straight?" (interview, 13 December 2013).

7 At the 1986 Annual Conference of the USITT Engineering Commission in Oakland, California, a project started that resulted in USITT DMX512 – Digital Data Transmission Standard for Dimmers and Controllers. Some revisions were made in 1990. http://www.usitt.org/content.asp?contentid=373

8 Salter, *Entangled*, p. 77.

9 Interview with Shiro Takatani, 15 December 2013. *OR* by dumb type – Visual design: Takatani Shiro, Koyamada Toru, Fujimoto Takayuki – Sound design: Ikeda Ryoji, Yamanaka Toru.

10 Interview with Takayuki Fujimoto, 15 December 2013.

11 Interview with Takatani.

12 Erik Davis blog, http://techgnosis.com.

13 Nathan Shedroff, "Experience Design Introduction," 2001, http://www.nathan.com/ed/ (accessed 9 April 2013).

14 Richard Schechner, *Between Theater and Anthropology* (Philadelphia: University of Pennsylvania Press, 1985), p. 35.

15 Davis, *Experience Design and the Design of Experience*, unpaginated.

16 Ibid., unpaginated.

17 Woodrow Hood and Cynthia Gendrich, "Memories of the Future: Technology and the Body in dumb type's *memorandum*," *PAJ: A Journal of Performance and Art* 25 (1), 2003: 20.

18 Woodrow Hood and Cynthia Gendrich, "Noise and Nudity: Kyoto's Dumb Type," *Theatre Forum*, Winter-Spring 2001: 9.

19 Ibid.

20 Ibid.

21 Ibid.

22 Interview with Takatani.

23 Hood and Gendrich, "Noise and Nudity," p. 10.

24 Davis, *Experience Design and the Design of Experience*, unpaginated.

25 I am thinking of Peggy Phelan's superb description of the work of Francesca Woodman in this regard: "To accept that her death survived her work, we need first to see it as something not enveloped entirely by the creative energy of her art. Woodman's use of photography as a way to rehearse her death allows us to consider her art as an apprenticeship in dying, rather than the thing that somehow outlasts or conquers death." Peggy Phelan, "Francesca Woodman's Photography: Death and the Image One More Time," *Signs* 27 (4), Summer 2002: 1002.

Whiteout Dumb Type

Postmodernism and the Birth of New Media Dramaturgy

Peter Eckersall

> Our private and corporate lives have become information processes just because we have put our nervous system outside us in electric technology.[1]
>
> *Marshall McLuhan*

In *Art as Far as the Eye Can See* Paul Virilio asks: "In an age when our view of the world has become not so much objective as teleobjective, how can we persist in being? How can we effectively resist the sudden dematerialisation of the world where everything is seen, déjà vu—already seen—and instantly forgotten?"[2] In foregrounding his concern with the accelerated pace of change in society Virilio explores the question of memory in relation to technology and the subsequent lack of a longer perspective of distance, personal or historical. What happens if memory itself is dematerialised to the extent that we can no longer see the past? What happens if we are no longer able as cultures and communities to create moments of critical awareness about our situation and environment?

According to Virilio, the intensifying effects of speed, telepresence and mediatisation curtail such an awareness and instead produce what he calls a "telescopic distancing and the remoteness of optical sensation … doubled with a TELESUBJECTIVITY that largely falsifies our relationship with things."[3] Virilio argues that our view of art has been transformed as a consequence of this, overtaken by an "economy of culture" that favours an ever-accelerating turnover of visual displays, hence placing art in a state of permanent transit and attuned to sensationalism and mass marketing rather than giving attention to the critical and aesthetic project of art itself.[4] He describes a situation where art is everywhere, and yet, paradoxically, it is also becoming much harder to see.

The dematerialisation of memory is a good place to start for a discussion of dumb type's hybrid media performance work *memorandum*. Made in 1999, *memorandum* is one of their last major performances. The piece's concern with what might be termed an existential collapse of memory into image—in effect to stage the postmodern experience of memory for the spectator—was provocatively realised in immersive, fragmented scenes combining image, dance, monologue and sound. I am interested here to explore how this combination of performance modes was connected to a strand of postmodern media arts in Japan that were at the same time deeply critical of postmodernism. Dumb type created iconic images and forms of presentation that are now part of the global history of postmodern art. However, the influence of postmodernism on the company's work has not been adequately explored. In this essay, I will briefly introduce the context of postmodernism in Japan and consider *memorandum* through this lens. I connect this to the idea of whiteout, a term that aptly describes the concentrated effect of media in the performance that is overwhelming to the point of erasure. From this perspective, we can see how *memorandum* explores the postmodern condition of memory without a past and the consequences of this for our sense of being. How the company depicts this condition by mixing image and sensory immersion with live performance affords insights into the formation of new media dramaturgy (NMD), giving much needed attention to the development of these hybrid media-performance practices in relation to questions of politics and cultural production in the postmodern era and beyond.

* * *

It is easy to discern how telescopic distancing and postmodern critique resonates with the experience of art in contemporary times, where the difference between art and commodity has lessened to such a degree that, wilfully or not, we often confuse the two. Notwithstanding the importance of this topic (and with writers such as Chantal Mouffe, Claire Bishop and Boris Groys providing exemplary analysis), my concern here is not with the contemporary moment.[5] Rather, it is with the history of these ideas and forms of performance and how vital it is now to think about the historical context of this moment and to reflect on when these ideas began to shape our present nuanced and at times contradictory relations with artistic practices. This leads us almost inextricably to the contradictory aesthetics of postmodernism where typically more is less and everything is reified and consumed. Virilio is one of a generation of influential thinkers writing on its political effects and his work is germane for its analysis of vectors of globalisation, media technology and the intensification of social life as an economy of speed. For Virilio, the virtue of these ideas was explored in his 1977 work *Speed and Politics* (cited above) where this intensification was shown to transform political agency. Other critiques of mediatisation contributed to the emerging debate about postmodern politics, performativity and cultural economy, as expressed in influential texts by Jean Baudrillard, Fredric Jameson, Michel Foucault and Judith Butler, amongst others.

I will return to Virilio's work, but first of all I would like to briefly touch on some of postmodernism's key points: Baudrillard's formidable theorisation of the simulacra, Butler's notion of the performativity of gender, Jameson's writing on the schizophrenic nature of late capitalism, and Foucault on biopolitics—all now tied to the exigencies of postmodernism. The invention of new media performance with its dramaturgical strategies of mixing live and mediatised bodies, using hacking and sampled images, teleportation and remote sensing, and experiments with digitally mediated immersive environments are some of the most visible instances of showing our evolving understanding of its cultural impact. Also relevant to consider is the influence of Gilles Deleuze and Felix Guattari in their reconsideration of 1960s politics by seeking to amplify its avant-garde tendencies. The emphasis they place on terms such as assemblage, network and deterritorialisation as a way of describing cultural production and subjectivity can be seen in the mixed media and proto-posthuman dramaturgical practices that evolved in the work of groups such as dumb type.

For Baudrillard, Butler, and Deleuze and Guattari, performance itself was important. I do not wish to seem to group their ideas into a singular methodology, but, for each of them, in various ways, performative gestures became the basis for reconsidering the everyday in their writings. They explored how performance is involved in the production of images, capital, gender, and so on. Each asserted a vision of how activist intellectual practices coupled with a theorisation of performance could form the basis of new kinds of resistant politics. Hal Foster has spoken about how a "postmodernism of resistance" aims not only to resist the "official culture of modernism but also the 'false normativity' of a reactionary postmodernism." In doing so, he argues that artists should seek "to question rather than exploit cultural codes, [and] to explore rather than conceal social and political affiliations."[6] The idea of such a postmodernism of resistance is helpful in seeing how dumb type developed their critical dramaturgical practices. These were practices that embraced the idea of displaying social and political affiliations, for example. Also of note is the question of how these were developed in *memorandum,* not so much as deconstructive practices that focus on the rights of marginal communities and identity practices (as was the case in *pH* and *S/N*, for example), but what I read as new here is the experience of concentration and intensification: how the nature of postmodern existence is not taken apart in this work but magnified. Arguably, here lies a connection between the evolution of new media performance aesthetics in the work of dumb type and a new kind of critical strategy bringing the ideas of postmodern resistance and NMD into a productive conversation.

Before developing this idea further, we need to briefly consider the impact of postmodernism in Japan, a place where the signs of postmodern architecture and art seemed to be everywhere. In fact, some scholars suggested that Japanese cultural history itself, with a reputation for absorbing influences from China, Europe and, in the post-war era, the United States, was inherently suited to postmodern analysis. As the art historian Inaga Shigemi put it: "Postmodern Japan is a system without structure floating on a flow of bits of mass-information, which are not destined to accumulate."[7] While dumb type were known as a company with many international influences and connections, we can also say that with their interest in Japan and its relationship to globalisation their work uniquely explored the Japanese experience of postmodernism. Their iconic media landscapes and pioneering use of media technologies were helping to develop a picture of the 1980s and 1990s Japanese arts as one of the important postmodern scenes.

Masayo Miyoshi and Harry Harootunian have argued that the influence of postmodernism in Japan was about pacifying dissenting groups and upholding a national myth of unity and cultural homogeneity: "the nation's critical and intellectual space is now painlessly absorbed into its productive space, calming the disconnected and silencing all the dissenters."[8] Indeed, this commentary touches on the wider criticism of postmodernism, especially the sense that its inventive commodification of all dimensions of social life and consequent loss of diversity makes life feel hollow and without sensation. In Japan, the 1990s is described as the lost decade (*ushinawareta jūnen*) during which time an overwhelming sense of inertia was underscored by rising social problems. The sense of pacifying entrapment was not experienced as a violent rupture, but with more of a feeling of confusion about what had happened. Events like the Aum Shinrikyo gassing of the Tokyo subway in 1995, or the increased incidence of young people isolating themselves from society by staying in their rooms (*hikikomori*), were emblematic of the wider atmosphere of despondency. The seeming lack of capacity to respond to these conditions symbolised a strong sense of postmodern malaise. But again, here the negotiation of postmodern forms or modes in art and architecture is a bit different from a sense of atomisation that is linked with postmodern malaise. Dumb type's postmodern and new media performance sought to show this condition as much as it also sought to activate the sensory experience of being in postmodernism as an act of resistance.

During the 1990s, the most active time for dumb type's performance activities, Asada Akira and Karatani Kōjin co-edited the journal *Hihyōkūkan* (*Critical Space*), probably the most important Japanese language source of critical debates about postmodernism and its effects on art, literature, society and politics (also mentioned in Yoshida's essay in this volume). A lack of perspective on questions of history and memory in postmodern culture was frequently a topic of discussion in the journal. Asada's concept of "infantile capitalism" as a notion of political economy concerned with play, diversion and non-material forms of production is also an important criticism of Japan's postmodern culture.[9] As I have argued elsewhere, this idea was reflected strongly in the theatrical trends of the 1980s, during which time the activist spirit of radical theatre of the 1960s dissipated.[10]

How much was dumb type connected to the postmodern scene and critiques of it? The answer is, quite a lot. It is well known that dumb type developed an interdisciplinary practice mixing dance, performance art, sound, video, text, bodies and projections. People associated with the postmodern art scene also worked with dumb type. Asada undertook dramaturgical and critical roles for the group at various times and his influence can be seen in the formation of dumb type's anti-capitalist outlook. The translator Alfred Birnbaum, who is credited as a conceptual collaborator in the programme for *memorandum,* was also an early translator of the novels of Murakami Haruki. His sensitivity to Murakami's ambient languid style and fragmented depictions of time and place compares to dumb type's fragmented anti-theatrical dramaturgy. In mixing the unhurried gestures of "everyday life" with a storm of mediatised images, their dramaturgy compares to the postmodern tactics of Murakami's early novels, which often showed moments of a banal domestic existence contrasted with moments of unexplainable violence. Such abrupt breaks in the rhythm of the work are especially heightened by digital effects in *OR* and *memorandum*. We can see this when moments of visual stillness and inert bodies are contrasted with the full sensory impact of screens, sound and frenetic movements. The company also included quotations from texts by Baudrillard and Foucault in their work, and references to Foucault and Butler in relation to *S/N* have been described elsewhere in this volume.

Critical perspectives in relation to dumb type's work seem to turn on a fine sense of ambiguity ("overstuffed with nothing") that arises from the intensification of postmodern culture at the expense of authentic experience—Harootunian's take on the intellectual space as absorbed and disconnected, for example. Similarly, in Virilio's essay, the interplay between the telescopic and the televisual highlights technologies of remote sensing and optics and discusses how this gives rise to an ambivalent relationship to politics. The two technologies are centuries apart, yet arguably it is only with television that the optical lens is superseded as the primary technology for viewing. The telescope magnifies and gives a view of the horizon. The medium of television is more detached. Images resulting from particles dispersed across a screen surface are not optical per se but atomised. Television is supposed to be an intimate media, shot in close-up and domestic. Yet televisual production fundamentally underpins the banality of the mediatised political economy that is partly responsible for the sense of failure that haunts politics today. It flattens intimacy into a blandness that is overwhelmingly crude; think twenty-four-hour reality TV. For all their promising vistas, both technologies truncate experience into narrow bandwidths and segment, or pixilate, the visual range of perception; they narrowcast and mask the events of contingency and context that lie just beyond our view of the horizon.

This becomes an argument about the politics of a mediatised visual field that is everywhere, and which is also effectively reduced and making us less able to see the sudden dematerialisation of the world. Dematerialisation is a result of over-sensation, as when snow-blindness is caused by the saturation of too much white light. The idea of a dematerialised aesthetics is one that is tangible but more sensed than seen: a whiteout effect that is a mark of dumb type's approach to dramaturgy, and, by extension, forewarning us about the effects of sensory overload.

Between Seeing and Already Seen: Dumb type's *memorandum* and the Question of Memory

Memorandum is perhaps dumb type's most complex mediatised work, aiming to stage the experience of memory and questioning how memories might be realised in the space of live performance. Combining "elements of multimedia, dance and fragmented narrative, memorandum explores the hazy dimensions of recall that ground and disquietly erode our experience minute-by-minute. The set is simple—almost an abstraction. A bare stage is bisected by an impenetrable but translucent wall, a screen onto which will be projected a barrage of images."[11] Data technology is compared to the Cartesian dyad of memory/mind and body in the work, and *memorandum* shows how the distance between body and mind and sensation and movement collapses into a data-driven postmodern event.

Dumb type called *memorandum* "a non-elegy recall, an impossible investigation into the unstable neurophilosophical events of memory itself."[12] As this shows, the work explores ideas of memory through an interweave of brain science and philosophy—hence the reference to neurophilosophy, a field related to cognition studies and seeking to understand how ineffable experiences of the world work in the brain. The philosopher Patricia Smith Churchland describes neurophilosophy as a focus on the interface between brain science and philosophy that directs us to questions such as:

> Are mental states identical to brain states? Are mental states reducible to brain states? What sort of business is reduction? What are emergent properties and are there any? What, if anything, is special about the subjective point of view? Are conscious experiences physiologically understandable? What are representations and how can a brain represent the world outside itself?[13]

These questions relate to *memorandum* in several ways. Firstly, with the concern to try and better understand the haptic and sensory demands of the piece for both performers and spectators, *memorandum* aims to explore how images and sounds create feelings. It asks on what terms are uncanny déjà vu-like experiences of memory connected with consciousness and the brain. In this sense, we can say that the work considers the nature of emergent properties of memory and perhaps suggests that mental states that connect us to memory exist in tandem with brain states.

This is how I interpret the two kinds of sense memory that are dramaturgically embedded into the performance. The first is explored through the production of image-scenarios that elicit emotions and uncanny effects; the sense of yearning that accompanies the experience of déjà vu, for example, and the flashes of uncanny nature in the projections. The second sense is not associative in an affective way; rather, we experience the effect of neurological triggers and involuntary responses to stimuli that work directly on our sight, sound and sense of embodiment. This is shown in the use of strobe lighting effects and the projection of rapid-eye movement imagery that is designed to physically overwhelm the audience. *Memorandum* utilises immersive environments, subliminal images and energetic choreographic sequences to create physical sensations as an analogue to memory. The bio-political effect of these agents (seen in the fact that they are working directly on the body) is one of the key insights of the work. In the "interface" of mind and body, we do not so much see an idea of power *represented*; rather, it is insistently *felt in the body,* activating us in ways beyond our conscious control. In other words, the way that the work aims to trigger perception is not symbolic but directly expressive. This in turn leads to the realisation of how the concepts and politics associated with the performance are not only processed cognitively but also felt.

An important distinction between dramaturgy's concern with poetics and metaphor and NMD's focus on the materiality of performance is shown here. What I am pointing to is an idea of how NMD restructures the means of communication in performance. A conventional dramaturgical perspective considers the dynamic tension and/or poetic potentials of performance, whereas here we see the existence of a network of assemblages of power. There is an emphasis on the importance of somatic activity; to borrow from Rosi Bradotti, this situation suggests "a more complex political economy that connects bodies to machines ... intimately, through simulation and mutual modification."[14] This idea moves on from postmodernism's concern with appropriation and commodity and into a field of inquiry that considers new ideas for politics and even new forms of life, something that we know members of dumb type were interested in exploring. A good example of this is how Furuhashi proposed that dumb type aimed to explore how "the times demand an evolution in our humanity."[15] The vision he had for the company combined an understanding of how humanity might enable new ways of living through developing inclusive and non-judgemental interpersonal relations and technologically mediated forms of representation. In this way communities could find coherence and fluidity, they could embrace diverse performative practices and even contradiction through the somatic flows of technological mediation. The new awareness that *memorandum* brought is the way that such an idea was shown through the active and visible somatically embodied dramaturgy.

But this point does not take away from the deep critical stance that *memorandum* develops in relation to information and the perilous state of society that is explored through showing what a postmodern collapse of history, identity and memory looks and feels like. The intense spectacle of whiteout mediatised data that is a recurrent image in the work is perhaps the most powerfully realised of the dramaturgical strategies in pointing this out.

Sequences of *memorandum* are given names such as:

» Initialise
  — store/clear previous images
» Random memory scan
  — cascade of white noise and REM-speed visual feedback
» Flash-frozen cascade
  — centrifuge
  — break-up of personality into dataloops
» On a clear day
  — real mirage
  — emerging to oceanic frieze exhausted of meanings[16]

These are all descriptions of the systems and actions of the data economy and its effects. Memory is shown as a form of decay, fragmenting into fleeting glitches and granular forms. Of course, we all know that the actuality of what we remember becomes fuzzy with the passing of time. But this piece explores a parallel "mirage state" of this fact where programmed memories and their deterioration and mutation exist as facsimile data recordings, downloads, links and uploads. This depiction of the postmodern idea of memory without origin links also the awareness of how memory is used as a tool to reboot history as a flattened depoliticised idea of nostalgia. History begins again as a consensus narrative without complications. It is a catalysis for the forces of acceleration and vanishing in the same moment. From these terms, we can see how the idea of data production and a focus on its political consequences is chief among the concerns of this work. In other words, this is exactly as Virilio observes in his comments in relation to the technological production of memory and its lack of critical distance.

Taking this further, I suggest that *memorandum* anticipates a post-historical and considerably deterritorialised idea of memory as seen in the following passage of voiced text written by Stefaan Decostere that accompanies an array of abstract images in one of the key scenes in the work. The scene is called "Twilight in the forest of memory—dance with self," directed by the choreographer and dancer Sunayama Noriko.

> All out / Tear the armor from my body / Don't be afraid of my skin / Make my joints supple / Make me insensitive / Erase my memory / In one go, hit me / Body to body / Hold me back / Leave me / Mercy, please / Look in my mirror / Follow me / Relieve my pain / Be kind / Kiss me / Without lips / Keep on seducing me / Free at last / Give me peace / Stop my heart / Use me up / Make my blood flow / Carve into me / Lick my metal tongue clean / Make me immortal / Create me anew / Lick me clean / Alone / So randy / Taste me / Try me / Change me / Again and again / …
>
> Welcome to the next level / Just float / The best is not good enough / Make me a god / Simulate me / Get a kick out of me / Drive me mad / Drop me / Stay away / Come closer now / Believe blindly / Incorporate me / Shave me bald / Color my lenses black / Kick me / Everywhere / Destroy me / Zap me away / Forever / Drop dead / Look at me / Here / Be silent / Stand still / Caress me / Don't leave me cold / Set me to zero / At once / Take me seriously / Dance with me.[17]

In the scene, dancers perform slow erotic movements in a fictional nightclub. It is a space of images linking with desire and languid transformations. The text includes some remarkable comments on the possibilities for entering the production of subjectivity in a new way, freed from the daily exigencies of reality and reimagined as a new kind of bodily assemblage. There is a constant shifting between surfaces and interiority that harks to Deleuze and Guattari's concept of the Body without Organs: "You never reach the Body without Organs, you can't reach it, you are forever attaining it, it is a limit. People ask, So what is this BwO? ... On it we sleep, live our waking lives, fight—fight and are fought—seek our place, experience untold happiness and fabulous defeats; on it we penetrate and are penetrated; on it we love."[18] This scene presents the central dilemma of *memorandum*: that is, a questioning about the exact nature of the relationship between existence and memory. While a BwO endlessly creates potentials, to only exist in partial fragments is also the limit point for memory where our sense of existence disappears.

One version of the work called *Cascade* (2001), but sharing much of the image texture and immersive aesthetics of *memorandum*, was an installation. The spectator entered the work at one end of an enclosed corridor and was able to see rapid, pixelated images of nature, city buildings, transit and objects that were flickering and dazzling the senses. The score magnified the experience of disorientation. With so many images literally "cascading," memory was seen in terms of fragments, disassociations, piling on a coded idea of information to the point of an acute sensory overload. The presumed experience of dying, when scenes from the totality of one's existence are recalled in a rapid jumble in the mind's eye, seems a good way to describe this. At the same time, the collapse of time into what Deleuze calls "time image"[19] seems more to the point. Time image is about the materiality of time and draws attention to the fact of duration. Notes on the dumb type website speak of *memorandum* and *Cascade* both having "a flow of time: repetition and recurrence instead of uniqueness and conciseness."[20] This is comparable to the idea of time image in that there is no longer a chronology or the capacity to reflect on things in sequence. It begs the question of what happens to memory if we are no longer able to remember an event as something historical, something recalled from the past, and instead the fragments of memories cascade in the present. Is there a comparison to be made between the idea of dematerialisation and the flattening of information? Is this, in fact, the new threshold of memory in postmodern times?

* * *

Dumb type's statement on *memorandum* suggests that this is the case: "Who can say what memory was before photography existed? What will come to replace cumulative direct experience as new technologies continue to overtake the threshold of cognisance, the speed of human recognition?"[21] Returning to their idea of the work being a non-elegy recall, this takes *memorandum* into an idea of memory that is outside the body and around us.

At the beginning of *memorandum* the audience sees the performer Kawaguchi Takao writing a note to himself that is filmed from above and projected onto a large screen.[22] His writing is biographical and these written memories soon blur into a vast projection of people walking in a city space. A flattened voiceover includes the phrases: "all out / erase my memory / welcome to the next level / just float / lead blindly / set me to zero." The scene suddenly shifts to a series of pixillating images of city, nature and data that is all mixed as an intense and unstable pattern of fragments. Watching this is disrupting and the frequency of images and sound work in tandem to unset and overload the senses. In writing about *memorandum,* Asada calls this "information integrated in the extreme, is cancelled out, close to absolute zero."[23]

Just such an idea is shown in the final sequence of *memorandum*. A performer stands behind a translucent screen in a swimsuit. We can see that they are stretching in preparation for taking a swim but the detail of the scene is opaque, an effect caused by the soft focus of the screen in front of the figure. Suddenly the performer dives backwards and immediately the fractured datascape from the earlier scene returns. After a brief frenetic burst that is an absolute assault on the senses, the scene comes to an abrupt end. The body is gone and the space is totally dark, still and silent. As the *memorandum* production notes state:

> The safe and sheltering forest of memory is no more. Nostalgic reminiscences of happy days past, sweet dreams of future memories to come—all are poised without critical mass on the brink of never, swimming headlong down a horizon-less maze toward no vanishing point.[24]

In other words, just as the media message that too much sensation is never enough, the non-elegy recall of dumb type's whiteout dramaturgy hits us with the urgent need to rethink memory in an age of never remembering. Remember or exist in a sublime state of nothing is the memo: "Erase my memory / In one go, hit me / Body to body / ... Relieve my pain." In making us experience the overwhelming sense of vanishing, the body is also activated and challenged to remember in new ways.

Notes

1 Marshall McLuhan, *Understanding Media: The Extensions of Man* (New York: McGraw-Hill, 1964), p. 52.

2 Paul Virilio, *Speed and Politics*, trans. Mark Polizzotti (Los Angeles: Semiotext(e), 2006), p. 121.

3 Ibid., p. 78.

4 Ibid., p. 126.

5 See, for example, Chantal Mouffe, *Agonistics: Thinking The World Politically* (London and New York: Verso, 2013); Claire Bishop, *Artificial Hells: Participatory Art and the Politics of Spectatorship* (London and New York: Verso, 2012); and Boris Groys, *Art Power* (Cambridge, MA: MIT Press, 2008).

6 Hal Foster, "Introduction," in *The Anti-Aesthetic: Essays on Postmodernism*, ed. Hal Foster (New York: The New Press, 1998), p. xiii.

7 Inaga Shigemi, "To Be a Japanese Artist in the So-Called Postmodern Era," *Third Text* 33, Winter 1995–96: 24.

8 Masayo Miyoshi and Harry Harootunian, "Introduction," in *Postmodernism and Japan*, ed. Masayo Miyoshi and Harry Harootunian (Durham, NC, and London: Duke University Press, 1989), p. xi.

9 Asada Akira, "Infantile Capitalism and Japan's Postmodernism: A Fairytale," in *Postmodernism and Japan*, ed. Miyoshi and Harootunian, pp. 273–78.

10 See Peter Eckersall, *Theorizing the Angura Space: Avant-garde Performance and Politics in Japan, 1960–2000* (Leiden: Brill, 2006).

11 http://www.epidemic.net/en/art/dumbtype/proj/memorandum.html (accessed 24 May 2015).

12 www.epidemic.net/en/art/dumbtype/index.html (accessed 24 May 2015).

13 Patricia Smith Churchland, *Neurophilosophy: Toward a Unified Science of the Mind-Brain* (Cambridge, MA: MIT Press, 1989), p. 2.

14 Rosi Bradotti, *Posthumanism* (Cambridge: Polity, 2013), p. 90.

15 Cited in Eckersall, *Theorizing the Angura Space*, p. 143.

16 http://www.epidemic.net/en/art/dumbtype/proj/memorandum.html (accessed 24 May 2015).

17 Dumb type, *memorandum* excerpt, cited in Woodrow Hood and Cynthia Gendrich, "Memories of the Future: Technology and the Body in dumb type's *memorandum*," *PAJ: A Journal of Performance and Art* 25 (1), 2003: 15.

18 Gilles Deleuze and Félix Guattari, *A Thousand Plateaus*, trans. Brian Massumi (London and New York: Continuum, 1987), p. 167.

19 Gilles Deleuze, *Cinema 2: The Time Image*, trans. Hugh Tomlinson and Robert Galeta (Minneapolis: University of Minnesota Press, 1989).

20 *Memorandum and Cascade*, exhibited at the House of World Cultures, Berlin, http://archiv.hkw.de/deutsch/kultur/2001/dumbtype/dumbtype_e.html (accessed 24 April 2015).

21 Dumb type, *memorandum*, program notes, www.epidemic.net/en/art/dumbtype/index.html (navigate: projects: memorandum; accessed 24 April 2015).

22 Kawaguchi has been exploring the idea of personal biography in his own works for the last decade as well as in *memorandum*. In these works he writes down memories from his life that are transformed into physical sensations, which in turn trigger light and sound effects. An example of this is the work *Tablemind*, made with Manabe Daito in 2011.

23 Critical Space Archive, http://www.kojinkaratani.com/criticalspace/old/special/asada/shicho03.html (accessed 24 May 2015).

24 Dumb type, *memorandum*, programme notes. www.epidemic.net/en/art/dumbtype/index.html (navigate: projects: memorandum; accessed 24 April 2015).

pH, dumb type (1990).
Photos © dumb type
& Emmanuel Valette.

pH, dumb type (1990). © dumb type.

S/N, dumb type (1994). © dumb type & Emmanuel Valette.

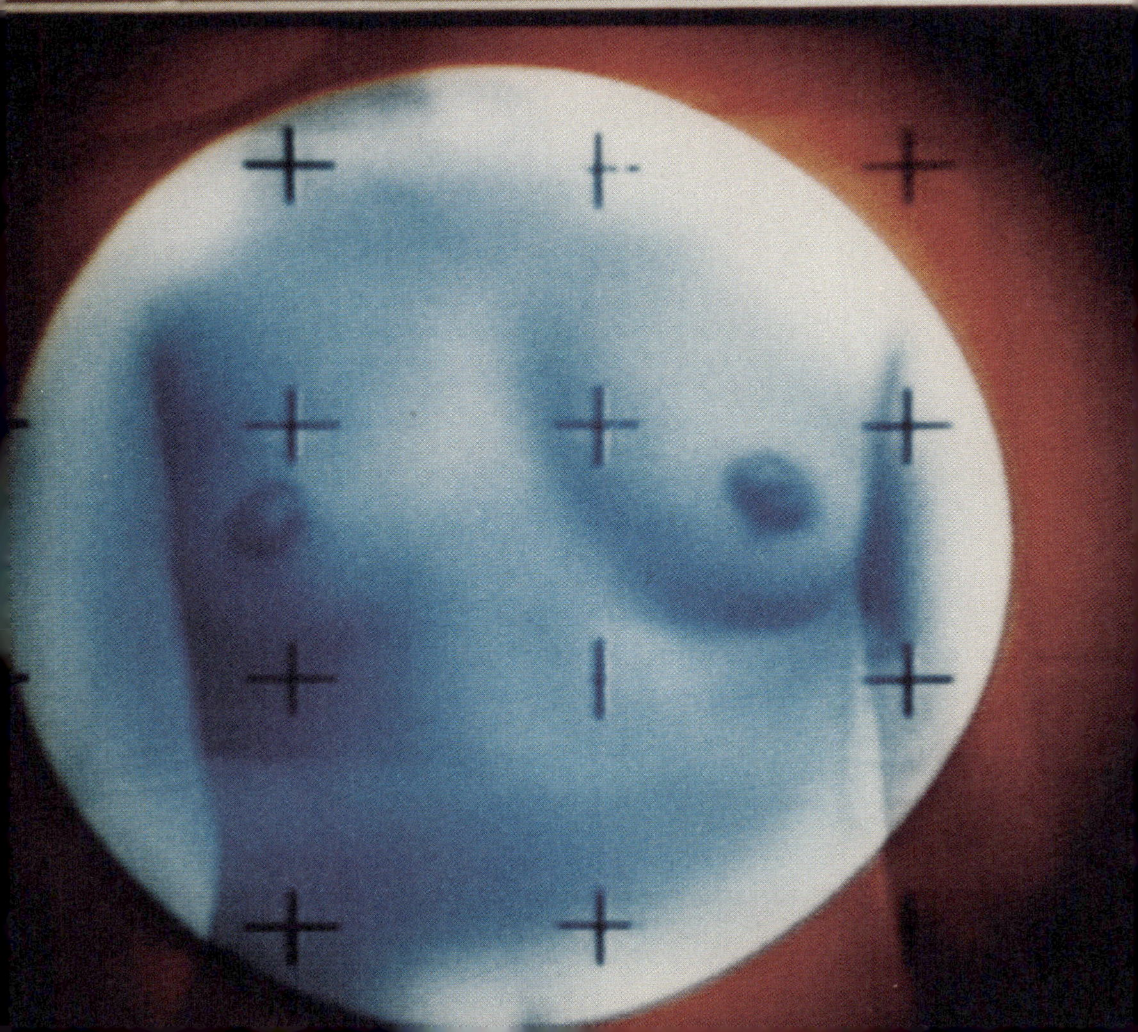

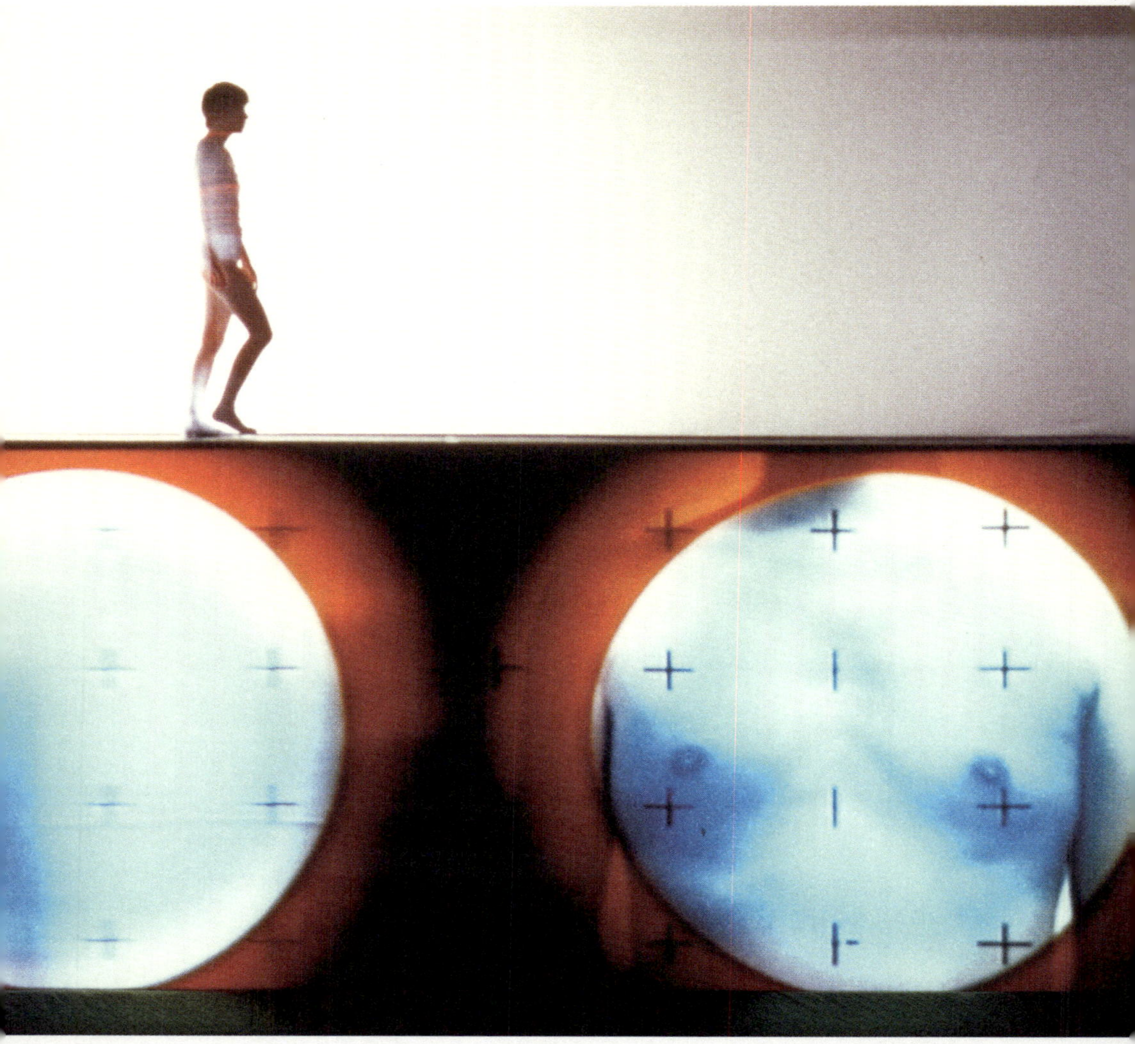

S/N, dumb type (1994). © dumb type.

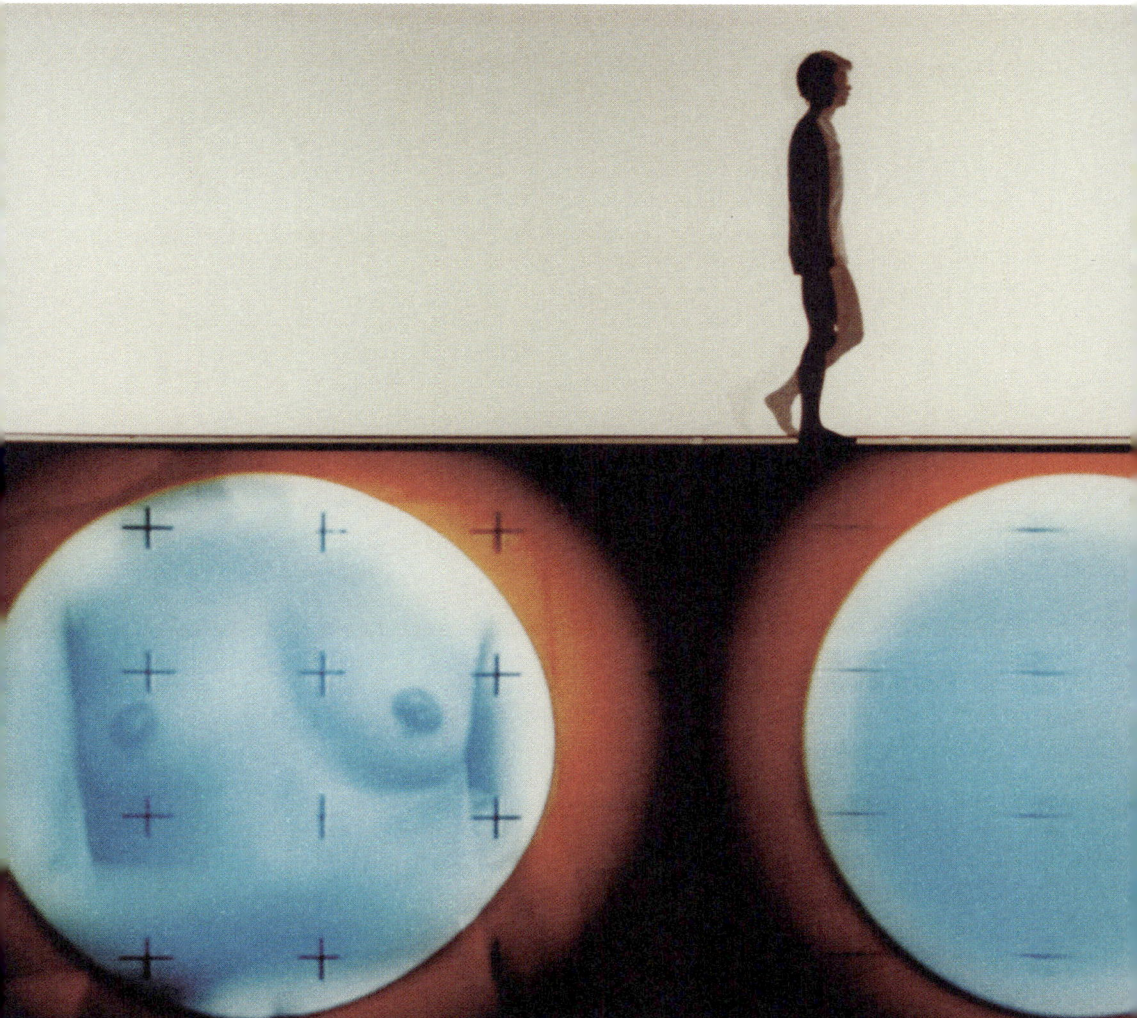

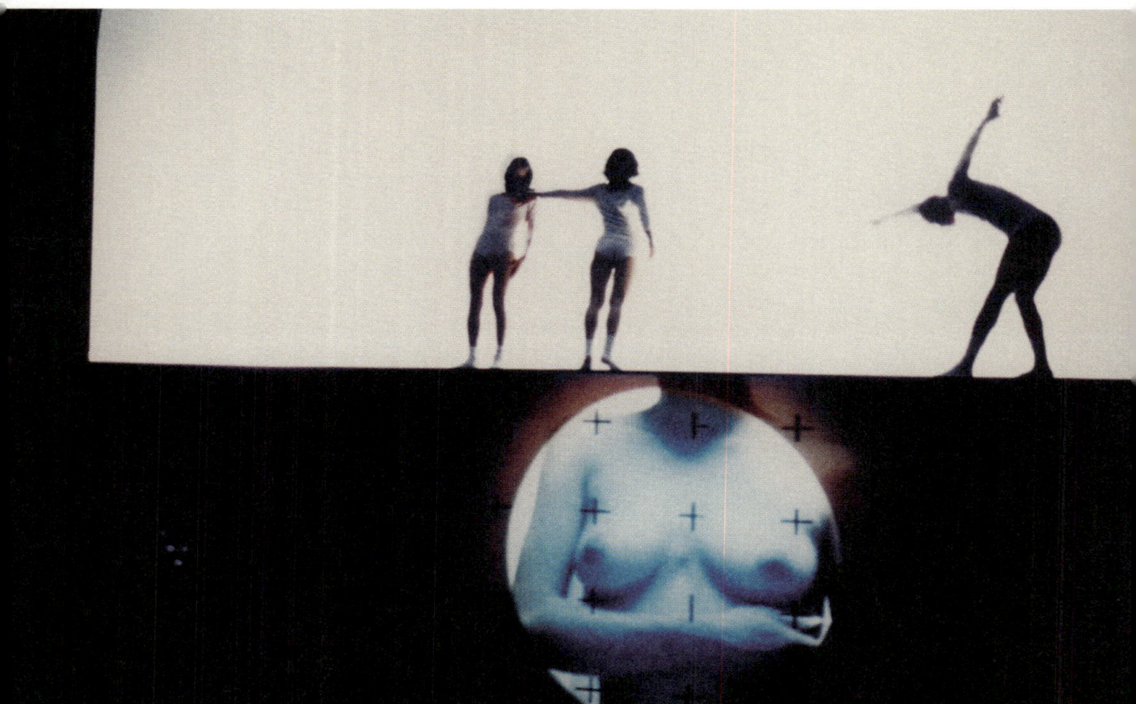

S/N, dumb type (1994). © dumb type & Emmanuel Valette.

S/N, dumb type (1994). © dumb type.

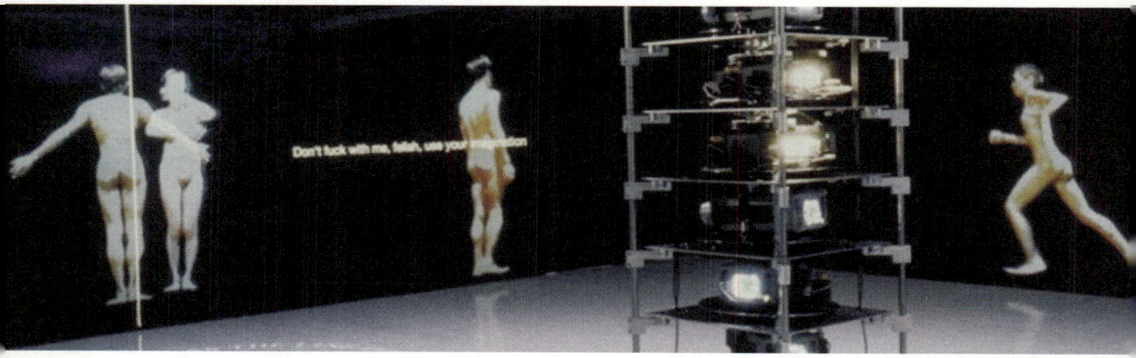

Lovers, an installation by Teiji Furuhashi and Tokyo Canon Artlab (1994). © Teiji Furuhashi and Tokyo Canon Artlab.

Voyages, dumb type (2004). © dumb type & Kazuo Fukunaga.

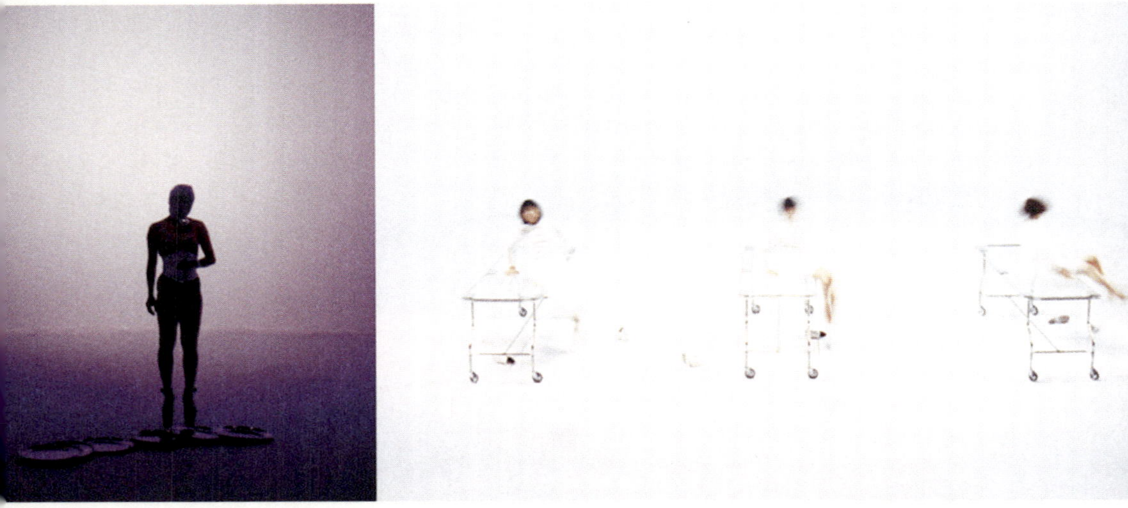

OR, dumb type (1997). © dumb type.

OR, dumb type (1997).

memorandum, dumb type (2000). © dumb type.

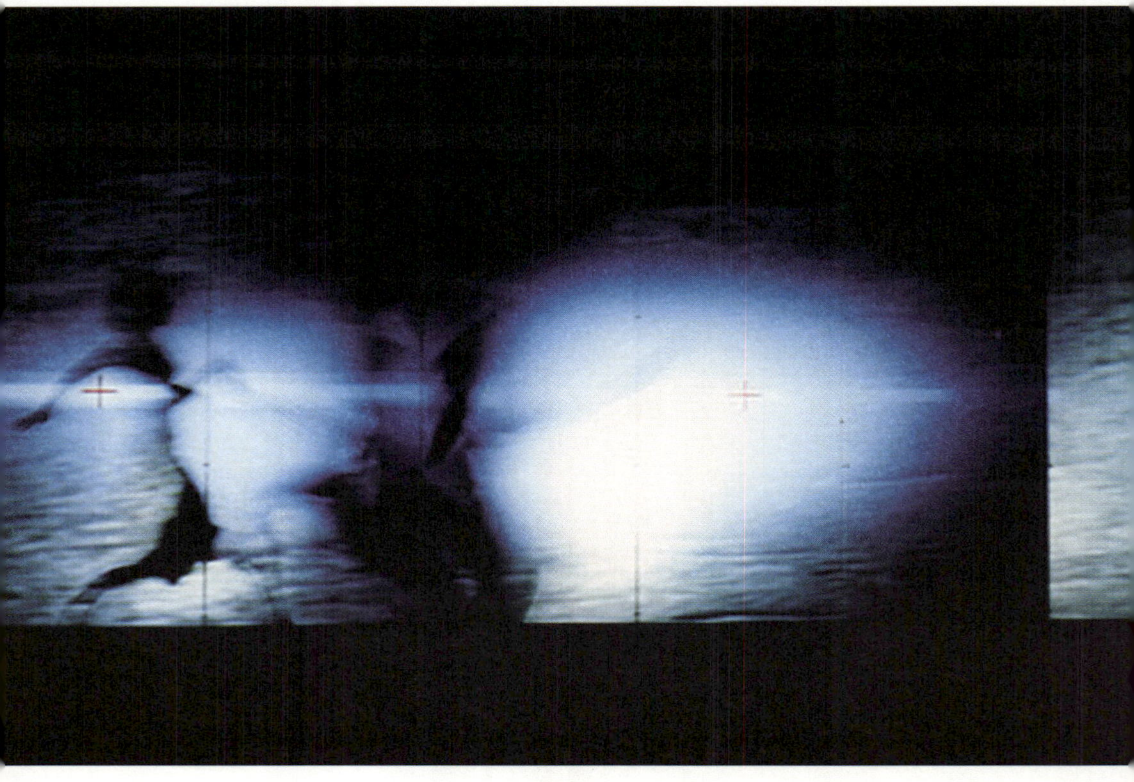

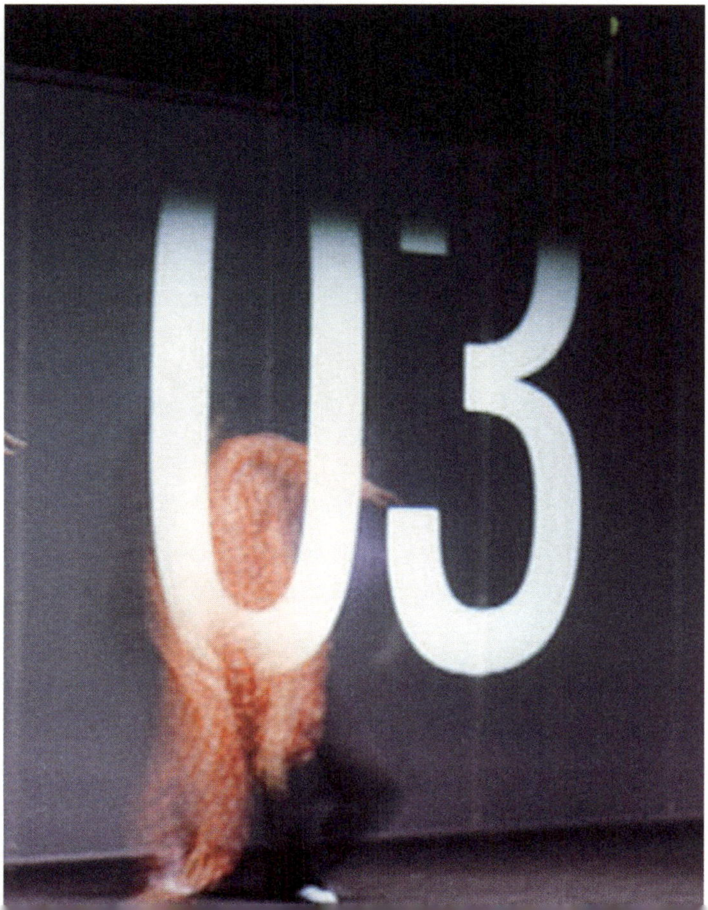

memorandum, dumb type (2000).

Re-thinking the Audience

Dumb Type, New Media, New Dramaturgy and the Spectator

Andreas Regelsberger

In this short essay I would like to examine the role of new dramaturgy and new media in regard to the audience in dumb type's works, focusing mainly on the two productions *OR* (1997) and *memorandum* (1999). Both were produced during dumb type's second creative period, after the experience of a major tragedy and severe setback in 1995 when Teiji Furuhashi, the founder and one of the central figures of the group, had died of complications related to his HIV infection.

1.

OR—which, according to the program, stands for both "Operation Room" and "Orientation"— premiered at the Festival VIA in Maubeuge in France in 1997 and has since toured throughout Europe, the United States and Japan. In the summer and autumn of 1998, it ran at the Barbican Centre in London, in Milan, at EXPO '98 Lisbon, Le Festival d'Automne in Paris, in Stockholm (the 1998 Cultural Capital of Europe), at the Kampnagel Theatre in Hamburg and the Zürcher Theater Spektakel in Switzerland. In late autumn of 1999, *OR* toured to four US cities: Portland, Seattle, Minneapolis and Chicago. Hence, the number of the show's spectators abroad must have greatly exceeded those who saw the production in Japan. *OR* tackles questions about life and death and is based on a concept of Furuhashi.

Before the performance begins, earplugs are handed out to the audience in anticipation of some of the acoustic effects that are to follow. The stage is filled with a large white floor and surrounded by a white semicircular wall that pushes back deep into the stage space, all lit by a bright, bluish light. The lights fade to black and the performance begins with a series of electronic beeps and a single vertical bar of light scanning the entire back wall, effectively transforming the space into a giant heart monitor. Blistering flashes of light burn images of the rapidly entering and exiting performers onto the retinas of the audience, giving the performers a visual afterlife even though they are no longer on stage. These bursts of light are accompanied by near deafening explosions of sound that ring in the ears. This opening sequence, titled "Edge," effectively confuses your senses, mixing what you may have really seen or heard with almost aural/visual hallucinations as the images remain burned onto your eyes and the sound continues to ring in your ears. A real sense of dread and excitement ensues about what is coming next.[1]

On stage the performers assume the roles of doctors, living and dying patients, and dead bodies. Later in the performance, some text is projected onto the back wall: "How much the science can control the borders of life and death," invoking the central theme of this show.

A sequence called "Crying Room" follows the opening section. Three men lie down on medical devices that resemble sickbeds, gurneys or dissecting tables, and die, covering themselves with white sheets. Each body is later approached by a woman. The women administer all kinds of tests to see if the men are really dead. Each woman deals with her dead man in a different way. The first woman uses a long rope and ties the body to the bed, as if to make sure that he won't come back to life. Another woman undresses her man and dresses him like a rock star, giving him sunglasses, leather pants and an electric guitar. As these two women finish their tasks, they leave the stage. The remaining woman, who has continued checking her man's body for signs of life, begins to quake and cry. The man rises slightly and a low, guttural wail comes from his body. However, it is the woman's face and body that give physicality to his wailing. The man's sound intensifies, as do the woman's convulsions.

A woman is first zipped into and later released from a white bag—which could be a body bag or a uterus—and is reanimated by some assistants. After coming back to life, she walks away, naked, in a robot-like fashion.

In the original concept for the production, written by Furuhashi before he passed away, it says:

> Explaining the issue around the border of life and death.
> And how technology is involved in to distinct this border now.
> Idea came up from my experiences
> in the hospital when my mother (cancer) died in August,
> and my brother (traffic accident), my lover (AIDS) in the past.
> How much the science can control this border.
> How much our mind can control this border.
> This is the border, which all the humans have to confront some day.[2]

Furuhashi was inspired in this production by the experience of the loss of his mother. In an interview, he said:

> My mother died last month of cancer. When her heart suddenly stopped, you could see that from the life support machine. It was there in the room. I was screaming to the doctors to come and they started, "Boom, boom." Beat. Attack to the heart. And air was in her mouth. Observing the beat from inside her body. … I couldn't distinguish what was the border between life and death. I had to rely on the technology to know when she died. … It was a very big experience for me. I am trying to explore that border. … I'm very trapped in exploring that idea.[3]

After Furuhashi's death, the collective expanded this idea into the fully realised performance, which opened up the series of questions about death and dying that the piece, as a whole, meditates upon. The performance programme reads:

> It is about the state of "white out," like in the blizzard,
> where you are deprived of ability to see,
> where you can't recognize anything,
> where you don't know where you stand any more,
> where you may not know whether you are alive OR dead.
> But what distinguishes one from the other?

> Where is border?
> What is death?
> What is it?[4]

Even though Furuhashi played a central role in dumb type's earlier productions, the group should probably be considered more as a conceptual collective as the creative processes are usually based on brainstorming and collective recalling, a process that marks a shift away from the solo performance artist.

As the Belgian dramaturge Marianne Van Kerkhoven (1946–2013) notes about processuality as a main characteristic of a collective work:

> One of the fundamental characteristics of what we today call "new dramaturgy" is ... a process-orientated method of working; the meaning, the intentions, the form and the substance of a play arise during the working process.[5]

In his own words, dancer and dumb type member Takao Kawaguchi remarks about this process:

> It's like a melting pot; anybody can put anything in the pot and cook. And then gradually when the steam comes up together, then each person takes the response in each field.[6]

Or, as Toru Koyamada, another dumb type member, says: "Dumb type's philosophy is to sample the source."[7]

It was during this period, when dumb type was touring with *OR* in Europe and the US, that they embarked upon the conceptual process for their next production, *memorandum*.

2.
memorandum

During the process of formulating *memorandum*, the members of the group came to the realisation that the acts of brainstorming and recalling are actually functions of memory and they decided to pursue this idea. *Memorandum* is thus a perfect example of a self-referential approach to producing a work. The basic premise of *memorandum* is to question the concept of memory and to investigate its relation to the technology that we use as a means of digital documentation of our memories. In about ten sequences loosely linked together in a very associative way, as our memory itself works, we witness scenes from, among others, *Goldilocks and the Three Bears,* Hawaiian vacations and nightclubs.

In *memorandum,* the stage space and floor is black, in contrast to the dazzling white of *OR,* the previous production. The set is, again, quite simple; a bare stage is separated by a translucent curtain, which functions as a screen onto which a large number of images will be projected. Amidst a cascade of white noise and REM-speed visual flashes, the performers' movements are broken down into displaced gestures in silhouette; they almost seem to dissolve into these images.

3.

The occasionally extreme and intense use of strobe and dazzling light (Takayuki Fujimoto), together with the dense video projections (Shiro Takatani), the projected texts by Stefaan Decostere and the sometimes deafening soundscapes (Ryoji Ikeda and Toru Yamanaka) are a challenge for the audience. In the performance of *OR* that I saw in 1997 at Kampnagel in Hamburg, many of the members of the audience got up and left early on. Some critics singled this out and characterised dumb type's works as an "assault on the senses" or a "visceral attack."[8] Yet, in these assaults or attacks there lies an extraordinary possibility for the audience. We are neither witness to a story that is being told to us, nor do we become part of it. The advanced use of multimedia, sound, light and performance all together creates a very special atmosphere where the audience has no choice but to submit and allow themselves to be immersed in these highly sensual yet clearly conceptual worlds.

Where we witness speed, acceleration and power (Paul Virilio), the idea of simulacra and simulation as well as the loss of reality (Jean Baudrillard), and the idea of the cyborg as a chimera of machine and organism (Donna Haraway), things may become complex, but ultimately the somewhat haptic dramaturgy employed by dumb type leads to an activation of our bodily sense of performance. With our senses affected in this very direct way, we find ourselves in the space between life and death, and experience the disturbing feelings Teiji Furuhashi himself wrote about and the disorientation of deceptive and illusive memory.

Notes

1 See Cynthia Gendrich and Woodrow Hood, "Noise and Nudity: Kyoto's dumb type," *Theatre Forum* 18, Winter/Spring 2000: 8.

2 Cited in Gendrich and Hood, "Noise and Nudity," pp. 4–5. As Gendrich and Hood note, this original "demonstrates some of the language and translation complications" faced.

3 Laura Trippi, "Dumb Type/ Smart Noise," *World Art* 2, 1996: 28.

4 Dumb type, *OR*, 1997, http://www.epidemic.net/en/art/dumbtype/proj/or-spect.html (accessed 4 February 2017).

5 Marianne Van Kerkhoven, "On Dramaturgy," *Theaterschrift* 5–6, 1994: 18.

6 See Gendrich and Hood, "Noise and Nudity," p. 8.

7 Quoted in Peter Eckersall, *Theorizing the Angura Space: Avant-garde Performance and Politics in Japan, 1960–2000* (Leiden: Brill, 2006), p. 145.

8 See, for example, Gigi Berardi's review "dumb type," in *Dance Magazine* 74 (2), February 2000: 96.

Two Memoranda

Was That a Question Thrown to Us?

KUMAKURA Takaaki

Shifting and Transformation

Artists shift. They are constantly moving. Of course, this also includes artistic collectives.

Since their establishment in 1984, dumb type have been changing constantly. While their membership, artistic practices and scope of activities have varied, they boldly kept challenging contemporary historical moments. Among the many signs of transformation, the shifting qualities of their work seen between the performances of *pH* and *S/N* broke mediocre expectations and confronted us with a totally unexpected new staging and idea of performance. *S/N*'s bold vision and potency annoyed some, while others were deeply impressed.

With *OR,* dumb type's work shifted again, this time in different ways to the changes seen between *pH* and *S/N*. While they sharpened their thinking about boundaries between life and death and established a new digital "aesthetics," in a sense the shift also decisively betrayed the essential quality of the thought explored in *S/N*. This transformation was welcomed by some as a new departure for dumb type, and, as with the earlier shift in thematic and practice, others were disappointed.

And now there are two "memoranda" that appear simultaneously: the Japanese premiere of the performance of *memorandum* and the publication of *memorandum,* the collection of the writings of Furuhashi Teiji. I wonder what it is that the company wants to tell us by presenting these two items *at the same time.* Are they throwing a big question out to us? And can we only stand still, immobilised and dazed in the face of such an enormous ideological, aesthetic and ethical difference in these works by dumb type, yet works that are made under the same name?

S/N — Creating "Artless-Wise" Culture

Dumb type's formation in Kyoto in 1984 and the development of their signature performances modelling text and body language go side by side with the development of the so-called "bubble economy" of the 1980s and the "postmodernisation" of culture. This was the time of the "small theatre boom" in Japan; however, dumb type diverged from the small theatre model in at least two ways. Firstly, while in a conventional theatre group the members often share a common destiny and work with a hierarchical division of labour under a charismatic director's aesthetical and political leadership, dumb type had a cross-sector and fluid manner of communication among each member's independent "speciality." Such specialisations and interests ranged from visual arts, music, dance and design, to architecture and computer programing. Furthermore, they introduced a model of non-hierarchical collaboration without a leader as the principle organiser of their activities. Secondly, they extended the communication among these "specialisations" to include media and engaged in a freely changeable idea of "multimedia" creation, not only conceived as performances, but also as installations, concerts, video art, CDs and the medium of print.

Along with deepening this multimedia collaboration, dumb type drew international attention by presenting works one after another such as *036 Pleasure Life* (1987), *Pleasure Life* (1988) and *pH* (1990–1995), works which made an issue of the hyper-reality of high-consumption societies at the time and the "new world order" caused by the collapse of Cold War structures. Nevertheless, no matter how much these creations were open to a spirit of media-wise collaboration, they were essentially and consistently created within the framework of "art" institutions.

However, this changed when Furuhashi announced his HIV-positive status. In the face of this incurably real situation, dumb type must have recognised the powerlessness of their previous creative language. This was an absolute reality, leaving the group dazed and wondering if the grammar of their "art" contained any creative strength. Yet, presumably after a long struggle, they undertook a major transformation in their work and began to make work as a "high-wire" act—with a sense of precarity and openness. They opened up "art" to an affirmation of realistic things, hoping to deconstruct and redefine art at a ground-zero level of expression. Hence, they developed this "artless-wise" process as a non-stop shifting between two vectors that they called the "creation of work" and the "creation of place."[1]

The project *S/N* (1993–96) was first presented as an installation work and an experimental "seminar show" that later developed into a performance work. *S/N* not only brought accusations against the force of the scientific, medical and political discourses around AIDS, sexuality and minorities by utilising a mixture of high-technology aesthetics, bare physicality and explorations of the political nature of text; it also incorporated a sophisticated use of "low" popular performance forms such as drag shows and striptease. It was a miraculous work, which took the risk of being at a zero point of artistic "technique" in that it intentionally staged scenes in a "clumsy" way and showed "reality" itself as a form of "object," thus enhancing the experience of objectification.[2]

S/N says: I am "out," therefore I am. We can truly love each other only through persistently being OUT, disclosing each other's body and barely tearing ourselves from the "silent common consent" such as science, art and gender that equals the molecular power of relationships of these discourses. Of course, such love with OUT cannot be realised through ordinary communication with an audience in a theatre. Therefore, the group's activities came out of the theatre and were disseminated in various "places" in the midst of real urban space, mostly in locations in Kyoto.

The first of these was Art-Scape, which explored a new style of art centre as a place for the collection and distribution of information about art and AIDS, fostering interactions with people and place to organise seminars and workshops. Another, Weekend Café, was established in a corner of a student residence at Kyoto University as a place for people to meet and talk. It was held on every second weekend, running late into the night, and hoped to redefine the cafe as a culture generator. There was also the AIDS Poster Project, a non-profit organisation for disseminating information and educating people about HIV and AIDS through visual media.

With these places, dumb type and their collaborators tried to foster an "artless-wise" culture, with a slippage between art and activism (ART–ACT), even if they did not know how it would turn out. As a non-profit organisation, they could expand their network not only in the field of art but also in exploring possibilities of reviewing the current state of nursing care, education and medical services.

On 29 October 1995, Furuhashi Teiji passed away. Close attention was subsequently paid to dumb type, with a mixture of emotions and with expectations and anxiety. With Furuhashi gone, the group had lost one of the cornerstones of their philosophy and aesthetics, and people wondered what kind of challenges the group might face. Then *OR* emerged.

OR — Digital Fascism of the Hyper-Modernist

OR (1997–99) was developed as a series of multimedia presentations, through installation, performance, a concert and a CD. Not surprisingly this work was a condensation and crystallisation of the emotions and thoughts of individual members who had each witnessed Furuhashi's illness and death, and the work was conceived as an "examination" of the "grey humour lying in the zone between life and death."[3]

Let us look at the performance. Pulses of sound and electronic flashes, suggestive of *S/N,* sharply lacerate the clinic-like performance space. Heavy bass sounds shake the whole theatre and are felt in our internal organs while flashing bursts of intense light take our sight away. The digital aesthetics broke from those previously seen in *S/N*. Here, it was rather the aesthetic amplification of the infinitely inorganic and cold rhythm of medical instruments. The bodies of the performers were physically exposed to this destructive power, fighting against it until they were exhausted. But what was mostly apparent was the impactful force of these operations on the audience and how their bodies were affected at the organic level. A flood of electromagnetic and sonic waves, beyond human physical perception, transported the audience to the edges of life and the depths of delirium.

A "grey humour" lying in the zone between life and death was seen in various short scenes or playlets, falling in tone between humour and seriousness. Their dramaturgical techniques were intentionally deployed in a flimsy way. This was overwhelming when compared to the marvellously realised "clumsy" reality exhibited in *S/N*. The words in *OR* were also flimsy. This is not to say that there was no script or text; rather that the signification of the text was empty, and, more than anything, there was no noise of words, or words as noise. There was only the emptiness of signals ensuring transparent communication.

The highlight of *OR* is the scene toward the end of the performance depicting a car travelling south from Switzerland to northern Italy. Scenic images are projected onto the entire curved wall of the stage and a female performer stands motionless in its centre. The speed gradually accelerates, starting from a super-slow motion. Images and sound are made into digital fragments that increase rapidly like cancer cells. Our bodies and our senses are taken over by the crescendos of discontinuous rhythm, confusion and the reintegration of forms.

While ordinary digital representation tries to simulate the analogue, in *OR* the visual and acoustic intensification of digital signals multiplied without the intelligible sense of reality. The aesthetics of hyper-modernism implanting digital representation with self-referencing is seen. There was a complete absence of noise and the overgrowth of signals, only hyper-visual and hyper-acoustic digital signals remained. I wonder if we see in this sequence a master realisation of a third type of a "body without organs," as theorised by Deleuze and Guattari.[4] The first body without organs educes the empty bodies (still not replete with strength) of masochists, drug addicts and those with schizophrenia. The second is a body sated with an underlying strength of desire (e.g. in courtly love or the Tao). With the third body without organs, the body has become like cancer cells that spread and proliferate; this is the very "stratum," the tissue of the organ-ised body.

At this point, it is possible that the sense of discontinuity and an overgrowth of functionality could direct us to thinking about an organisational hierarchy of fascism. Is it any wonder that the speeding car and jet engine noise, the technologies that fascinated the Italian Futurists with their admiration of Mussolini, appeared in *OR*? Is it a coincidence that the journey on the screen was heading to Italy? The body without organs as an idea of digital fascism and hyper-modernism: could that be the aim of the high-tech aesthetics of *OR*? After all, we are not sure if the performer standing centre stage, motionless, directly in front of the screen in this new aesthetic is a muse or a sacrifice.

At the end, perhaps the examination of "grey humour" at the boundary between life and death in *OR* collapsed the contiguous vectors of *S/N* that opened signal to noise, IN to OUT, Thanatos to Eros, and "artwork" to "place." Furthermore, before we knew it, the collective that was supposed to keep seeking the new possibilities of networking through the not-for-profit system had made dumb type into a business corporation.

Two Memoranda — Was That a Question Thrown to Us?

In the process of such philosophical, aesthetic, political and economic transformation, it was not surprising that some members of dumb type left the group. For people who truly understood the philosophy of *S/N*, a work that fundamentally questioned "if art is possible"[5] when facing the im/possibility of love with AIDS, the new-found fascination for a digital hyper-modernism based on "fascistic/menacing communication"[6] must have been a harsh brunt to bear, one that went to the heart of an ethics of creation.

And then there were the two versions of *memorandum.*

The performance *memorandum* is basically an extension of *OR*. The digital fascism increased its destructive strength more delicately and skilfully. According to a company statement, *memorandum* explores "the hazy dimensions of recall that ground and disquietly erode our experience minute-by-minute" and the "dancers drift in a slow sensual subconscious slidestep through the 'forest of memory'." I wonder if dumb type wanted to create a multimedia version of *Remembrance of Things Past* with this new work. What is the reality?

Imageries of empty urban-scapes are projected across the stage. Suddenly they are shuffled hyper-visually and hyper-sonically with dazzling speed. Every part of our brain is rapidly scanned and memories are reverse-transferred into a rapid overload of digital signals. Breaking through the criticality of the brain. White-out. We are brought into a new world. "Welcome to the next level," says a voice, "just float."

Hereupon dumb type has created a new aesthetics of sublimity, or, more correctly, a techno-logic of hyper-sublimity. In the eighteenth century, Immanuel Kant conceived of an aesthetics of the sublime: in facing the awesome power of nature, he praised the greatness of human reason.[7] At the end of the twentieth century, with an avalanche of digital "things-in-itself," dumb type attempts to crash through this sensibility, understanding and *nous*, i.e. human beings. Excessive nature arouses fear, but as long as we are physically safe, the encounter is determined to be sublime. dumb type's digital "thing-in-itself" crashes "human beings" with a physical terror and tries to achieve a hyper-sublimity.

However, the impulse force of the technology of hyper-sublimity is loosened by the philosophical and formative flimsiness of the playlet scenes enacted by the performers. These short scenes sound like the re-edited versions of the individual memories of the performers.[8] Mannerism and narcissism rule in these moments. (I use the term "mannerism" not in its correct usage in art history but as *maniera* = attachment to technique.)

Hawaiian dance, American popular songs, a star-filled night sky, white paper circles, props such as a bucket, a stool, a trunk, stylish costumes and semantically empty text: they have all become design and decoration without formative tension. The mannerism and stylistic beauty is in some aspects reminiscent of, for example, the choreography of Sankaijuku's "reverse orientalism,"[9] even though its appearance is very different. I wonder if dumb type has also fallen into the trap of Japanese mannerism.

The most shocking scene from *memorandum* is the comedy-like play by the performers dressed in animal suits, the burly bears fooling around. I wonder what we should see, feel and think in this fairy tale that is neither comical nor weird. What is projected in the scene might be a narcissistic imagination that can only retrogress to a fantasy of the old days. This makes for an illimitable breakaway from the darkness of the collective memory of society and from the thickness of human history. I wonder if dumb type has begun to share a mental climate similar to something that recent Pappa Tarahumara performances have fallen into.[10]

Digital fascism, mannerism with reverse orientalism, and narcissism, freed from world history. I wonder if the performance of *memorandum* could be a masterpiece, in no way inferior to *S/N*, in its brilliantly simulated depiction of Japanese society, and, more broadly, humankind at the present moment in showing us our near future. Some critical interpretations do see the work in this light. However, I can never think of a critical eye in a work of simulation or the diagnostic as comparable to *S/N*; *S/N* brought noise, dissimilation and prompted awareness. It seems more likely that *memorandum* is an uncritical work that destructively intoxicates us to the assimilation of fascism, mannerism and narcissism.

And what about *memorandum*, the collective writings? This little grave of Furuhashi's words consolidates his artistic, philosophical and existential processes that were so much a part of *S/N*. A runaway from a "castle named art." Leaving the capitalist distribution system. Independence from a company structure. Empathy with the punch line of the joke, and a Kansai sense of humour. A reality that can be shared with others only after collapsing the fantasy of one's "self." Evolution of communication. Invention of a new human being. Rejection of narcissistic sublimity. The necessity of sincere self-criticism, etc. Furuhashi's thoughts and vision, though not always shared with dumb type after *OR*, are revealed throughout. But these philosophies and this vision cannot be attributed to Furuhashi alone. In the process of creating *S/N*, dumb type fostered them as a group. I think we empathised with its impressive example as a "work" (of art) and as an action of a "space."

Two *memoranda*. But is the philosophical, aesthetic and political "conversion" (dare I use this word?) that sets the two apart really only a problem for dumb type? If those of us who praised *S/N* also praise *OR* and the performance *memorandum* in the same way—that is, with no awareness of this "conversion" or with blinkers on—this shows that we have lapsed into a serious philosophical dementia and critical neglect. Perhaps dumb type is encouraging us to awaken from the dementia of non-criticism by presenting the two *memoranda* at the same time. Or am I reading too much into this?

Walter Benjamin once saw political aestheticism in Marinetti's fascism and the aesthetics of war.[11] A closed-door aestheticism and "art for art's sake" symbolised by the principal character Jean des Esseintes in Joris-Karl Huysmans' *À rebours* (Against Nature) was an easy target for the Futurists in their "anti-art" manifesto. However, in reality, its essence was an inheritance for the Futurists, its meaning twisted by Marinetti and transformed into a design of social aesthetics, political aestheticism and an aesthetics of praising war. The person who drew attention to this dangerous and problematic conversion from aesthetic fascism to an aesthetics of fascism was no other than Benjamin.

A new aestheticism in "virtually" closed-door cyberspace and a state of "art for art's sake" are now converted into a digital fascism *of* micro-society as theatre. It depends absolutely on our critical abilities whether this state will be developed as political aestheticism *in* a macro-society and take hold.

Notes

* This essay was originally published in *BT (Bijutsu Techo)*, February 2001, pp. 104–111) and is translated by Naomi Ota and Peter Eckersall. In the Japanese publication the editors included the following introduction to Kumakura's essay. The text below is by unnamed editors and was not written by Kumakura. As it provides some relevant background to the essay, we include it here:

> At the same time as dumb type presented their eagerly awaited Tokyo performance of *memorandum*, a book, also called *memorandum* and which was a collection of manuscripts, letters and other writings by the former key member of dumb type, Furuhashi Teiji, was published posthumously. There is a sense of a gap here, an opening between these two "memorandums" located in the interval of the late twentieth and early twenty-first centuries that these events mark. This is generated by disparities in the formation of the dyads body/technology, information/memorandum and virtual space/theatre space. For dumb type, this gap or place should be a productive one. And thus, with this in mind, we examine the history of dumb type in the late twentieth century and their directions now.

1 Project plan of dumb type in 1993.

2 Dumb type, *Memorandum teiji furuhashi* (Tokyo: Little More, 2000), p. 79.

3 Brochure for the performance *OR*.

4 Gilles Deleuze and Félix Guattari, *A Thousand Plateaus* (Japanese version), trans. Uno Kuniichi (Tokyo: Kawade Shobō Shinsha, 1994), pp. 171–90.

5 Dumb type, *Memorandum teiji furuhashi*, p. 22.

6 Ibid., p. 80.

7 Immanuel Kant, *The Complete Works. Critique of Judgment, Vol. 1* (Japanese version), trans. Eiji Makino (Tokyo: Iwanami Shoten, 1999), p. 136.

8 Brochure for the performance *memorandum*, p. 8.

9 Ueno Chizuko, "Orientarizumu to Jendaa (Orientalism and Gender)," *Matemalist Fascism, New Feminism Review*, Vol. 6, ed. Kanō Mikiyo (Tokyo: Gakuyō shobō, 1995), pp. 108–31. Put very simply, "reverse orientalism" is a position of imagining the reversal of categories of principal and subsidiary to display one's own minor identity in a nationalistic manner.

10 Translator's note: Pappa Tarahumara is a mixed-media performance and dance group founded by Koike Hiroshi in 1982.

11 Walter Benjamin, *Fukusei Gijutsu Jidai no Geijutsu Sakuhin*, trans. Takagi Hisao and Takahara Kōhei (The Work of Art in the Age of Mechanical Reproduction [1935]) (Tokyo: Shoubun-sha, 1970), pp. 44–47.

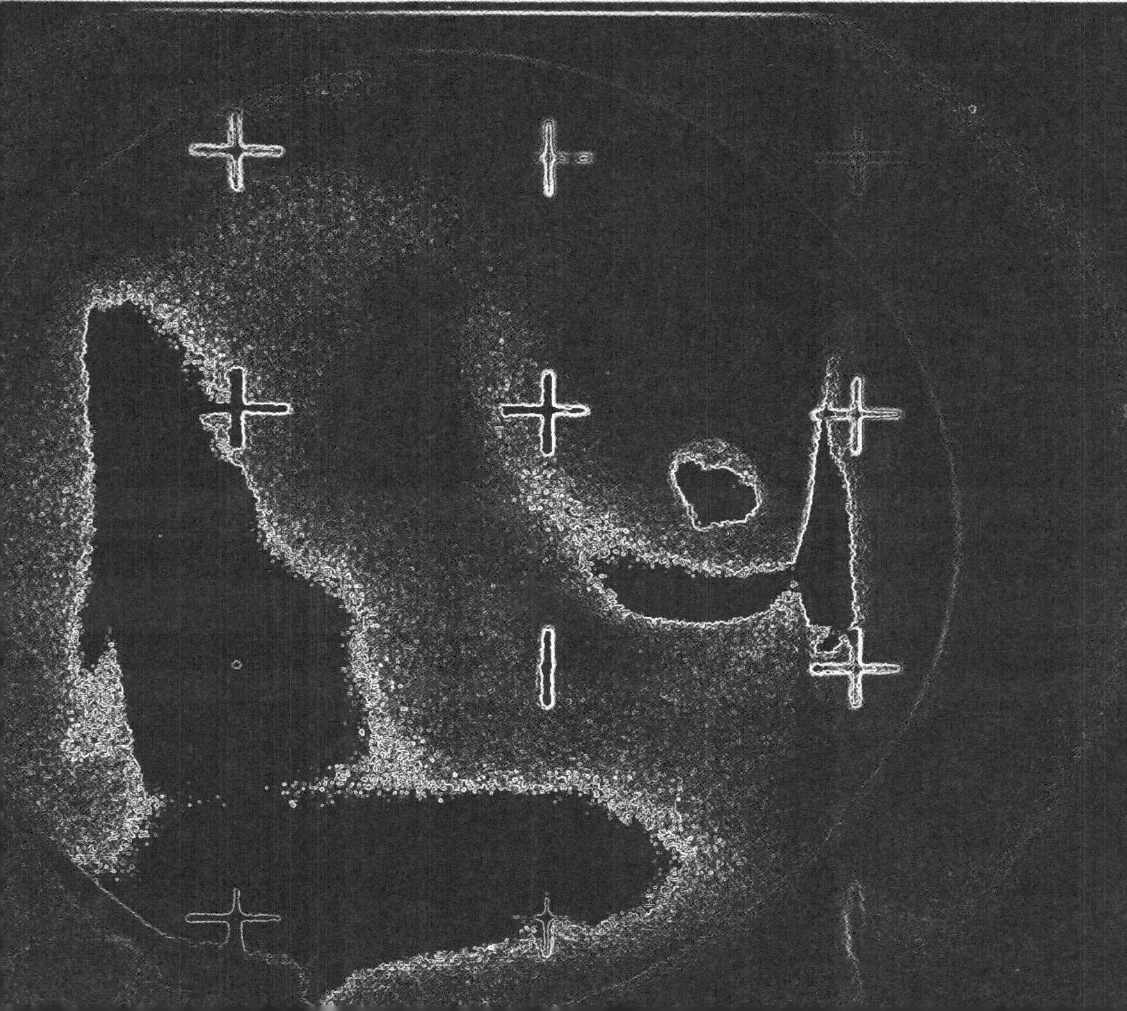

Bridges

Lovers

Corporeal Projections and Ocular Demands

Stephen Barber

This essay focuses on *Lovers* (1994), Furuhashi Teiji's first (and last) moving-image installation work, viewing it within the framework of the histories of immersive, moving-image projection environments involving human figures in performative movement. *Lovers* has an intricate rapport with previous experiments in immersive moving-image projection in relation to performance and choreography, and, in turn, illuminates the intimate interweaving of performance with other media such as film and digital forms. I also examine a film-projection experiment, *The Birth,* that was shown at the Japan World Exposition festival in Osaka (better known now as "Expo '70") and which involved the work of the ankoku butoh choreographer Hijikata Tatsumi. Finally, I look back to 1893, 101 years before *Lovers,* to examine the originating event for all projections of moving-images within specially designed, enclosed spatial environments: the English moving-image innovator Eadweard Muybridge's project to create the first ever space for the projection of moving-images to a public audience, through the construction of his "Zoopraxographical Hall" at the World's Columbian Exposition in Chicago, a project which, like *Lovers,* shows images of naked human figures walking, in sequential movement and in intersections and encounters. The aim of this essay is not to situate *Lovers* within a static lineage of immersive moving-image projections, but, rather, to show that the preoccupations driving such experiments form enduring and transformational ones that manifest themselves in very distinctive and dynamic ways, and which can challenge and overturn their audiences' preconceptions of the corporeal and ocular dimensions of performance.

In 1998 I had the experience of being present as a spectator within the spectral moving-image environment of *Lovers*. Developed by Furuhashi in collaboration with an innovative digital arts agency operating in Tokyo, Canon ArtLab, *Lovers* was installed within a range of arts museum spaces internationally in the years following its first appearance. It was initially shown at a gallery space for performance and moving-image experiments, the Hillside Plaza in Tokyo, from 23 September to 3 October 1994. The Hillside Plaza was used, during the period 1990 to 2001, for many other moving-image installations, including a retrospective of the work of the well-known Japanese filmmaker Iimura Takahiko. The space still exists, but is now used to host corporate events and receptions. This first installation of *Lovers* belongs to a particular moment in the development of Japanese digital art, from the early 1990s onwards, in which technology corporations such as Canon and NTT actively sponsored work, or provided environments for performance-focused experiments with emergent digital moving-image and virtual-reality technologies, often working closely with digital artists and performers to provide them with funding and technical support that were otherwise scarce. By 1998, NTT had opened a large-scale arts museum of contemporary digital technology, the InterCommunication Centre in Tokyo's Shinjuku district, and *Lovers* was also exhibited there as part of the exhibition "Possible Futures" in 2005. My own experience of seeing *Lovers* was in another Tokyo venue, Spiral Hall, in 1998, three years after the death of Furuhashi, and also at the end of that distinctive period of arts curation that encompassed performance and experimental moving-image technology. The Canon ArtLab would dissolve in acrimony after a curatorial dispute in 2001, and the NTT Intercommunication Centre also experienced severe operational difficulties in the same era, although it does still exist. Digital arts curation then became subject to entirely different imperatives through the following decade, the 2000s, and into the current moment.

In an interview from 1995, Furuhashi evokes the theme of *Lovers* in the context of its projection technologies: "In conventional terminology, the piece is called a multimedia installation. It uses life-size images of nine naked performers which circle the room round the viewer; five laser discs; and seven video projectors. It deals with the theme of contemporary love in an ultra-romantic way."[1] Two of the most significant elements of the design of the installation are, firstly, that its projected sequences surround or immerse the spectator (intimately so, since *Lovers* was usually exhibited within relatively constrained confines), and secondly, that the spectator's body and eyes actively participate in determining the projection of walking and intersecting figures. A short promotional film by the Canon ArtLab, made at the time of the Hillside Plaza installation, emphasises this second aspect of the work: "Sensors in the centre of the space are activated by the visitors' presence, triggering words and images to move and react on the wall. Sensors that dot the ceiling are triggered to project messages down on to the floor, creating boundaries."[2]

When I experienced *Lovers* in 1998 at Spiral Hall in Tokyo as that soundscaped environment of bodies in slow motion walking, running and embracing while simultaneously evanescing, I was struck by the sense of a volatile process of infiltration between the projected and spectatorial bodies in the space, especially during the moments at which, as the spectator approached the projected bodies they abruptly vanished, and another figure, that of Furuhashi, moved towards you before falling backwards. Among the English-language texts that appeared within the projections, I noted one that read: "Do not cross the line"; and another, "A jailbreak across ordinary fields is harder than over walls and wire fences." That second text brought to mind the experience of Jean Genet (a great hero of transvestite and transsexual culture in Japan, from the 1960s onwards), during his incarceration as a child in the 1920s at the French rural prison of Mettray (a prison surrounded by open fields, rather than by walls). In one of his texts, Genet wrote: "One of the finest inventions of the [Penal] Colony of Mettray was to have known *not* to put a wall around it—it's much more difficult to escape when you have to cross a bed of flowers."[3] Genet's final book is titled *Prisoner of Love*, the same title as a love song associated with James Brown. The preoccupation in *Lovers* with "prisoners of love" and "love songs" interconnects that work with dumb type's *S/N* performance of the same era, with its focus on the potential forms of *future* love songs. That "love song" preoccupation materialises in *S/N* in the form of a song sung by Barbra Streisand, "People Who Need People," as well as inciting the spectator's eye and body to traverse boundaries. Genet filmed the eyes of prisoners and wardens, peering through spyholes, in his 1950 film with the same title, *Un Chant d'Amour* (or, *A Love Song*). Fearing that a needle, directed from the far side of the cell door, will pierce his eye and blind him, the character of the warden in that film is still compelled by sexual desire for his prisoners to look through that aperture. What he sees are not prisoners in misery, but instead prisoners who are engaged in a choreographed sexual frenzy—they dance wildly, or are masturbating—and two prisoners communicate with each other via the wall between two cells through which a hole has been drilled, and cigarette smoke is blown from mouth to mouth through that aperture. A future "love song" may involve an opening-up of flesh, in the cutting of two wrists and the mixing of blood, as in *S/N*, or else the piercing of an aperture, as with that of a film camera lens, in conjuring into existence the intersecting and intercrossing bodies of *Lovers*, which then intimately surround their spectators.

The contemporary status of *Lovers* is a potentially precarious one; it must be projected in order to exist. It holds sparse traces, as a future "love song," since it is now exhibited and projected with relative infrequency, at least in contrast to its international prominence in the second half of the 1990s. But since it was acquired as an "artwork" by several museum collections in that era, it therefore exists multiply, in editions of its constituent materials and sequences, and the corporeal presences they hold, ready for revivification. Its originating materials may also be stored archivally, but archives of projection experiments are notably fragile and risk undergoing transmutations and disintegration. This current interstitial status of *Lovers* connects with an alternative title (or subtitle) sometimes used for its projections in the 1990s: *Dying Pictures, Living Pictures*.

A similarly liminal projection experiment that left behind a precarious residue took place a quarter of a century before *Lovers*, in the form of the project conceived for Osaka Expo '70, *The Birth*, that involved the celebrated originator and choreographer of the ankoku butoh performance art form, Hijikata Tatsumi. Placing Furuhashi and Hijikata together necessarily generates a salutary site of disjuncture and tension, since Furuhashi was not a great admirer of ankoku butoh, commenting in 1995: "I can't get into the mysterious profound butoh atmosphere, that profound look and mood. I'm more into how to invent the profound moment with cheap-looking materials and movements from daily life ... And my choreography is more influenced by people dancing disco."[4] To trace any valid intersection between the work of Furuhashi and Hijikata, it is necessary to go back to the very beginnings of Hijikata's work, around 1959, to investigate what he originally envisaged for his emergent performance art. In his manifesto "To Prison" that was inspired by the work of Genet, Hijikata wrote: "To a production-oriented society, the aimless use of the body, which I call dance, is a deadly enemy which must be taboo. I am able to say that my dance shares a common basis with crime, male homosexuality, festivals and rituals because it is behaviour which explicitly flaunts its aimlessness in the face of a production-oriented society."[5] In the late 1960s, Hijikata and his dancers notoriously worked in nightclubs and discotheques, such as the Club Space Capsule in Tokyo's Akasaka district, in spectacles that prefigure Furuhashi's transvestite spectacles of the mid-1980s in Kyoto nightclubs.

A more tangible connection is that of the involvement of both Furuhashi and Hijikata in immersive, 360-degree projection experiments featuring moving-image sequences of human figures in performative movement. Hijikata had been closely involved in a succession of performance collaborations with experimental filmmakers, such as Takahiko Iimura and Donald Richie, throughout the early stages of his work. At the end of the 1960s, he participated in a large-scale project involving a newly developed, immersive moving-image technology for the recording and projection of images: "Astrorama." For many years, all surviving evidence of this project appeared to have vanished. The Astrorama technology generated a spatial moving-image installation, *The Birth*, installed at the "Midori-kan" (the "Green Pavilion") at the Osaka Expo, which ran from March to September 1970. The Midori-kan itself was constructed by an alliance of Japanese technology corporations to display innovations in image-projection, among other technological developments, and was sited within the extensive grounds of the Expo that formed a sub-city at Osaka's peripheries. The event, together with the Tokyo Olympic Games six years earlier, marked Japan's new ascendancy in both media technology and the visual and performing arts and attracted vast crowds (over sixty million spectators) and international attention. World fairs and Expo events have often constituted spectacular showcases for experimental projection technologies, most notably at the event held in Chicago in 1893. As a result, Osaka Expo '70 formed an ideal context for the developers of the Astrorama projection technology, Goto Inc., to show off their new development, which was inspired, at least in part, by IMAX technology, and was intended for large-format, 360-degree immersive projections that surrounded their audiences within specially designed spaces.

The inclusion of many contemporary Japanese performers, musicians and artists as participants in Expo '70 was an attempt to emphasise the event's aura of innovation. The influential performance art group of the mid-1950s Gutai took part (in one of their final spectacles before the group's dissolution), and two of Hijikata's previous collaborators, the architect Isozaki Arata and the artist Yokoo Tadanori, were closely involved in conceptualising Expo '70 and issuing invitations to participants. The Astrorama film of Hijikata's performance had been shot in June of the previous year, on location on the slopes of the volcanic Mount Atosanupuri (also known as Mount Io) in north-eastern Hokkaido; the volcano, close to the caldera Lake Kussharo, remained active and emitted sulphurous steam. Hijikata's performance was shot over six or seven nights by the team of twenty-one Astrorama technicians, including their supervising director Akiyama Tomohiro. Hijikata appears in only one sequence of the ten-minute film, as a magician or shaman who conjures up the world as part-miracle, part-malediction; at the end of the sequence, Hijikata moves directly towards and then leaps over the Astrorama film-camera. The film's scenarist, the poet Tanikawa Shuntaro, had specially requested Hijikata's appearance as a monstrous, grotesque figure, present at the world's origination directly through the medium of dance. Other sequences for the film showed primal natural landscapes and fragments of cities about to be destroyed. A further sequence, shot in the Meguro district of Tokyo, at Hijikata's studio—the "Asbestos-kan"—depicts his company of dancers, naked and shot directly from above rather than frontally. That sequence was then superimposed with images of hell from paintings by Hieronymus Bosch and others.

The Astrorama film-camera had five separate lenses, each shooting simultaneously with the intention of creating sequences that would be multi-dimensional and sensorially engulfing. The sequences were recorded on a special 70mm celluloid film stock (an extremely large format) whose exacting development process required it to be sent to specialist laboratories in Hollywood for processing. In the Midori-kan at the Osaka Expo, the Astrorama film was screened using an ambitious system that projected five film-reels simultaneously onto the internal dome of the Midori-kan across five huge screens, thereby generating a 360-degree, immersive environment for its audiences. It was certainly not one in which the projected human figures in motion could be approached intimately as in *Lovers*. An estimated fifteen million spectators visited the Midori-kan during the six-month run of Expo '70, but most passed quickly through the pavilion as part of tour groups rather than amassing to experience the projection as a collective, static audience. That abbreviated, tangential experience of traversal (both an ocular and physical transit), experienced by the spectators of Hijikata's performance on film, is familiar to visitors to digital-image installations at contemporary art museums.

After Expo '70 closed, in September 1970, most of the extravagant pavilions were abandoned and left to deteriorate into ruins, despite the vast expense entailed in constructing them. Several years later, the site, including the Midori-kan, was almost entirely razed and converted into a suburban commemorative park for the citizens of Osaka, with Expo '70's emblematic "Tower of the Sun," designed by the artist Okamoto Tarō, standing at its entrance. The Astrorama projection technology proved too complex and expensive for the massive commercial exploitation that its designers had envisaged, with the result that it became obsolete immediately. The original celluloid film-cans containing the film of Hijikata's performance were stored away and forgotten until researchers from the Centre for the Arts at Keio University in Tokyo relocated them, forty years later, in the Osaka storage facilities of the Sanwa Midori-kai alliance of technology corporations, whose previous incarnation had sponsored the Midori-kan. The film had been preserved over those four decades more through oblivious neglect than active conservation; its status was that of the stored away detritus of the now defunct Astrorama projection technology, rather than that of a vital moving-image document of Hijikata's performance work. In that sense, the Astrorama film survived as an aberrant form of archival entity. If *Lovers* had been preserved in the same way, it would have been as a manifestation of mid-1990s video and laser-disc technologies (and of their imminent obsolescence), rather than as a unique work of performance art. To revivify the Astrorama projection of Hijikata's performance, in its spatial and immersive dimensions, would involve reconstructing the vast environment of the Midori-kan, whereas recreating the space of the *Lovers* installation forms a less challenging project requiring only the reactivation of its archived components.

Finally, I move further backwards in time, to the very first moving-image projection, within a space created especially for spectators, of sequences of walking, running and intersecting human figures. The projection took place at another Exposition event, the 1893 World's Columbian

Exposition in Chicago, for which the moving-image innovator Eadweard Muybridge constructed a building that was part performance exhibition space, part proto-cinematic space in order to project his sequences of figures in movement. As with the projection environment of Hijikata's filmed performance *The Birth*, almost all traces of the projection space for Muybridge's experiment have been lost. Only a few photographs exist of the facade of Muybridge's building, the "Zoopraxographical Hall," and none of the interior of the space itself.

Muybridge was the first moving-image innovator to envisage a specially constructed space, to be entered by spectators who, in conditions of darkness, would then experience moving-image sequential projections of human figures performing acts of walking, of encountering one another and even embracing; an experience intimately close to that of the spectators of *Lovers*, a century later. Muybridge's work as an inventor focused on the performative gestures and movements of the human body, especially in situations of crisis and malfunction. He experimented with the ways in which those gestures connected with moving images, in the form of projections that could surround their spectators, and thereby instigate unprecedented visions and sensations. He began experimenting with immersive, 360-degree image-environments as early as 1878, fifteen years before his Chicago projections. At that time, his focus had been on urban space, rather than on human figures. He assembled large-format photographic panoramas of San Francisco, and installed them within an art gallery space in such a way that they surrounded their viewers, inducing a sense of topographic disorientation. During the same period, he also began experimenting with moving-image projection for spectators, using sequences of images transferred onto glass discs; he constructed a projector, which he called the "Zoopraxiscope," to animate those images. In 1884, he was commissioned by the University of Pennsylvania in Philadelphia to use multiple, high-speed cameras to capture images of human bodies, as well as animals, in sequential movement. Over a span of three years, he created more than twenty thousand sequences, including those of figures who pivot and turn rapidly, as also occurs in the *Lovers* installation. Muybridge directed and choreographed his human models specifically as performers, who undertook pre-set acts of performance rather than isolated gestures or improvisations. The filmmaker Hollis Frampton has commented on the excessive nature of Muybridge's project and its axis in acute repetition: "Quite simply, what occasioned Muybridge's obsession? What need drove him, beyond a reasonable limit of dozens or even hundreds of sequences, to make them by thousands? ... Time seems, sometimes, to stop, to be suspended in tableaux *disjunct* from change and flux. Most human beings experience, at one time or another, moments of intense passion during which perception seems vividly arrested: erotic rapture, or the extremes of rage and terror came to mind."[6]

In his specially constructed projection-space at the Chicago Exposition in 1893, Muybridge projected his Philadelphia sequences, along with newly created sequences, from glass discs. He had been planning a large-scale projection tour across Japan, India and Australia, but abandoned this in order to participate in the Chicago Exposition, which appeared to offer him an unprecedented arena to demonstrate his innovations. Since no pre-existing building constructed uniquely for the projection of moving-images preceded it, Muybridge had to imagine that space entirely for himself. His plans for the building's facade indicate that he envisaged a spectacular form, with classical columns, inspired in part by ancient Greek and Roman theatre architecture; the building stands in splendid isolation in his plans, without the presence of other, competing Exposition attractions. His projection-space was around fifty by eighty feet in dimension and was constructed from brick, iron and wood. When Muybridge describes the building in promotional material prepared for the Exposition, he gives the impression that it appeared almost magically or spontaneously, without human intervention. He refers to himself in the third person: "He delayed his Far Occidental expedition and returned to Chicago to find a commodious theatre erected for this special purpose on the grounds of the Exposition, to which the name of Zoopraxographical Hall had been given."[7] Almost nothing is known about the interior space of Muybridge's building. In the absence of any writings on the subject by Muybridge himself, or any eyewitness accounts, it is simply not known whether he projected his sequences immersively around the interior walls of the space. Since he possessed only one projector, he would have needed to rotate it, in mid-projection, through revolutions around the space, in order to do so. All that is known with certainty is that Muybridge himself stood alongside his projection surfaces (or screens), as a corporeal and vocal presence, and narrated his sequences of figures-in-movement to his audiences. It is also certain, from attendance figures for the Exposition's many attractions, that the project was a disastrous failure in financial terms; Muybridge drew only a very few spectators into his projection space.

As with the Osaka Expo '70, the Chicago Exposition was an immense undertaking, lasting for six months. Its total attendance was around 27 million, around half that of Expo '70, but the number of exhibitors with whom Muybridge was competing was huge: 65,422. Every exhibitor in Chicago had a new technology or a new spectacle of some kind to display, often with far greater promotional resources and within much more extravagant buildings than Muybridge. In that architectural and promotional context, Muybridge's projection-space generated only a negligible presence, despite its extraordinary ambition and innovation as a seminal site for moving-image projection in the form of an experimental laboratory for future visual technologies. Less than halfway through the duration of the Chicago Exposition, Muybridge's projection-space was closed, then rapidly reoccupied by another exhibitor with a new attraction, the "Pompeii Theater and Panorama," containing a painted panorama of Pompeii during its destruction by the volcanic eruption of Mount Vesuvius. As with the Osaka site of Expo '70, that of the Chicago Exposition would also rapidly disappear; it was first abandoned, then largely destroyed by a fire several months after it had closed. Muybridge undertook no further experiments in moving-image projection after his experience in Chicago. Instead, he scaled down his activities, returned to his hometown of Kingston-on-Thames in England and bequeathed his entire personal archive of projectors, images and documents to the town's library on his death in 1904.

The traces and survival of immersive moving-image experimentation around projected bodies in performative movement—from Muybridge's 1893 projections of human-figure sequences, through the 1970 Astrorama immersive projections of Hijikata's choreographic work, to Furuhashi Teiji's 1994 *Lovers* installation, and extending into the present moment—are often precarious, their status subject to erasure or reactivation in new, contrary forms. They depend upon memories and documentation, which are flawed, partial or even non-existent. Archives of performance projections often comprise fragmented detrita, fissured by time and imprinted by disparate approaches to documentation, rather than source materials for acts of flawless reconstitution. Such archives themselves possess engulfing spectatorial demands, and precipitate transits in flux across the histories and spaces of performance. They also indicate that whatever appears to be a contemporary, immediate new-media technology conceived for incorporation within performance can, very rapidly, appear obsolete and vanish, but then resurge aberrantly in a new manifestation, often with original and compelling imperatives for its future spectators. All resilient performance-traces demand attention, even when their resilience is the result of accident or chance. In exploring the dynamics of innovations in performance cultures, and the preoccupations and intentions of their creators, such as those which drove Furuhashi's *Lovers,* it is always essential to view together the event of performance and its surviving moving-image documentation, together with the pivotal role of the human body which intimately interweaves them.

Notes

1 Furuhashi Teiji, "Interview with Carol Lutfy," *Tokyo Journal* (Tokyo), 1995. http://renfield.net/tj/9509/converse.html (accessed 10 May 2017).

2 Canon ArtLab promotional film, *Lovers* (Tokyo: Canon ArtLab Productions, 1994). The short promotional film, which would have been distributed by the Canon ArtLab in the mid-1990s in video cassette format to prospective art museum exhibitors of Furuhashi's artwork, has been made freely accessible on YouTube: http://www.youtube.com/watch?v=ZAaYEZN7EwI (accessed 10 May 2017).

3 Jean Genet, *L'Ennemi Déclaré* (Paris: Gallimard, 1991), p. 223.

4 Furuhashi Teiji, "Interview with Carol Lutfy."

5 Hijikata Tatsumi, "To Prison," *TDR: The Drama Review* 11 (1), Spring 2000: 44–45.

6 Hollis Frampton, "Eadweard Muybridge: Fragments of a Tesseract," *Circles of Confusion* (Rochester, NY: Visual Studies Workshop, 1983), p. 79.

7 Eadweard Muybridge, *Descriptive Zoopraxography* (Philadelphia: University of Pennsylvania, 1893), p. 2.

Turning Catastrophe into Art

On Dumb Type's *S/N* and Tadasu Takamine's *Cool Japan*

Shintarō FUJII

I will discuss here two thematically related artworks: *S/N* (1994), a performance work by dumb type, and *Cool Japan* (2012), a visual art exhibition by Tadasu Takamine, a former dumb type member. The first was created after Teiji Furuhashi, dumb type's principal member, told others in the group that he had been diagnosed with HIV. *Cool Japan* was conceived after the Great East Japan Earthquake in 2011 and the ensuing Fukushima nuclear crisis. I argue that, despite the evident differences in form, these works can be interpreted in the same light—that is, in terms of their relation to a catastrophe that destabilises society, and through their critique, by means of art and imagination, of predominant social representations of the catastrophe.

S/N

S/N started as a work-in-progress project.[1] It changed radically after Teiji Furuhashi (b. 1960) told the other members of dumb type in the fall of 1992 that he had developed AIDS-related symptoms (he died in October 1995). Inevitably, in the wake of this news, *S/N* turned its focus to the question of life and death, sexuality and its consequences, *eros* and *thanatos*. Like other dumb type performances, *S/N* uses a non-linear, fragmentary narrative structure to combine multimedia devices such as video projections and electric music, refined scenography and lighting, and dance-based corporealities in a highly sophisticated manner. Yet *S/N* is singular in its incorporation of some very personal and private matters (sex, sexuality and mortal disease), in its use of direct, verbal and theatrical sequences, and in addressing critiques of mainstream social representations, especially the media discourses surrounding the AIDS crisis. It was as much a political act as an aesthetic one, for, to this day, Furuhashi remains one of the very few homosexuals in Japan, artist or otherwise, who died of AIDS after having publicly declared that he was suffering from the condition,[2] and *S/N* is still considered one of the most innovative and influential works, not only by dumb type but of contemporary Japanese performing arts.

As for its dramaturgy, *S/N* is composed of seven eclectic scenes, independent from one another in terms of both form and content. The scenes are nevertheless loosely connected in their questioning of binary social distinctions such as sex and gender, sexuality or nationality, which determine the way our societies are organised and thereby the way we are. The eclecticism can be observed also in terms of the composition of the cast, which includes not only "mainstream" Japanese but also a gay deaf-mute (Alex), a gay Black American (Peter), a gay person with AIDS (Teiji) and a "sex worker," or a prostitute who has intentionally chosen this profession to serve her artistic and political project (BuBu de la Madeleine). Dumb type was, for Furuhashi, a collective and thus political challenge, where everyone was "personally and artistically equal."[3] Moreover, *S/N* is a bilingual performance that uses both Japanese and English.[4] Yet, even the Japanese used in the show is far from standardised, in contrast to the traditional conventions of theatre: by turns, it is spoken with a Kyoto accent and an American accent, pronounced with difficulty by the deaf-mute and written out and projected onto the white wall. As for the scenography, although the projection of images demands a rather conventional frontal relationship between the stage and the audience, the scenic space is composed of several heterogeneous parts: a large acting area on the level of the stage floor, a white vertical wall behind it that serves as a screen, another narrow, horizontal acting area on the top of this wall, and the invisible space behind it, into which performers occasionally fall from the top of the wall. The *way S/N* shows and tells is just as meaningful as *what* it shows and tells, if not more.

The performance begins with a scene that uses the method usually associated with documentary theatre, in which the performers, in this case Alex, Teiji and Peter, appear as themselves. The stickers on their suits literally label them as "male," "homosexual," "Japanese," "American," "deaf," "HIV-positive," etc. Indeed, Peter says, "I am sorry to tell you but we are not actors. We are this. He is male, Japanese, deaf, homosexual. And he is male, Japanese, HIV-positive, homosexual. And I am male, black, American, homosexual. And how are you?" This challenges theatrical convention by perplexing the audience, who are accustomed to being presented with fictional, as opposed to actual, situations. As Furuhashi quips in the scene, "We are here in a theatre, where no one knows what belongs to reality and where people gather to escape from such 'reality'."[5]

As is suggested by the title *S/N*, which refers, among other things, to the ratio between signal and noise,[6] between what is worth listening to and what should be ignored or eliminated, much of the performance is about questioning the dichotomy between the majority (the *unmarked*, in linguistic terms) and the minority (the *marked*), such as nationals and foreigners, male and female, heterosexual and homosexual, physically sound and handicapped. What the performance seems to stress is that the voices of the minority are often turned into noise or silence, that their existence is rendered invisible by mainstream discourses, sometimes with the help of the apparently neutral scientific discourses. This is encapsulated in the repeated projection of "Conspiracy of Silence / Conspiracy of Science / Conspiracy of Scientia."[7]

There was a concomitant silence about homosexuality in general and AIDS in particular, even though so many things had been said about it. This was certainly the case even in Japan, where the number of AIDS-related deaths and the consequent activist movement for public sensitisation and political pressure were considerably less important than in Europe and North America. Especially before HAART (highly active antiretroviral therapy) was successfully put into practice, a strong fear was projected onto homosexuals—all the more so because HIV is invisible—thus reinforcing the existing homophobia in Japan. Much, but not enough, was said about the problem. Dominant discourses tend to marginalise alternative ones and force the minority into silence or into "abstractions you would like to see,"[8] to quote the expression used by Alex on stage. Of course, this problem is not limited to homosexuality and AIDS, and Takamine's *Cool Japan* addresses it in the context of the Fukushima nuclear crisis, in which fear was projected onto invisible radioactivity.

S/N is about questioning the aesthetic and political relationship between the visible (the valuable, the powerful) and the invisible (the valueless, the powerless) and possibly reversing this relationship. The performance brings to light what otherwise remains invisible, or at least marginalised. It gives a voice to those who are deprived of one. It works powerfully, firstly on the visual and aesthetic level, with the projected images and the use of the flashing strobe light. More strikingly, however, the visible is used to put into question the power politics that define what should or should not be socially visible. For instance, although it cannot be denied that the naked bodies, whether live on stage or projected as images, stimulate our scopophilia to a certain degree, they also make us imagine an anonymous power in the background that controls or censors what is made visible to us. This power is suggested by the shadows cast on the eyes and genitals of the naked bodies and by the removal of faces from the frames of the images. Moreover, the group's search for aesthetic precision and perfection by means of the technology is relativised by the presence of the rather clumsy bodies of non-professional performers. The words spoken by Alex, the deaf-mute, articulated with difficulty and barely audible, become all the more powerful as this sort of voice is seldom heard in our society. An irony, a critical gap or distance arises with regard to what the artists show and tell, what they want to show and tell, and what the audience will see and hear. Spectators are asked not to take at face value what they see and hear, because it is not what they really want to show and tell ("no one knows what belongs to reality"). *S/N* may well have been influenced by minority activism in the United States, but the performance's activism should be understood not as propaganda but as an attempt to activate the awareness of the audience. I would argue that a similar intellectual irony characterises Takamine's works.

Cool Japan

Tadasu Takamine, born in 1968 and eight years younger than Furuhashi, graduated in 1991 from the Lacquer Craft Department of the Kyoto City University of Arts, the same university that Furuhashi and many other dumb type members attended. Acquainted with the collective since the 1980s, Takamine participated in two performances by dumb type: *S/N* (1994) and *OR* (1997). He recalls his participation in the group repeatedly in his writings, saying that, despite his difference in age from other dumb type members, it was a crucial experience that shaped his sensibilities as an artist.[9] In 1997, shortly after the premiere of *OR*, he left Kyoto and dumb type to continue his graduate studies at the Institute for Advanced Media Arts and Sciences (IAMAS) in Gifu City. He has since been very successful as a visual/performance artist and participated in various collective exhibitions both inside and outside of Japan, including the Venice Biennale (Japanese Pavilion, 2003), and in several solo exhibitions, such as "Big Rest" (Sendai Mediatheque, 2008), "Good House, Nice Body" (21st Century Museum of Contemporary Art, Kanazawa, 2010), and "Too Far to See" (Yokohama Museum of Art, 2011).

Before turning to *Cool Japan*, I would like to discuss two other relevant works by Takamine. He has become known particularly for a performance/video piece, *Kimura-san*, created in 1998 and the scandal it provoked. It features and is titled after a severely disabled Japanese man called Kimura-san (Mr. Kimura), a performer from the performance group Taihen that is composed solely of people with various disabilities. This man, a victim of the arsenic-contaminated milk product that caused a great scandal in the country in 1955, cannot talk, walk or eat by himself and needs twenty-four-hour assistance (Takamine had been assisting him on a voluntary basis since 1993). By showing the artist helping Kimura-san masturbate until he eventually ejaculates, the video depicts in a quite explicit and provocative way that disabled people have or need a sexual life. The work's sexual explicitness probably makes many viewers uncomfortable; moreover, it features a homoerotic relationship between a disabled person and the artist, even though neither of the two are (said to be) gay. The essential point of the work was to question what "disability" means today. The work also revealed that taboos still exist in contemporary art, despite the illusion that all taboos have been broken and anything is allowed, and it denounces the hypocrisy of a society that empowers disabled people in some ways but at the same time turns them into "abstractions [we] would like to see."

In Japan, the public authorities, in the name of neutrality, tend to avoid working with artists or projects that may offend certain sensibilities (especially those of conservative politicians and pressure groups); and public "obscenity" still constitutes a misdemeanour (in *S/N*, the black shadows cast on the eyes and genitals of naked bodies imply such intervention on the part of the authorities). Museums, galleries and artists are sensitive to these questions and sometimes autocensor (this may be another reason why activism in art is rare in Japan).[10] Takamine worked again with disabled people in 2008 for *Big Rest*, an exhibition organised at Sendai Mediatheque in which blind people guided the visitors through installations, imposing upon them a different mode of approach, communication and reception.

Takamine has continued to work with social taboos. *A Lover from Korea* (2003) started from a question his girlfriend—now wife—asked him, "What is this antipathy you show towards Koreans?" Although she was born in Japan to a Korean father and a Japanese mother, according to the law on nationality in force at the time of her birth, Japan does not recognise her as a Japanese national.[11] This led Takamine to question the idea of nationality, the principle that determines who does or does not belong to a national community, an issue the Japanese seem no longer to consider important.

Cool Japan can be understood as an extension of Takamine's previous works—it does not hesitate to disturb, to address social taboos and offend certain sensibilities, and to make visible the social unconscious. It was curated by Mizuki Takahashi and held at Art Tower Mito, a large gallery, theatre and concert hall complex located in and operated by the city of Mito, from 22 December 2012 to 17 February 2013. The title refers ironically to "Cool Japan," one of the key projects of Japan's foreign and trade policy, which aims to promote cultural export and thereby improve the country's image. It imitates "Cool Britannia," a similar "national branding" policy conducted in the UK under Tony Blair's government in the 1990s. It probably also refers to the necessity to cool down the nuclear reactors, firstly, and, secondly, the nationalistic fever that grew out of the recognition of the 11 March 2011 event as a "national" tragedy. Indeed, Takamine sees in this catastrophe something that affects the way the Japanese represent themselves as a nation.

Composed of eight different rooms loosely connected by the theme of the recent nuclear crisis, the most important characteristic of *Cool Japan* is that none of the works it includes are truly of Takamine's own making. The artist says that this exhibition has a "strong documentary aspect"; indeed, for most of the works presented, Takamine's role is that of a documentarist or an editor who weaves the discourses of others into a text, rather than that of a creator who conceives original artworks per se.[12] The first room, called the "Cool Japan Room," contains a wall painting resembling manga drawings that was composed by an illustrator commissioned by Takamine. Several pieces of sculpture representing six men and women (some of whom are "actors" in the anti-nuclear movement) are inspired by Auguste Rodin's sculpture *The Burghers of Calais*.[13]

The earthquake and tsunami of 11 March and the consequent nuclear crisis revealed that most of the information we had about nuclear power had been manipulated. For example, the Japanese government and electric companies conjointly provided heavy financing for scientific research on nuclear power; in return, researchers provided results that supported and justified existing national policies and projects while minimising or concealing their potential danger. And this point of view was diffused largely through the mass media. There was again a "Conspiracy of Silence / Conspiracy of Science / Conspiracy of Scientia." Much has been said about the matter, but as if only to mask the essential questions. And as a result of the more direct involvement of the Japanese government, nuclear power has become even more problematic than AIDS and homosexuality, which have never really been on the Japanese national agenda. The anti-nuclear movement, although given only minimal media representation, existed well before the crisis: the "Lost Lawsuit Room" shows headlines from the different newspapers reporting the sentence given by the different courts of justice in the country, which have categorically denied all the calls for suspension of the exploitation of nuclear power.

Takamine's irony is most evident in the "Room of Free Expression." The 11 March catastrophe was the occasion for many Japanese to rediscover "national" virtues (patience, discipline, orderliness, self-sacrifice, etc.). On torn white sheets of paper, Takamine displays numerous comments he collected from the Internet and social media in the wake of the catastrophe. The comments represent attempts to reconfirm Japanese nationhood, but in fact they contain a rather heavy dose of racism and pure nonsense.

In the "Japan Syndrome Room," which could be considered the centre of the exhibition, visitors see three highly theatricalised and performative video projections, created at three different places (Kansai, Yamaguchi and Mito) during three different periods.[14] In each video, the "actors" re-present, as if in the theatre, certain conversations they held in the respective towns.

For example, in a scene that represents an encounter in a seafood products store, we hear the following:

> Customer: Do you prepare [the frozen cod] here?
> Shop assistant: Yes we do.
> Customer: Where does it come from originally?
> Shop assistant: It is actually written on the back, but basically it comes from places like the United States and Russia. …
> Customer: Has the radiation had any effect?
> Shop assistant: Radiation er … no problem at all. This is not from this year or last year [it is from the year before the earthquake].
> Customer: Oh is that right?[15]

Their tone is that of everyday life, and the conversation contains nothing aggressive or accusatory. Again, *how* the work shows and tells seems more important than *what* it shows and tells. In this filmed performance, the decor is simplified to a few elements in cardboard that vaguely evoke places, and all the actors wear the same clothes—nothing distinguishes the shopkeeper from the customers. This device indicates the partial abandonment of mimetic representation (it is impossible to represent such a catastrophe by means of art), but it also reveals the theatricality of social reality, that our social reality is a theatrical construction in a cheap, shabby setting, a result of the calculation and manipulation involved in the political *mise en scène*.

Conclusion

Both *S/N* and *Cool Japan* deal with the politics of the visible and the invisible in the midst of a catastrophe, public in the case of *Cool Japan* and personal in *S/N*. They both allude to texts and images from mainstream discourses to question the legitimacy of these; they look at a visible crisis with an invisible cause—in one case a virus, and in the other radioactivity—as well as media representations of the crisis, which becomes all the more unsettling because of the cause's invisibility. These works question, through their visual representations, the role of the visible, which in fact often serves as a screen to conceal what does not fit into its framework, to divert public attention from the undesirable fact or object, and to marginalise further the already marginalised minority. They both use irony, which presupposes a cleavage between what they show and tell, what they want to show and tell, and what the audience will see and hear. The ironic gap also exists between the scenes and between the rooms—that is, between the loosely connected elements of the artworks. It is this interstice, this critical distance, that solicits the spectator's imagination and intelligence.

In this sense, both *S/N* and *Cool Japan* are works of art created in response to catastrophe that constitute self-reflexive, aesthetic and political critiques of the visible, and which deploy artistic means to make us imagine the invisible. They remind us of the theatrical origin of the word "catastrophe": in ancient Greece, it simply meant a "reversal" in the course of the dramatic action, synonymous with *peripeteia*; but with time it began to refer to the event that brings about the tragic ending. These two examples succeed in effectuating yet another reversal of "catastrophe"— that is, in making the invisible visible, turning chaotic weakness into creative force, and having the disaster become their, and *our*, guiding star.

Notes

1 *S/N* was first presented in the form of an installation in September 1992 (it was shown at the Musée d'Ixelles in Brussels, Fukui Fine Arts, Yokohama Museum of Art, the Guggenheim Museum, San Francisco Museum of Modern Art and Art Tower Mito), and then as a "seminar-show" in March 1993 (at Artspace Mumonkan in Kyoto and Shônandai Cultural Centre near Tokyo). It then developed into a performance that premiered at the Adelaide Festival in Australia on 8 March 1994. Furuhashi died on 29 October 1995, while *S/N* was on tour in Brazil. The tour continued, with Furuhashi being replaced by recorded images. The script of the performance is reprinted in a Japanese theatre review magazine: Dumb type, *S/N Performance/Text #1*, in *Theatre Arts* 1, 1994: 177–91.

2 It should not be overlooked that in Japan, since the 1980s, activism, both politically and artistically, has become weakened and marginalised. The LGBT movement is not an exception: Furuhashi once said in an interview that Japanese society tolerates gays as long as they do not disturb (Teiji Furuhashi, "Artist Teiji Furuhashi interviewed by Carol Lutfy," in Dumb type, *memorandum teiji furuhashi* (Tokyo: Little More, 2000), p. 118. In this context, *S/N*, which might look quite "soft" to a European/North American audience, was, in this context, an exceptional sign of engagement.

3 Furuhashi, "Artist Teiji Furuhashi Interviewed by Carol Lutfy," in *memorandum teiji furuhashi*, p. 124.

4 It reflects the fact that Furuhashi was quite familiar with American culture, and especially the New York gay milieu and its radical activism during the AIDS crisis. He had spent some considerable time in New York (his boyfriend lived there), which also explains the activist aspect of the performance. Besides featuring deaf, Black American and HIV-positive homosexuals, the projection of poetic and political messages ("I dream ... my gender/nationality/blood/rights ... will disappear") have similar effects to those of the works of Barbara Kruger or Jenny Holzer, or, alternatively, a rather didactic sequence on the importance of safe sex.

5 These lines are not included in the text published in *Theatre Arts*.

6 According to the performance text, other intended meanings are: some/none, south/north, society/nature, sign/name, state/nation, system/network, sense/nonsense and science/necromancy (Dumb type, *S/N Performance/Text #1*, p. 181).

7 Ibid., pp. 189–90.

8 Dumb type, *S/N Performance/Text #1*, p. 179. In Japan, it is true that TV reserves a certain visibility for gays, but mainly for feminised ones and transvestites—that is to say, only as long as they are easily distinguished from the rest of the male population.

9 Tadasu Takamine, *A Lover from Korea* (*Zainichi no koibito*) (Tokyo: Kawade Shobō Shinsha, 2008), pp. 99–100 and pp. 141–43; *Too Far to See* (*Tōkute yoku mienai*) (Tokyo: Film Art, 2011), pp. 50–63.

10 For example, the public projection of *Kimura-san*, planned for 2004 at Yokohama Museum of Art, was abandoned after the organisation running this municipal museum consulted the city authorities as well as police officials and decided that the public presentation of this video, with its sexually explicit scenes, may have been against the law. See the report of Tetsuya Ozaki on the *Real Tokyo* website, "A Blunder at Yokohama Museum of Art," http://www.realtokyo.co.jp/docs/ja/column/outoftokyo/bn/ozaki_093/ (accessed 30 June 2014). However, Jonathan Watkins reveals that even at the Hayward Gallery in London, the planned projection was dropped in 2001 because of Kimura's disability (Tadasu Takamine, *Too Far to See*, pp. 182–93).

11 The definition of Japanese nationality is based on filiation (*jus sanguinis*). The law has since been amended, and now a child will be granted Japanese nationality if at least one of the parents is Japanese (before 1985, this had to be the father).

12 *Tadasu Takamine's Cool Japan*, exhibition catalogue (Mito: Art Tower Mito, 2013), pp. 68–69.

13 As Rosalind Krauss points out, even the original by Rodin, which exists in twelve casts (one of them belongs to the National Western Art Museum in Tokyo), had already taken on a multiple character. See Rosalind Krauss, "The Originality of the Avant-Garde," in *The Originality of the Avant-Garde and Other Modernist*

Myths (Cambridge, MA: MIT Press, 1986), pp. 151–70. Moreover, the sculpture, completed in 1889, a century after the French Revolution, commemorates the six citizens of Calais who were victims of Edward III of England during the Hundred Years' War and thus carries a heavy symbolic value in terms of moulding French national identity.

14 These were first created and shown in Kyoto (23 September–16 October 2012), in Yamaguchi (23 June–1 July) and then in Mito. They form a part of a series of performance works under the title *Japan Syndrome*, created each year at the Kyoto Experiment festival from 2011 until 2014.

15 Cited in Edan Corkill, "One Foreign Resident's Cool Japan," in *Tadasu Takamine's Cool Japan*, p. 81.

Bodies that Matter

S/N and the Art Activism of BuBu de la Madeleine and Akira the Hustler/Yukio Cho

Fran Lloyd

The opening scene of dumb type's *S/N* performance is about corporeal bodies, how they try to perform, enunciate, and how they are labelled: "male," "Japanese" "deaf" "homosexual," "HIV+." Central to the performance are questions about language, constraints of nationality and borders, of gender, sexuality, ethnicity, "normative" bodies and "living with AIDS." "I am sorry to tell you we are not actors. We are this... And... how *are* you?" This direct address to the audience by the dumb type performer and dancer Peter Golightly sets the terms of engagement that are intimately interwoven throughout the performance, making a vital link between the bodies of the performers and those of the audience. Interconnected through the swift moving plethora of sound, movement, light effects, and corporeal and text projections that disrupt fixity, these visceral bodies are the vital medium of the performance, the site of emotional and political enactment, physical exertion, disruption, danger, disappearance, and of questioning that is orientated toward future possibilities. Crucially, these bodies are about change, and effecting change, through their physical actions and enunciations which compel the audience to feel their bodies as part of, and enmeshed within, the shifting signal/noise ratios of *S/N*: information, codes of behaviour and inter-corporeal subjectivities.

In reflecting in this essay on the performative and transformative affects of *S/N* for the dumb type collective, I propose that dumb type's *S/N* erodes the boundaries of the public and the private, and interconnects art and the everyday, the aesthetic and the social, through the performative enactment of the personal as political and the political as personal. These artistic strategies are, I argue, at the heart of the *S/N* project. They set it apart from previous dumb type performances and are key to its continuing power to address diverse audiences through the eighty-five minute film record of the performance at Tokyo's Spiral Hall in 1995, re-edited in 2005 by dumb type member Shiro Takatani.[1] I focus on the ongoing impact and continuing realisation of dumb type's *S/N* artistic strategies through an analysis of the art activist activities and collaborative performances of the Japanese artists BuBu de la Madeleine and Akira the Hustler/Yukio Cho from the 1990s to the present day. Both artists were profoundly affected by *S/N* and its impact propelled their subsequent art activist practices.

S/N, unlike the earlier dumb type touring live performances *Pleasure Life* (1988) and *pH* (1990–93), was developed through a series of public seminars combining live performance with invited panel and audience discussion around the central themes of AIDS, HIV, love and sex. This discursive and direct questioning process, unusual for both early 1990s Japanese theatre and live art performance, was one way of breaking the silence surrounding AIDS in Japan and of gauging audience responses and eliciting feedback. It also established a vital link between the personal and the public by situating the performance-in-process within the wider social and political sphere of post-bubble Kyoto and Japan. The trigger was Teiji Furuhashi's letter of 11 October 1992 to dumb type members and friends ("Teiji Furuhashi's New Life: Life with a Virus, In Commemoration of the Announcement of My HIV Infection") where he stressed the need "as an artist … to do something more and become involved," and requested sole directorship of *S/N*.[2] An exceptional request given the collective's stress hitherto on their non-hierarchical processes and structure, it was a decisive moment of coming to terms with the implications of this new life for both individual dumb type members and their friends and for the group's collaborative methods.

The development of *S/N* was emotionally and physically challenging for dumb type. During the intense period of its development, members of the collective and friends were trying to establish the implications of what HIV infection meant amidst the general lack of information or support available in Japan and the misconceptions and prejudices that abounded.[3] Gathering as much information as possible from individuals and organisations within Japan and abroad, these disparate sources informed their extensive debates and activities in Kyoto. In this sense, *S/N* was a coming together of the intensity of these explorations as they were unfolding between October 1992 and March 1994, when the *S/N* live performance premiered at the Adelaide Festival of the Arts.[4] *S/N* remained an "ongoing-work-in progress," as the dumb type visual and media artist Koyamada stresses, a "complex living experience" where changes were made during the collective's tour to different countries that concluded with the last *S/N* performance in Paris in 1996, after Furuhashi's death.[5]

Alongside live performances of *S/N*, the collective also developed a number of art installations, such as the digital projections of *Love/Sex/Death/Money/Life*, that brought components from the *S/N* performances into the exhibition spaces of the art gallery. The projected words of LOVE, SEX, DEATH, MONEY and LIFE, in changing configurations, on screens or direct to wall, effectively combined a minimal conceptual aesthetic with an incisive comment on contemporary life, meticulously reconfigured for each differing gallery site.[6]

BuBu de la Madeleine performed in *S/N* in the sixteen countries it toured to from 1994 to 1996.[7] Trained at Kyoto City University of Arts in the early 1980s alongside many future dumb type members, she joined the group in 1992 on her return to Kyoto. By contrast with the anonymous role performers enacted in *pH*, in *S/N* BuBu is introduced by her self-elected artist name during the second talk show sequence ("Love Song"), and is invited to join a discussion about love and sex through a live video link that projects her "phantom" image onto the installation wall on stage.[8] During the initial conversation about love songs, BuBu recounts her experience as a sex worker and "safer sex professional" and then directly asks Furuhashi about his "personal life" since he became HIV positive. The ensuing conversation is powerful and moving in its directness as Furuhashi describes the importance of touch, hugs, kisses and making love like everyone else. The tenderness of the "Love Song" conversation is heightened by its placement within the performance. It immediately follows the eerie, moving projections of circular images of male and female torsos onto the wall—impersonal objects of surveillance or targets—accompanied by pulsating sounds and the flickering bodies of the performers moving across the narrow, high platform of the projection wall where the sense of bodies in danger is visceral. Immediately after the "personal" public conversation about love between BuBu, Furuhashi and Golightly, the immaculately made-up Furuhashi enacts a lip-synch

dumb type
S/N
Performance, 1993–1996. Photo by Kazuo Fukunaga. Courtesy of Ota Fine Arts Tokyo.

drag performance of "People" by Barbra Streisand, "People, people who need people," followed by the onslaught of computer generated voice and projected text statements "Talking about AIDS," drawn from early 1980s and 1990s newspapers and journals.

To borrow Judith Butler's term, the performance is about "bodies that matter" in the double sense of performative bodies that are produced, made sense of and valued within the "constraints of certain highly gendered regulatory regimes," and those excluded and deemed not to matter.[9] Seen through the lens of Butler's theoretical work on performative gender, the visceral and projected bodies of the *S/N* performers enact subversions of identity, fully aware of the power of bodies of knowledge that work to constrain, misrepresent or limit their presence. While the often projected words "Conspiracy of Silence: Conspiracy of Science" reference Foucault's regimes of power, the physical border of passport control in "Censor Me" hinders movement (scene three), and performers imagine such borders disappearing.[10] Caught in the glare of flashing lights, they enact staccato movements on the narrow ninety-centimetre-wide walkway, four metres above the ground. At intervals they run across the high platform, undress, fall backwards and disappear: "I dream … my gender will disappear. I dream my … nationality will disappear." Described by Kōjin Nishidō as an "aesthetics of annihilation," the bodies of the audience physically sense these moments of dropping and the intense, changing signals and noises that are the stuff of life.[11] Our inter-corporeal subjectivities are heightened and raw. We experience humour, joy, loss and danger in fast succession

dumb type
S/N
Performance at Adelaide Festival, 1994. Video still, Epidemic Video, 2012.

Available on YouTube: www.youtube.com/watch?v=2UbRQZ5LpN4

and the power of sound and light to communicate the vulnerability of the moving bodies. This enactment of the interweaving of the personal into the public sphere and the public into the personal, tests our emotional, conceptual and corporeal limits. It prises open the intersecting worlds of technology, science, medicine, philosophy, the body, drag culture, sex clubs, and much more, in relation to lived bodies and their corporeality.

If *S/N* tested the limits of the performers both physically and emotionally during its inception and performance, it was also transformative in other ways. For BuBu, as for many dumb type members and associates in Kyoto, this performative project generated the need to be actively involved in the issues it raised beyond the realm of art performance spaces, theatres and galleries. The concerns of *S/N* affected everyday life and eroded the boundaries between performance and life, the aesthetic and the social. BuBu became involved in the various projects centred on Art-Space, the communal building dumb type moved their base to in 1992.[12] These collaborative activities included the non-profit organisation AIDS Poster Project (APP), which gathered images and posters on HIV/AIDS and commissioned new works. The poster project was shown in August 1994 in the exhibition hall at the 10th International AIDS Conference in Yokohama, an event that attracted 10,000 visitors and was widely acknowledged as a wake-up call for Japan whose government had invested relatively little in support and prevention.[13] Under the umbrella name of LOVE+, a coalition of Japanese activist groups (made up of Kyoto's dumb type and the AIDS Poster Project, Visual AIDS Tokyo and Stop AIDS Sapporo) organised an accompanying conference on AIDS and Activism, where the American activist and art historian Douglas Crimp first presented his paper on "De-moralizing Representation and AIDS."[14] Part of the wider international activist network in Yokohama, BuBu also participated in the workshop discussion on the specific challenges facing Asian sex workers.[15]

In Kyoto BuBu participated in women's groups, and club performances and parties that helped raise awareness of the issues surrounding HIV/AIDS in Japan and benefit funds to support various campaigns. For example, APP hosted the monthly "Club Luv+" in Kyoto where BuBu performed as part of the "OK Girls" with dumb type choreographer/performer and sex-worker Norico Sunayama,[16] and where Yukio Cho performed as Akira the Hustler.[17] The performative spaces of the drag clubs of Kyoto and Osaka and the popular monthly *Diamonds Are Forever* drag queen parties, initiated by Simone Fukayuki and Furuhashi in 1989 on the latter's return from New

The Biters
48 Ways to Make Love
Reproduced from *BuBu de la Madeleine Art Works 1993–2005*.
Courtesy of Ota Fine Arts Tokyo

York's East Village, were sites of gender transgression and entertainment.[18] For BuBu and Yukio Cho, amongst others, they became important sites of activism and a testing ground for performative practices that parodied gendered binaries and norms of masculinity and femininity. Echoing Judith Butler's proposition of the subversive potentiality of drag, gender was revealed as scripted, rehearsed and performed.[19]

Yukio, born in Tokyo in 1969, trained as a fine artist in oil painting at Kyoto City University of Arts, graduating in 1995 after a BA and MA. Yukio was introduced to dumb type when he was a student through Megumi Matsuo, director of the Voice Gallery on Kyoto's Kawaramachi Imadegawa, where Yukio was working part-time while dumb type occupied the adjoining space. Through Megumi and dumb type, Yukio became involved in the group's activist activities, including the Poster Project and Club Luv+, and in 1998, as Akira the Hustler, he became a co-member of the sex-worker performance group The Biters, with BuBu and Mikado (Noriko Sunayama). In a highly theatrical manner that directly addressed the audience, the group employed their personal experience as sex workers and artists to promote the pleasures of sex through performance, video and writing that played humorously with gendered and sexual stereotypes, parodied sex manuals (*48 Positions for Love Making*) and provocatively advocated a politics of equality and respect for male and female sex workers.

Viewing their performances as a form of art activism, The Biters' often outrageous performances presented their highly stylised and exaggerated "gendered" bodies as both subject and object, and playfully refused both a moralising tone and the enactment of victimhood. They performed in clubs, theatres and in public and commercial galleries, alongside their involvement in activist organisations. Notably, in 1998, their video work and photographic performance documentation were exhibited in "Donai Yanen! et Maintenant! – La création contemporaine au Japon" at the École Nationale Supérieure des Beaux-Arts in Paris, organised by Éric Mézil, and in solo exhibitions at the Tokyo gallery Ota Fine Arts. Extending and interweaving their aesthetic and social practices further, both BuBu and Akira the Hustler each produced a *Whore's Diary* in 2000 recounting their experiences as sex workers.[20]

Alongside performance and activist work post-*S/N*, BuBu also collaborated with the Tokyo-born feminist artist Yoshiko Shimada. Their initial connecting point was Furuhashi, who Shimada had met through their respective participation in the exhibition "The Age of Anxiety" curated by Louise Dompierre at the Power Plant in Toronto, Canada.[21] The exhibition opened in September 1995, just a month before Furuhashi's death on 29 October, and included his solo work *Lovers* (1994), an elaborate four-wall projection presenting life-size images of naked bodies, including his own, appearing and disappearing on the walls, alongside and interspersed with projected statements on the gallery floor that were triggered by the movements of the visitors and which challenged the audience: "Do not cross the line ... Do not jump over the line." Shimada's multi-layered installation work developed for the exhibition and entitled *Look at Me/Look at You* (1995) employed projection of a different kind. The walk-through installation consisting of mirrors, full-size wedding costumes, photographic portraits and a wall installation of condoms, centred on contemporary perceptions of Korean women seen through the lens of Japanese colonial history and the sexual abuse of Korean comfort women forced to serve the Japanese Imperial Army's needs. The work, like *S/N*, brought to public attention some highly controversial subjects that the Japanese government had sought to ignore.[22]

Shimada, like Furuhashi, had lived outside of Japan. Trained as a printmaker at Scripps College in the US in the early 1980s, she had also lived in Berlin from 1993 producing work that critically examined the mismatch between the official or public histories of Japan's recent imperial past, the Emperor system and the active role of Japanese women in supporting colonial expansion.[23] On Furuhashi's suggestion, Shimada and BuBu met and from 1998 they collaborated on a number of art activist projects. Coming from different artistic trajectories, they developed a body of collaborative work comprising drawings, paintings, photographic and video work that documented their performative preoccupations with undermining dominant social and cultural narratives and representations surrounding sexuality, femininity and masculinity, the representation of woman's bodies, and questions of power and submission.

BuBu and Shimada's *Made in Occupied Japan* (1998), a performance recorded on video, was generated by the artists' personal experience. For Shimada, who was born in 1959 in Tokyo, the experience was of growing up

Yoshiko Shimada
Look at me/Look at you
Installation, 1995. Exhibition view at Ota Fine Arts, Tokyo. Courtesy of Ota Fine Arts Tokyo.

near a US air force base in her hometown of Tachikawa, a former Japanese Imperial Army base, and as becomes clearer in her later work, the marriage of one of her aunts to an American black GI who chose to settle in the US.[24] For BuBu, earning a living as a sex worker and a representative of Japan's sex workers at the International Congress on Prostitution in Los Angeles in 1997, the theme was personal, political and ethical. Following the surrender of Japan in August 1945, the country was occupied by the American military from 1945 to 1952. The GI occupiers bought services from Japanese women who were trying to survive in the difficult post-war years, and, paralleling her own experience as a sex worker, questions about hostile public attitudes to prostitution and the silence on such matters as sex workers rights underscored the work.[25]

BuBu + Shimada
Made in Occupied Japan
Photo collage, 1998.
24.8 × 32.9 cm. Courtesy of Ota Fine Arts Tokyo.

The resulting work is a series of vignette enactments by the two artists that capture aspects of occupied Japan: the re-enactment of General MacArthur and Emperor Hirohito's first meeting in August 1945, based upon the iconic photograph reproduced worldwide that marked Japan's surrender; transactions between an American soldier and Japanese sex worker; and enactments of the stereotypes of the housewife and prostitute.[26] Based upon the imaginative interweaving of their personal gendered experience within the narrative of Japan's history, the collaborative enactment of *Made in Occupied Japan* presented an overlooked and politically contentious history of war and sex within Japan and foregrounded complex ethical

BuBu + Shimada
1945, Made in Occupied Japan
Photo, collage, 1998. 91 × 91 cm.
Courtesy of Ota Fine Arts Tokyo.

questions about power. By playing out roles of woman as housewife, lover and sex worker, issues of negotiated survival come to the fore and the inadequacies of the dominant binary of victim/oppressor most frequently drawn along the gendered lines of male/female and their implications for the post-war Japanese nation. Resonant with the central artistic strategy of *S/N*, the work of Shimada and BuBu opened up these uncomfortable past and present spaces by asking personal questions about where the individual stood, whether as artist or viewer. Negotiating a shared space with their audiences through the directness and intimacy of the performance, their performative works offered new perspectives and understandings of the

BuBu de la Madeleine
The Flags of All Nations
Pen, conté and felt-tip pen, 2001. 10 × 15 cm.
Courtesy of Ota Fine Arts Tokyo.

interconnectivity of bodies and subjectivities and the questioning of how an individual might act in such circumstances.

Part of this shared space included holding open discussion sessions and workshops that focused on engaging a wide range of audiences in dialogue alongside their exhibitions and performances.[27] In the United Kingdom in 2001, this included BuBu's performance of the unveiling of the flags of many nations, an act first performed in *S/N* that interwove the practices of feminist art performance with those of the sex club industry.[28]

In documenting her work from 1992 to 1998, including collaborations with BuBu, Shimada entitles the publication *Art Activism*, which she defines as follows: "Art Activism is one space in which the personal becomes political. ...art has the power to change people's perspectives. I don't mean as propaganda, but as something that makes viewers re-think their own existence ... by presenting my own position. I think this anxiety brings the possibility of a change of point of views."[29]

Such collaborative and dialogic methods that place emphasis on dialogue as an ongoing dynamic and social process of meaning-making by multiple voices, akin to Mikhail Bakhtin's ideas, have remained central to the activities of BuBu and Akira the Hustler/Yukio as artists and activists since the 1990s.[30] Both have continued to be involved in promoting sexual awareness of HIV/AIDS and in gay community projects. BuBu worked for MASH (Men and Sexual Health), an HIV information centre within the Osaka dista community space,[31] and developed and organised art events and a Club party as part of the cultural programme from 2003 for the Seventh International Congress on AIDS in Asia and the Pacific held in Kobe, Japan, in July 2005.[32] Yukio/Akira the Hustler was a co-founder of the Rainbow Ring in 2003, a gay NGO that runs the Akta community centre in Tokyo's Shinjuku district. The interweaving of art and social activism is embodied through the visual material generated by the NGO and through participatory projects. For example, the *Living Together* project, initiated in 2004, started as a collaborative project between Rainbow Ring and Place Tokyo (Positive Living And Community Empowerment), another NGO providing support to people with HIV. As part of this project, sponsored by the Japanese government's Ministry of Health, Labour and Welfare from 2006, Yukio/Akira the Hustler created a number of awareness-raising activities that enabled the sharing of the realities of HIV-positive individuals with those unaware of them. Under the banner "We, both HIV-negative and HIV-positive, are already living together," events included the once-a-month

Living Together Project
REAL
Tokyo, 2008.
Courtesy of Akira the Hustler.

Living Together Lounge, comprising diary readings accompanied by background music set to the tempo of the average heart beat to create a supportive and relaxing environment for both the reader and audience, followed by a club night.[33]

In January 2008, when *Living Together* was presented at Tokyo's Ota Fine Arts gallery, the multimedia installation presented the personal stories of those involved in the project. The exhibition space also became a performative site where the audience were invited through the "living together table" to contribute to these stories and thereby through participatory action to co-produce part of the installation. Akira the Hustler described the exhibition as one "which visualizes the voices of HIV-positive people, who still hesitate to have a say or come out to the outside, their families, boy/girl friends and those who support them."[34] Employing dialogic and collaborative strategies of direct address to the audience through the focus on specific bodies and experiences that erode the boundaries between the private and public, and interconnect the aesthetic and the social through the performative enactment of the personal as political and the political as personal, the exhibition brought ongoing social issues and concerns into the gallery space as part of Japanese contemporary culture.

In his more recent film and three-dimensional painted clay works, first shown in the international exhibition "Love's Body: Art in the Age of Aids" at the Tokyo Metropolitan Museum of Photography in 2010, Akira the Hustler focuses on the every day relationships as an affirmative act of living together.[35] As Michiko Kasahara, the curator of the exhibition, observes: "The importance of basic human action of touching and relating even amidst the numerous difficulties imposed by the age of AIDS."[36] This concern with social interaction was developed further in "Ordinary Life" at Ota Fine Arts in 2012, an exhibition of painted clay figures and two-dimensional work, where the emphasis was placed on the symbolic device of the red string that connects living beings of differing ages and sexuality, and on private and public communication as an act of agency and an alternative to fear and silence.[37]

Seen within the wider frame of performance in the twenty-first century, the art activism of BuBu de la Madeleine and Akira the Hustler has migrated across the boundaries of art and life. Their many activities in the public sphere have, as Adrian Heathfield argues in relation to performance in general, "become a means through which to test the foundations of and borders of identity, to bring the self into new relations with its 'outsides',

Akira the Hustler
Living Together
22 January – 16 February 2008. Installation at Ota Fine Arts, Tokyo.
Courtesy of Ota Fine Arts, Tokyo.

and 'others'," and thereby shown its capacity to "generate new forms of relation, collaboration, and community."[38] If the work of BuBu de la Madeleine and Akira the Hustler can now be seen as part of the wider global "social turn" identified by Shannon Jackson as a meeting of performance practices, post-studio art and social movements, the roots of their practices were in the Kyoto-based development of dumb type's *S/N*.[39] With *S/N*, as I have argued, the live performance was generated through the strategy of beginning with the personal—both the personal of themselves and of others, the "how are you?" of *S/N*—in order to focus on the specific effects and affects of lived and gendered experience in the difficult economic and political climate of the immediate post-bubble years in Japan. It is the focus on bodies that matter, and the social and ethical implications

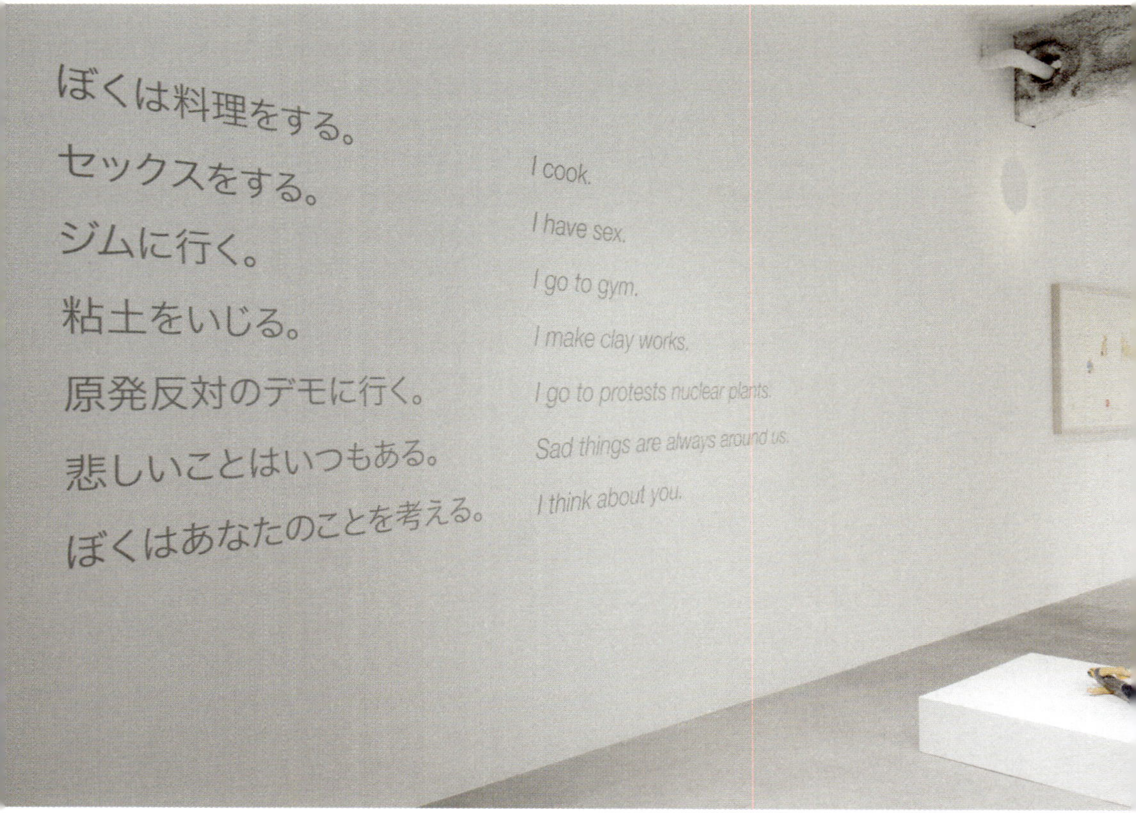

Akira the Hustler
Ordinary Life
8 September–13 October 2012. Installation at Ota Fine Arts, Tokyo.
Photo: Hiroyuki Takenouchi. Courtesy of Ota Fine Arts, Tokyo.

that this embraces that makes *S/N* a powerful collaborative performance which has resulted in such an ongoing legacy of art activism. Refusing to create homogeneous and singular categories that are the classic form of making "other," the artistic strategies central to *S/N* are recognising that we are all involved, directly or indirectly, in coming to terms with living in the contemporary world and that the interweaving of performance and activist art practices has the power to communicate and involve individuals as part of a wider social collective and to challenge ways of thinking about the self and others.[40]

Notes

1 *S/N*, Spiral Hall, Tokyo, 1995, filmed by Japan Satellite Broadcasting WOWOW. A 2006 Tokyo performance was used for the dumb type translation of the *S/N* text, "*S/N*, dumb type," in *Half a Century of Japanese Theater, 1990s Part 2*, ed. Japan Playwrights Association (Tokyo: Kinokuniya, 2000), pp. 257–86.

2 Shinya Yamaki, "Life with Art: Receiving and Passing on," in *Love's Body: Art in the Age of Aids* (Tokyo: Tokyo Metropolitan Museum of Photography, 2010), p. 182. The complete letter in Japanese is reproduced in Dumb type, *memorandum teiji furuhashi* (Tokyo: Little More, 2000), pp. 36–43.

3 See Satoko Itoh, "Japan," in Tadashi Yamamoto and Satoko Itoh, *Fighting a Rising Tide: The Response to AIDS in East Asia* (Tokyo: Japan Center for International Exchange, 2006), pp. 119–55; and Andrew Pollack, "Japan May Have to Face Up to AIDS," *The New York Times*, 7 August 1994.

4 For a 14 min 37 sec extract of *S/N* at The Adelaide Festival of the Arts released by Epidermic video, see http://www.youtube.com/watch?v=2UbRQZ5LpN4 (accessed 28 October 2014).

5 Toru Koyamada, "Notes on *S/N*," in the exhibition catalogue *Japanese Contemporary Dance Media 2005* (Tokyo: Tokyo Metropolitan Museum of Photography, 2005), p. 195. For an account of BuBu's response after the Paris *S/N* performance, see "La Dolce Vita, 2000," text, drawings and DVD film stills in *BuBu de la Madeleine, Art Works 1993–2005* (Tokyo: Ota Fine Arts, 2006, unpaginated).

6 The installation of *S/N #1* was first shown in 1992 at the Museum of Ixelles, Brussels, Belgium, and subsequently in "Japanese Art After 1945, Scream Against the Sky," at the San Francisco Museum of Modern Art and the Yerba Buena Center for the Arts, San Francisco, USA, in 1995. *S/N #2* premiered at the Art Tower Mito, Mito, Japan, as part of curator Yuko Hasegawa's "Mito Annual '93: Another World," 21 November 1992–7 March 1993. *Love/Sex/Death/Money/Life*, first presented at the Spiral Hall, Tokyo, in 1994, has travelled widely as a video installation, including: in Paris, Espace d'Art Yvonamor Palix (1995) and "Donai yanen! Et maintenant!" (1998), and in "Art, Performance and Activism in Contemporary Japan," Pumphouse Gallery, London (2012).

7 BuBu performed in *S/N* under her birth name of Izumi Kagita.

8 Katherine Mezur, "Fleeting Moments: The Vanishing Acts of Phantom Women in the Performances of Dumb Type," *Women & Performance: A Journal of Feminist Theory* 12 (1), 2001: 200.

9 Judith Butler, *Bodies That Matter: On the Discursive Limits of "Sex"* (New York: Routledge, 1993), p. xi.

10 As Butler discusses in *Bodies That Matter*, her work on performative gender was developed in dialogue with Michel Foucault's writings, notably *Discipline and Punish: The Birth of the Prison*, trans. A. Sheridan (London: Allen Lane, 1977) and *The History of Sexuality: Vol. 1*, trans. R. Hurley (London: Allen Lane, 1979).

11 Kōjin Nishidō, "Introduction, *S/N*, dumb type," in *Half a Century of Japanese Theater, 1990s Part 2*, p. 260.

12 Artspace Mumonkan in Kyoto, a site of live performance and alternative group meetings from the 1980s was the base of dumb type from 1992 to 2001. For Artspace projects, see the AIDS workshop publication, *AIDS, And Dance with Somebody* (MASH Osaka and Kyoto Prefecture, 2007, unpaginated).

13 10th International AIDS Conference ("The Global Challenge of AIDS: Together for the Future"); International AIDS Society, "List of Exhibitors, International Conference on AIDS" (10th: 1994: Yokohama, Japan), 7 August 1994. http://quod.lib.umich.edu/c/cohenaids/5571095.0084.045/2?page=root;rgn=full+text;size=100;view=image;q1=List+of+exhibitors (accessed 20 October 2014).

14 Douglas Crimp, in *Melancholia and Moralism: Essays on AIDS and Queer Politics* (Cambridge, MA: MIT Press, 2002), pp. 253–72.

15 See "Asian Sex Workers Discuss Experiences, Hardships," in *AIDS Conference News: Tenth International Conference on AIDS/International Conference on STD, no. 2* International AIDS Society, The Organizing Committee of the Tenth International Conference on AIDS/International Conference on STD, 8 August 1994, p. 5. http://name.umdl.umich.edu/5571095.0086.193 (accessed

20 October 2014).

16 See Katherine Mezur, "Sex with Nation: The OK (Bad) Girls Cabaret," in *Bad Girls of Japan*, ed. Laura Miller and Jan Bardsley (London: Palgrave Macmillan, 2005), pp. 175–89.

17 Jai Arun Ravine, "Photographs and Interview with C.Snatch Z. and Tomoaki Hata," *Drunken Boat* 14 (Summer 2011). http://www.drunkenboat.com/db14/5sex/hata/gloriously.php (accessed 5 January 2015).

18 "Interview with Teiji Furuhashi by Bridget Cooper," *Kyoto Journal* 16 (1), January 1991. Reprinted in Dumb type, *memorandum teiji furuhashi* (Tokyo: Little More, 2000), pp. 59–61. Gay nightlife and drag performance in Osaka from 1996 to 2004 are documented by the Los Angeles-based Japanese photographer Tomoaki Hata in *The Night is Still Young* (New York: Powerhouse Books, 2010).

19 Judith Butler, *Gender Trouble: Feminism and the Subversion of Identity* (New York: Routledge, 1990). Chapter 3, "Subversive Bodily Acts," focuses on the practice of drag as a way to destabilise the notion that there is an "original" gender.

20 BuBu de la Madeleine, *Whore's Diary*, DVD, 20 min 34 sec, 2000; Akira the Hustler, *A Whore's Diary* (Tokyo: Isshi Press, 2000). See also BuBu, "BuBu's Diary," in *Sex and Consumerism: Contemporary Art in Japan*, ed. Fran Lloyd and Melanie Roberts (Brighton: University of Brighton, 2001), pp. 47–56.

21 See *The Age of Anxiety*, exhibition catalogue, ed. Louise Dompierre (Toronto: Power Plant, 1995).

22 It was only in 1993 that the Japanese government publicly accepted responsibility for the coercion of comfort women with the Kono Statement. See C. Sarah Soh, *The Comfort Women: Sexual Violence and Postcolonial Memory in Korea and Japan* (Chicago: University of Chicago Press, 2009).

23 See Rebecca Jennison and Laura Hein, "Against Forgetting: Three Generations of Artists in Japan in Dialogue about the Legacies of World War II," *The Asia-Pacific Journal* 9, 25 July 2011: 30. http://www.japanfocus.org/site/make_pdf/3573 (accessed 2 October 2014).

24 Ibid., unpaginated.

25 While the term "sex workers" covers a range of practices, Japan's Anti-Prostitution Law, which came into force in April 1958, criminalised the act of committing sexual intercourse in exchange for actual or promised compensation. For details on the complexities of sex working in Japan, see Kaoru Aoyama, "The Sex Industry in Japan: The Dangers of Invisibility," in *Routledge Handbook of Sexuality Studies in East Asia*, ed. Mark McLelland and Vera Mackie (Routledge: New York, 2014), pp. 281–93.

26 See the photo essay "Made in Occupied Japan," in *Consuming Bodies: Sex and Contemporary Japanese Art*, ed. Fran Lloyd (London: Reaktion, 2003), pp. 109–26.

27 *Made in Occupied Japan* was exhibited in 1998 at Ota Fine Arts, Tokyo, and toured the UK in 2001 in the group exhibition "Sex and Consumerism." Other collaborative works by BuBu and Shimada include *Attack/Damage* (Itabashi Art Museum, Tokyo, 1998) and *Women in Camouflage*, a video work based on interviews with women who worked in the Japanese Self-Defence Forces, exhibited at the inaugural exhibition of the Kumamoto City Contemporary Art Museum in 2002.

28 University of Brighton, UK, 6 October 2001.

29 Yoshiko Shimada, *Art Activism 1992–98* (Tokyo: Ota Fine Arts, 1998, unpaginated).

30 See Mikhail Bakhtin, *The Dialogic Imagination: Four Essays*, ed. Michael Holquist, trans. Caryl Emerson and Michael Holquist (Austin and London: University of Texas Press, 1981).

31 http:// www.dista.be/ (accessed 12 October 2014).

32 *Seventh International Congress on AIDS in Asia and the Pacific, Congress Report, 2005*, Kobe, Japan, 1–5 July 2005, "Cultural Programme Committee," http://www.icaap7.jp/images/report.pdf, p. 76 (accessed 12 October 2014).

33 For a sociological study on the role of music in the Living Together Lounge, see Mia Nakamura, "Retelling, Memory-Work, and Metanarrative: Two Musical-Artistic Mediations for Sexual Minorities and Majorities in Tokyo," *Music and Arts in Action* 4 (2), 2014: 5–23.

34 http://www.otafinearts.com/en/exhibitions/2008/living_together/?p=works#works-7 (accessed 2 October 2014).

35 "Love's Body: Art in the Age of Aids" at the Tokyo Metropolitan Museum of Photography in 2010 featured the work of A. A. Bronson, Akira the Hustler/ Yukio Cho, Sunil Gupta, Felix Gonzalez-Torres, Hervé Guibert, Peter Hurjar, David Wojnarowicz and William Yang.

36 Michiko Kasahara, "Love's Body: Art in the Age of Aids," in the exhibition catalogue *Love's Body: Art in the Age of Aids* (Tokyo: Tokyo Metropolitan Museum of Photography, 2010), p. 167.

37 "Ordinary Life," Ota Fine Arts, Tokyo, 8 September–13 October, 2012. See http://www.otafinearts.com/en/exhibitions/2012/post_84/ (accessed 2 October 2014).

38 Adrian Heathfield, "Alive," in *Live Art and Performance*, ed. Adrian Heathfield (London: Tate Publishing, 2004), p. 10.

39 Shannon Jackson, *Social Works: Performing Art, Supporting Publics* (New York and London: Routledge, 2011), pp. 11–12.

40 For BuBu de la Madeleine's and Akira the Hustler's responses to the earthquake and tsunami in Japan in March 2011, see Akiko Mizoguchi, "In Flux: Eight Japanese Artists in the Aftermath of 3/11," *WSQ: Women's Studies Quarterly* 39 (3), 2011: 318–28.

Interviews

"I don't see a difference between machine-time and human-time"

Interview with TAKATANI Shirō, Kyoto, 15 December 2013

Peter Eckersall, Edward Scheer, FUJII Shintarō

TAKATANI The year I started at University was the year that dumb type started as a theatre club, after we decided that the name Karma wasn't really appropriate anymore. In that summer of 1984, we got together to come up with a new name: dumb type. This was a time when the theatre was changing quite a bit because of the influence of people like Terayama Shuji. It was also around the time when Bob Wilson, Laurie Anderson and other people came to Japan, when things were really changing very quickly.

I was studying architecture and environmental design, and when I chose to join this theatre club it was not because I wanted to be on stage or perform but because I was interested in exploring the use of space, light and video, experimenting with space and presenting people on stage differently.

At the time I was working mostly with slides and with light, because video projection was quite new and not so accessible at the time, but in sound there were a lot of possibilities already—with interactivity and creating new sounds just using microphones. But video was still inaccessible, so we used mostly slide projectors and 16mm film. When new technological developments occurred, the process changed.

I was very much influenced by film, Tarkovsky and Visconti for instance. We would all go to see these films and then discuss them and think "Oh, this scene was interesting," or "can we use colour like that?"

Another inspiration was the different kinds of media used in experimental music concerts. At the time, members were interested in presenting not a theatre performance per se but a time-based piece, all disciplines working together.

ECKERSALL So your influences are visual arts, architecture, music. Is this where the idea of time-based art came from in these early days?

TAKATANI It wasn't only about creating this time-based work, but more about doing something together with all these different people. Sometimes we'd do something in the gallery, if we were asked by the gallery, or we'd rent a small phone-booth-sized kind of box that we'd do something in. So there were different formats ... installations as well as performances. But the general idea was to collaborate with different people or to create something together. After becoming dumb type, that was the most important aspect of it.

ECKERSALL The key word seems to be collaboration. Was this something that just happened, or did you have a kind of manifesto about it or a politics of collaboration?

TAKATANI It naturally developed that way. We didn't discuss it at all.

Furuhashi-san or Koyamada-san, who were three or four years older, had very particular things that they wanted to explore...

SCHEER So what did you bring, in particular, to that collaboration when you first started working? Was it the design influence?

TAKATANI At the beginning it was just poster design, or set design, or lighting, in fact all kinds of things. At the university it was possible to make your own posters and tickets. So it was really fun to do all those things yourself.

ECKERSALL Also, I think a feature of your work from the very early days right through until now is the relationship to objects, and the way you bring objects into the theatre space and use them.

SCHEER Like these tables.

ECKERSALL Like these tables. Like the objects in *Pleasure Life*. We could talk about *pH* as a kind of object in one way. How do you think about objects in relation to your artistic practice?

TAKATANI When you are a set designer by training, you learn that only the front is important; the back of the object doesn't matter and it just has to be easily transportable. I was interested more in developing a kind of installation, something more sculptural, more machine-like, like a kind of an environment for the performers to be confronted with, rather than a theatre set.

So in *pH*, for instance, there is an object that you can look at from all sides; there is no backside to it that's supposed to be invisible. I'm thinking of the entire work as a kind of sculpture or an art piece that has to be seen from all sides, not something frontal. So that was the challenge for me.

SCHEER It's also a challenge to the conventions of theatre and the naturalistic fourth wall dramas. So, already with *pH*, the company was moving beyond theatre and into visual arts institutions and museums, and that work toured extensively, not in theatre spaces but predominantly in visual arts museums and other sorts of locations. Was that a deliberate gesture at that stage, to move out of theatre? Having been dumb type Theatre—becoming dumb type and moving away from theatre?

TAKATANI It's almost like the 'theatre' in dumb type Theatre was a bit of a mistake or an accident. The *idea* was to create installations and to work together as a group of artists, but the main *activity* at the time was making performances in the theatre space. So it was sort of a natural thing to put theatre in the name, maybe automatically... When we realised after a few pieces that that wasn't really what we were doing, we decided to let go of the word 'theatre' in the company name.

ECKERSALL Could you talk a little bit about the performativity of the objects, perhaps using *pH* as an example, and the way that they create a complex set of interactions with performers as well as with audiences?

TAKATANI There were two things I wanted to try. One was to not work in a proscenium arch stage theatre. Two, was to really involve the audience in the performance. I was also interested in the idea of old technology that we're not using any more—imagining people from the future looking back at the technology from the past. So to have that kind of perspective seemed like a good idea in *pH*; to have people look at it from above and sort of peep into this world from the past somehow. But then this whole construction was put back into a theatre space.

When *pH* was performed in New York, a reviewer wrote that it looked like Charlie Chaplin's *Modern Times* and that's kind of accurate, that's sort of what I wanted to do. *Modern Times* are not our times, just sort of similar... we were exploring what would happen when you look back at our times as modern times from the past.

ECKERSALL *Modern Times* is often understood by critics to offer a strong critique of technological determinism in which the human becomes alienated. Was that also an intention in making *pH*?

TAKATANI Yes, but it's another kind of technology—because in *Modern Times*, it's a human being that can't keep up with automation, the automatic process of labour actually. In *pH*, it's about digital technology and how it comes into our lives. It's like when you go shopping and the scanner goes beep, beep, beep—it's related to labour and consumer behaviour. In the film, it's about labourers in the factory, but for us it is more the way technology has infiltrated our everyday lives on all kinds of levels.

SCHEER But *pH* also looks forward, doesn't it, because it's about the "worldwide Infobahn," as the programme notes say. This kind of terminology was only just appearing at that time, and yet this work predates the Internet by some years. So, in a way, dumb type is one of the first major performance companies that deals with that new, not only digital but also networked experience of contemporary life.

ECKERSALL *pH* seems to look forward at the same time as looking back. Could I ask you to speak a little bit about the way in which your work with dumb type evolved over the decade from *pH* through *S/N*, which is perfectly located within digital culture, to *OR* and *memorandum*, and what kind of practices you developed as an artist? What happened to the focus on machines as object, for example?

TAKATANI One very simple element is that up to *pH* we couldn't afford to get video projectors. It was still new technology and very expensive. By the time of *S/N*, we were able to buy one and we also had an editing machine, so it was easier to work with video. Very early on we had developed a system to link video and sound, so that was an element that came into play in *S/N*. It was also the first time we worked with live camera images.

Technologically, there wasn't so much difference when moving into the creation of *OR*. But there was a feeling that this piece had to be based on visuals and sound more than on text or other elements—that it was the power of the visual image and the power of the sound that would push this piece along somehow. It was an experiment in seeing how much could be done with these two elements—or how they could really carry a performance, not text. It was also an attempt at creating a different space on the stage, not just an object put into space or a set.

As for the later works, *memorandum* was edited on the computer. It ended up being a piece where there was a screen as a central element and projections on the front and back of the screen. *Voyage* worked with modular scenes, different units that were combined into a temporal structure, which was a new way for dumb type to work.

SCHEER How was the making of *OR* for you? Did someone have to step in to the role of director to make that work happen after Teiji's passing? What happened to the company at that time and what were the key, rebalancing acts that had to occur to get dumb type back functioning?

TAKATANI Basically, at the beginning, the idea was collaboration; we were a collaborative group. So there was no leader and we all worked on the pieces together. After Furuhashi-san passed away, the idea that we would no longer make any work would have made our collaborative ethic a lie, this idea that we were all making it together. So we decided to continue to work together. I did the video, Yamanaka-san did the sound in *OR*, and also Ikeda Ryoji (who had come in for *S/N*), and it was very different from the previous shows, because it is very prominent. Furuhashi-san had been involved with the sound, with the video and with the performance aspect; he sort of had a general overview over what was going on... and did some of the final adjustments to the piece... like looking at it from the outside. But when he passed away that kind of person wasn't there, so it felt like the different roles that Furuhashi-san had were divided between different people.

The day *OR* opened, it was an hour and a half long, and then the next day it was only 45 minutes because we cut so much. But we were lucky enough to be working in Maubeuge at the time in France, and we were able to use the theatre for a whole month, which is impossible in Japan.

SCHEER I've heard *OR* being referred to as a moment of the body's disappearance from the theatre really, where it's all about what technology will allow. I'm not so sure if I agree with this reading, but I'd like to hear what you think. I see *OR* as being a very complex piece, which re-engages the physical through technology. But what's your sense of how that plays out? Do you have a sense of the body in relation to technology in that work?

TAKATANI I think you're right in your analysis. The violence of the sound and the light that the audience can experience is, for me, a kind of amplification of the identification of the audience with the actor or performer on stage. In theatre, the audience identifies with the actors on stage but the technology can help by amplifying this effect, by making the audience experience these things that the body on stage also experiences, and in that way also identify with the performer in a different, additional way. Not like in film when you're looking at the actors; on stage they look sort of small. And it wouldn't work if there were no actual bodies on stage. The bodies on stage support this whole system. Without them, this circuit of experience between the audience and the performer wouldn't work and there would be no identification process and nothing to be amplified by the technology.

Acting in film and acting on stage are different. If you're watching a film, you want it to look natural, but on stage, if people are natural, it's not enough to enable identification with the people in the audience. So technology can help to amplify this possibility for identification with the actors on stage. And maybe that's where the name dumb type really fits; because when we started, theatre was still all about projecting a lot of spoken text in big voices. We were exploring other ways for actors and performers to be on stage, not just by projecting spoken text.

ECKERSALL Could I ask you to speak about the scene in *OR* of the video sequence of the road trip?

TAKATANI The images came from a drive we took from Switzerland to Italy, sped up to only four minutes duration—and, in fact, the sound existed first. Ikeda-san wanted to make music that went really fast and then stopped. He made that music with the crescendo and we used it in the piece. So when we went to Europe, we rented a car and went travelling, and we thought the road scenes were really nice and filmed them from the window. We thought maybe we could use this footage with the music. So the video and the sound were edited together; and then we wanted a visual text to accompany this, so we asked Alfred Birnbaum to write a text that would fit this video of a trip from Switzerland to Italy.

ECKERSALL There's a very interesting fracturing of the image at one point, where the image pixelates, and the woman stands alone in front of the screen. What gave you the idea for that kind of resolution?

TAKATANI [LAUGHS] When the actress is placed in front of the screen, either she disappears into the image or the image disappears and the actress remains alone on stage. The effect was actually made so that the actress did not disappear into the image. In order for that *not* to happen, use of visual effects was necessary.

SCHEER Very interesting. What about the idea for these tables? Because they always seem very medical to me. Seeing them here in your house makes them seem like designer objects. They're very beautiful and functional, but seeing them on stage, they had a kind of austere, clinical look. With that sequence with the shroud on the body at the end, they seemed to represent a mortuary slab as well. You've achieved an enormous amount with the design of these objects, again, but which of those readings was prominent for you in the design process? What were you thinking of when you were designing these tables?

TAKATANI Yes, they are like a stretcher, or a gurney, the idea of getting someone to the hospital or a hospital bed. They're very cold images. That was the main image, of a stretcher.

ECKERSALL There is so much detail in them. I mean these are not theatre props. These screws, for example...

TAKATANI It's like what I was talking about earlier, not just a prop for a theatre but an object that's nice to look at from all sides—that is what I always want to do.

ECKERSALL Could I ask you to speak a little bit about the very rapid montage effect in *memorandum,* the sequences where the body and the video are almost in competition with each other, with the explosion of images in a very short time, both in the live performance and also in the installation version?

TAKATANI Well, if you take the scene in *OR* we were just talking about... you can run the scene very fast, but when it's a continuous story or a continuous line of imagery, there's a limit to how fast you can play it because otherwise it becomes difficult to watch. But when you think about memory, you can scan memory very quickly and you can do a search for certain things and all kinds of images can sort of come up one after the other and you can then link these images. This was the method that I used or developed for *memorandum.* So there's an unlimited amount of images in memory, both conscious and unconscious images, that you can search and go to one place, then start another search and go to another place... and you can just continue like that, with lots and lots of images. *Memorandum* is a performance about memory, so that's the starting point for this method that I developed and then used afterwards, for example, in the installation I made called *Frost Frames.*

ECKERSALL In *memorandum* your work is getting faster and shorter. Two days ago we saw the show you did with Ryuichi Sakamoto at Tokyo Intercommunication Centre. Spectators were encouraged to lie on the floor and to have a relaxation experience, watching flowers and hearing soft music. This show, I think, frames the visual experience differently. So what is that progression about, from fast to slow visuality?

TAKATANI Both are important—fast and slow—and, in fact, it's not too different; they are sort of the same. When you have different images following each other, it feels very fast... but in this supposedly slow piece, it's actually very fast as well. It's actually the same, if you think of it in terms of the amount of data involved or the speed with which the data changes.

Think about the cameras we use at the finish line in sports that freeze an image in time. It's the same process, actually.

ECKERSALL Dumb type's work was against nature, in a way, whereas these works focus intensely on natural environments: clouds, the outdoor environments in the projections, also in the panoramic works of the sky. Of course, "against nature" was a comment about sexuality—but, in a way, it's also kind of ironic.

TAKATANI The theme of this latest exhibition is to think about new technologies and what kinds of new perspectives or vision, or ways of seeing, we can introduce. In the catalogue there's an essay which says that when the photograph was invented it allowed people to see themselves from the outside for the first time, which introduced a whole new way of thinking, a new philosophy. So the question here is what kind of new ways of seeing, of observing new perspectives, the new technologies we have can offer us. If we're looking at time as a line, a timeline, or compressing a whole day into one scene, what kind of new ways of vision can we develop.

SCHEER Again, it looks to me like machine-time being brought into some kind of relation with the human experience of time. So machine-time and human perception have a different register, but they can be brought into a relation together through media art and through this exhibition, for example. I thought that's partly what you were doing, the way you used those lovely lenses and the old images. You know, the nineteenth-century wet collodion photography that takes ten seconds for the image to form. It's a very slow process—and now digital cameras, that aren't even taking images of the world anymore, they're making things up. So again, there's a whole continuum of image making in the exhibition; machine-time and human-time are brought closer together, which I think does go back to the dumb type kind of experience as well.

TAKATANI I don't see a difference between machine-time and human-time. It is a human experience of space and of society, and just by using technology you can cut it differently and offer a different slice of time by reorganising it and slicing it up differently, making different ways of looking at it. For instance, if you cut it up in bits, then you can see a reality that maybe you only unconsciously experience, or that you cannot have in memory, but by slicing it up differently you can see it in a different way. But it's real time that we're experiencing, not machine-time.

ECKERSALL You're listed as the Artistic Director of dumb type in the exhibition. Has the company changed its structure in recent times, or what is dumb type now?

TAKATANI The name still exists but everyone is busy doing other things, so there's no work being produced now... but there's all the material, the memory, the archive. There's no need to get rid of the name now. But if the name or the company stopped existing, then what do we do with all this material? So for now, I am the guardian of the archive of dumb type.

SCHEER I came here to Kyoto fifteen years ago, to the old dumb type office, and met you [indicating Takatani Yoko], and you gave me the VHS tape of the show reel, which I have played to my students so many times it's now unusable. I need to refresh the materials.

ECKERSALL I also came here fifteen years ago.

TAKATANI Really!

ECKERSALL Yoko was very kind to me. [To Takatani Yoko] You drove me through Kyoto and showed me the temple and took me to the Shinkansen.

YOKO I also joined dumb type when it was a university club, and, at the time, the first year students had to perform because the older ones told them to, but I performed for a few times and decided it was not my thing anymore and didn't perform after that.

I wasn't involved in the artistic side so much. I left for a while and came back as Furuhashi-san's assistant, doing the management and production.

ECKERSALL If you were both to think about the experience of dumb type and its contribution, what does it leave us with or give us? What would you say that its most important aspects are?

TAKATANI I think what came up earlier in relation to technology and how it offers possibilities to show a slice of Japanese society. I think that's a unique aspect of dumb type's work, the way in which it shows a slice of society.

YOKO The fact that very different, interesting artists, with different views and opinions, came together to make this work, is the most interesting aspect, I think.

FUJII It's very difficult to live as an artist, making performances in Japan, and especially in Tokyo. Perhaps here it's a little bit easier, and maybe there are more opportunities here... so what's the role Kyoto plays in your work?

TAKATANI I went to school here and just sort of stayed around. But maybe it's also not bad for the work to have been here and to have that distance from Tokyo, because the image I have from Tokyo is that people get tired or get pushed away, sort of used and abused and pushed aside, and then other people come in and take over. It's a very commercial system, and here there's a bit of a distance from all that. And when you're invited to perform somewhere, you can perform and then come back. You don't have to live in this system, but it's not that easy. Of course, it's not that it's easy in Europe either, even in some places where people are supported very well... or in America, where it's all about making money and if you're not making money then you just stop existing. So it's difficult to find a position in relation to this that works. But there's a feeling that it's necessary for people, like those in France who invited us, or those that came to Japan to see things. They invite us because they want people in their community to see this kind of work. It would be good if in Japan there would be more people like that as well, who go to see things at different places and invite these performances, because they feel that the people in the conservative theatres should see this kind of work. There are some people in Japan like that, but not enough; it would be better if there were more people supporting work in that way.

ECKERSALL Thank you so much for your time and your thoughts.

Punch Cards, *Pleasure Life* and *pH*

Interview with FUJIMOTO Takayuki, Kyoto, 15 December 2013

Peter Eckersall, Edward Scheer

ECKERSALL Fujimoto-san, can you tell us how you came to be working with dumb type?

FUJIMOTO I knew the people of the Karma Group through the volleyball team. Furuhashi Teiji was also in the same high school as me, same grade as well, so we knew each other before. I was also working as a stage assistant in a regular public theatre, so I was familiar with the theatre system. I was also drawing and painting, and after university I rented a studio. It was quite a big space, which was at a Kendo school. There was an apartment on the first floor and the ground floor was a big space... and when we graduated and we all started to make work, everyone moved into this first floor apartment because it was empty.

I was drawing in the downstairs space and we were living upstairs and performing in a space called the Orange Room. I was working in the theatre on the side, and knew most people from the volleyball team, so that was good. I went to see their first performance, *Plan for Sleep* (1984), and thought it was really great. So I started helping out. My contributions were not so much conceptual as practical or technical.

By then I was already working in theatre, building stage sets. There were four different theatres in Kyoto where the geisha or kabuki performances happened, and I was working in three of those spaces, wearing these black outfits. Not very dumb type-like, very different. But for Koyamada-san and me, it was like a student job.

ECKERSALL What's the first piece you worked on with dumb type?

FUJIMOTO *036 Pleasure Life*. The work was a kind of TV montage; it was the first time that we used video. Also, we made the original handmade fluorescent light structures and the technology wall. There was no moving light system at the time, but I had my friend make a motor system for the lights...

ECKERSALL With the clock.

FUJIMOTO The clock was controlled by the computer, and we were making the patterns for the punch cards that programmed the computers back then (it was 1987).

ECKERSALL How did you develop the technical expertise? Essentially, you're inventing systems and you need to have a certain amount of technical expertise. How did you develop that vocabulary?

FUJIMOTO Furuhashi-san had this image of what he wanted on the stage. There was also another person who was involved with dumb type, called Hozumi-san (Hozumi Yukihiro), who knew how to program code, and they got together and figured out what they wanted and if it was possible to build it using the computers they had. They had a system built that Furuhashi-san designed.

SCHEER How did Furuhashi-san convey the images to your friends? Say, for the concept of *pH*, did he make sketches?

FUJIMOTO There were conversations between Furuhashi-san, Koyamada-san, Takatani-san and me, and we talked about what we wanted, and, following these kinds of drawings, Takatani-san would develop the technical specifications or resources. But how we were going to execute this, or how it could come into being was not clear. With *pH*, I think Takatani-san drew up the plan for this, but I don't remember. It's a very simple system, with just the light and the switch.

ECKERSALL You must have had some anxieties when you were running a large show with these new technologies.

FUJIMOTO It happened a lot that it *didn't* work. In *pH,* we had the huge truss that looked like a scanning machine made by Takatani that was designed to go to this side, or that side, and follow where the dancers are...

ECKERSALL Oh wow, homemade?

FUJIMOTO Homemade and we all had to move it by hand. There was no computer.

ECKERSALL That could have been dangerous.

FUJIMOTO Well, we had a back-up system of sensors that was supposed to make it stop, but sometimes it didn't. In the beginning there was a lot of trouble with this truss system and Koyamada was constantly troubleshooting and fixing it. After a while we attached it to a computer, so then that was easier and we could run it with a single crew member. From the beginning, we had a computer system for the slide projectors so Takatani-san could control all the slide projectors himself. Tomari-san was on lights and Yamanaka-san was on sound, and I operated the truss system. There was 16mm film as well.

I was interested in the relationship between the performance and the technology at that point because it was so risky; you didn't know what was going to happen with these trusses. Apparently the performers were very nervous, because they felt like they could die in the system somehow. It was kind of a life and death situation for them.

This was before the first Apple portable computers started coming out, around '88–'89. By the time *S/N* came around, the first Mac notebooks were available so we could use CDs for the imagery. With the changes in the technology, I had more and more possibilities to play with.

SCHEER So *pH* was a pre-digital show, an analogue structure.

FUJIMOTO Yes, and also because of the 16mm films. Back then it was very difficult to get a good video projector, so they would make a video first and then transfer that to film, and use 16mm film in the show because it's better quality.

Furuhashi-san, Koyamada-san and Takatani-san were doing research all the time. For *pH,* they wanted to have the tennis balls thrown onto the space, so they searched through catalogues and found that there were machines for tennis, which were small in scale so they could use that. It also took time because there was no Internet or anything.

ECKERSALL If we look at the journey from *pH* to *S/N,* your technical dramaturgy, your aesthetic, becomes more projection-based, more visual and digital based. What was that like, to move from a kind of machine age where you're putting these machines into the space to creating works on digital machines with no moving parts anymore?

FUJIMOTO With *pH,* we had two tonnes worth of machinery that we were dragging from one place to the next. So that was really tough.

From around *S/N,* we wanted to be able to use the existing systems in the theatre rather than making our own—to make touring easier. From that point on, I became the lighting person, because Takatani-san started to work on the computer graphics and Koyamada-san was doing the stage management. The roles started to be divided, because for the lighting they needed someone who knew how the theatre systems worked and how to talk to the theatre staff on tour.

But the first image that we had about *S/N* was this wall that people would fall off. It's very much an object on stage and the piece deals with this relationship with the object, so it's kind of similar to *pH* in that way.

ECKERSALL And I think there's a conveyor belt on top of the wall? The audience can see the performers being moved rapidly along like on a moving walkway...

FUJIMOTO It's just a normal wooden platform. No machinery.

ECKERSALL That's great. So somebody's doing it by hand!

FUJIMOTO Yes, the dancers are just pretending that there is really a conveyer belt and they're not moving.

ECKERSALL Could I ask you to talk a little bit about the development of the technical work for *OR*? The development of the lighting systems and the sound systems?

FUJIMOTO There was new technology for this called DMX. Before that, different systems had to be operated independently, and the level of the lights could only be changed using individual dimmers. So before DMX and the digital dimmer came, lighting people had to remember what to do at certain moments, manually changing the switches. But with DMX, you could just plug a device into whatever lighting system you were using and eventually everything was automated. It was a completely different thing.

ECKERSALL The stroboscopic lighting in *OR* was synced to Ryoji Ikeda's soundtrack, wasn't it? Was that also something that was then possible for the first time?

FUJIMOTO We had this data flash system that could react when the sound reached a certain volume. So we played with different sound triggers for the light and with the interaction between them, and we developed a system where there was sound that you couldn't hear outside in the auditorium but which was triggering the lights. This was only possible because we were using the computer to develop these systems.

SCHEER The performance opens with a very powerful stroboscopic effect, the single beam of light.

FUJIMOTO That's video. We played with a very special light that you can't really see—a HID light. It's really bad for your eyes [LAUGHS].

The video and the sound were connected because we were using a system called Symphony that was used in the film business to make film sound and video work together. We used it so that the soundtrack could trigger the strobe lights.

ECKERSALL Could I ask you about your work with the lighting systems, and with the projections? When this technology became possible, people really had to develop a new way of lighting the stage. How did you develop your lighting systems in relation to projection?

FUJIMOTO In dumb type, part of the starting point for my work was the coming together of video and lights. It's not like in other companies, where maybe the lights are already there and then someone comes in with a video and they have to adjust the existing light or the other way around. From the beginning in dumb type, it was all as part of one thing, one design.

ECKERSALL When did you start using the LEDS in your lighting designs?

FUJIMOTO I never used LED in dumb type. We didn't have that then. The LED lighting system I used was developed by a small company in Japan. When I started using LED in 2003, I could ask them for specific things.

ECKERSALL Going back to *S/N*, were there multiple projectors to get those images?

FUJIMOTO There were four video players connected to four projectors for the video wall, and then for the text we used slides projected onto mirrors to make the text appear to turn. At the time, the slide technology was better developed than video, so if you wanted to project text in a video, it was going to always have the frame of the video. So with the slides, we could make the text move with no frame around it.

ECKERSALL And that would have been extremely complicated to light adequately so that you could see the slide and the video at the same time.

FUJIMOTO In *S/N*, the image was sort of divided... so if the light wasn't going onto the video wall, it was okay. The division was quite clear. The set designers did a lot to make this easier.

ECKERSALL Do you have a favourite piece, either with dumb type or since?

FUJIMOTO Probably whatever I'm working on now. I've recently started doing lighting for Noh performances, using LED, but the Noh performances are improvised. In traditional Noh theatre, the actors know all their pieces, so they don't rehearse, they just come together and improvise. Everyone knows their part. So it's a challenge to do this kind of lighting for these things because there are no rehearsals.

Chronology of Works

1984

The Admirable Health Method
Performance
Kyoto City University of Arts, Kyoto, JAPAN

An Asteroid Addition
Performance
Kyoto City University of Arts, Kyoto, JAPAN

1985

The Order of the Square
Installation / printed matter
10 locations, Kyoto, JAPAN

An Encyclopedia for Landscapemanias
Performance
Kyoto City University of Arts, Kyoto, JAPAN

Listening Hour #1
Performance / installation / video
Gallery Garden, Kyoto, JAPAN

Listening Hour #2
Performance
The Museum of Modern Art, Shiga, JAPAN

1986

Plan for Sleep #3
Performance
Orange Room, Osaka, JAPAN

Plan for Sleep #8
Installation / printed matter / symposium
Ryo Gallery, Kyoto, JAPAN

1987

Yes, the Salt of Passion – Part 6
Performance / installation – Collaboration with Hotel Pro Forma
Toga International Arts Festival, Toga, JAPAN

036 – Pleasure Life
Performance / video / printed matter
Artspace Mumonkan, Kyoto, JAPAN

1988

Pleasure Life
Performance
Quest Hall, Tokyo, JAPAN / The 1st New York International Festival of The Arts, Performance Space 122, New York, USA / Theater im Pumpenhaus, Münster, GERMANY / ICA, London, UK / The Royal Museum of Fine Arts, Copenhagen, DENMARK / ALTI, Kyoto, JAPAN

Plan For Sleep #1
Performance
Kyoto City University of Arts, Kyoto, JAPAN

Plan For Sleep #2
Performance
Artspace Mumonkan, Kyoto, JAPAN

Every Dog Has His Day
Performance
Artspace Mumonkan, Kyoto, JAPAN

Plan for Sleep #5
Performance
Osaka International Arts Festival, Osaka, JAPAN

Suspense and Romance
Installation / music concert
Tsukashin Hall, Osaka, JAPAN

1989

The Polygonal Journey #1
Performance – Collaboration with The Bridgehouse Collection
Artspace Mumonkan, Kyoto, JAPAN

Media Art Museum
TV – NHK
Quest Hall, Tokyo, JAPAN

1990

The Polygonal Journey #2
Performance – Collaboration with The Bridgehouse Collection
Northern Light Planetarium, Tromsø, NORWAY

pH
Performance / installation / video / printed matter
Spiral, Tokyo, JAPAN

1991

pH
Performance
Kyoto Municipal Museum of The Arts, Kyoto, JAPAN / ICA, Nagoya, JAPAN / "Granada Festival," Estadio de la Juventud, Granada, SPAIN / "Art in the Anchorage," Creative Time, New York, USA / Moda Hall, Osaka, JAPAN / Chapter, Cardiff, UK / Tramway, Glasgow, UK

1992

pH
Performance
Wiener Festwochen, Messepalast, Vienna, AUSTRIA / Centro de Arte Reina Sofia, Madrid, SPAIN / Theater im Pumpenhaus, Münster, GERMANY / "Zones of Love,"Museum of Contemporary Art, Sydney, AUSTRALIA

Metropolis – dumb type
TV production, 30'00"
Produced and broadcasted by Televisión Española, SPAIN

pH
Video
Sole d'Oro Award [TTVV-Riccione, ITALY] / Best Stage Recording, Studio Adaptation Award [IMZ – Dance Screen 92]

The Nutcracker
Performance – Collaboration with Mika Kurosawa
Aoyama Round Theater, Tokyo, JAPAN

Play Back
Installation / video
"Against Nature", San Francisco Museum of Modern Art, USA / Akron Art Museum, USA / MIT List Visual Arts Center, USA / Bank of Boston Art Gallery, USA

pH
Performance
Artspace Mumonkan, Kyoto, JAPAN

PLAY BACK
Installation / video
Seattle Art Museum, USA / The Contemporary Arts Center, Cincinnati, USA / Grey Art Gallery, New York University, USA / Contemporary Arts Museum, Houston, USA

pH
Video
WOWOW – Japan Satellite Broadcasting, JAPAN

Play Back
Installation / video
ICA, Nagoya, JAPAN

S/N #1
Installation
"The Binary Era," Museum of Ixelles, Brussels, BELGIUM

The Enigma of the Late Afternoon
Performance – Collaboration with HOTEL PRO FORMA
Glyptotek Museum, Copenhagen, DENMARK

S/N #2
Installation
"Another World," ATM Contemporary Art Gallery, Mito, JAPAN

1993

pH
Performance
Spiral Hall, Tokyo, JAPAN / "June-festival," Theaterhaus Gessnerallee, Zurich, SWITZERLAND

The "seminar show" for *S/N*
Performance & talk
Artspace Mumonkan, Kyoto, JAPAN / Shonandai Culture Center Civic Theater, Fujisawa, JAPAN

1994

Love/Sex/Death/Money/Life
Installation
Spiral (in the elevator), Tokyo, JAPAN

S/N #1
Installation
"Japanese Art after 1945: Scream against the Sky," Yokohama Art Museum, Yokohama, JAPAN / Guggenheim SOHO, New York, USA

1995

S/N
Performance
"VISAS Festival International," Le Manège Scène Nationale - La Luna, Maubeuge, FRANCE / "Luxembourg 95 – Ville Européenne de la Culture," Théâtre d'Esch, Esch, LUXEMBOURG / Cankarjev Dom, Ljubljana, SLOVENIA / Theater im Pumpenhaus – Münster, GERMANY / "Festival EXIT," Maison des Arts de Créteil, Créteil, FRANCE / "Kunsten – Festival des Arts," Théâtre Varia, Bruxelles, BELGIUM / "Züricher Theater Spektakle," Theater Werft, Zürich, SWITZERLAND / "Århus Festuge," Musikhuset, Århus, DENMARK / SPIEL.ART – Muffathalle, München, GERMANY / "Festival Internacional de Artes Cênicas," Teatro Castro Alves, Salvador, BRAZIL / "Festival Internacional de Artes Cênicas," Sesc Anchieta, São Paulo, BRAZIL

1996

S/N
Performance
"Tokyo Theater Fair 96," Tokyo Geijutsu Gekijo, Tokyo, JAPAN / ALTI, Kyoto, JAPAN / "Hong Kong Arts Festival," Hong Kong Culture Centre Studio Theatre, HONG KONG / "New Zealand International Festival of the Arts," Shed 1, Wellington, NEW ZEALAND / Teatro Central, Sevilla, SPAIN / "Festival EXIT," Maison des Arts de Créteil, Créteil, FRANCE

pH
Video
"Video Film Dance Festival," Ljubljana, SLOVENIA / Broadcast by RTBF Liege/Carre Noir, BELGIUM

S/N #1
Installation
Fukui International Video Biennale, Fukui, JAPAN / Kunsthalle, Vienna, AUSTRIA

S/N
Performance
"Adelaide Festival," Adelaide, AUSTRALIA / Musée d'Art Contemporain de Montréal, Montréal, CANADA / On The Boards – The King Theater, Seattle, USA / Landmark Hall, Yokohama, JAPAN

pH
Video
"Video Film Dance Festival," HONG KONG

Love/Sex/Death/Money/Life
Installation
"Fluctuations Fugitives," Espace d'Art Yvonamor Palix, Paris, FRANCE

S/N #1
Installation
"Japanese Art after 1945: Scream against the Sky," San Francisco Museum of Modern Art and Center for the Arts at Yerba Buena Gardens, San Francisco, USA

pH
Performance
"VISAS Festival International," Le Manège Scène Nationale – La Luna, Maubeuge, FRANCE / "Festival EXIT," Maison des Arts de Créteil, Créteil, FRANCE / "Today's Japan," Harbourfront Centre, Toronto, CANADA

S/N
Performance, CD
Spiral, Tokyo, JAPAN

Monkey Business Class
Performance – Collaboration with Hotel Pro Forma and Diller + Scofidio
Malmø Musikteater Storan, Malmø, SWEDEN / Albertslund Music Theatre, Copenhagen, DENMARK

1997

OR
Performance
"Festival VIA,"Le Manège Scène Nationale – Théâtre du Manège, Maubeuge, FRANCE / "Festival EXIT," Maison des Arts de Créteil, Créteil, FRANCE / "Ars Electronica,"Design Centre, Linz, AUSTRIA / Park Tower Hall, Tokyo, JAPAN / "Festival d'Automne à Paris," Maison des Arts de Créteil, Créteil, FRANCE

1998

Dangerous Visions
Concert – Collaboration with Art Zoyd + Lille National Orchestra
Lille, Maubeuge, Créteil, FRANCE

S/N #1
Installation
Voice Gallery, Kyoto, JAPAN

1999

OR
Performance
The Museum of Art, Kochi, Kochi, JAPAN / "Kyoto Arts Festival," Kyoto City North Culture Hall, Kyoto, JAPAN / "Donaufestival," Theaterhaus Alte Sporthalle, Krems, AUSTRIA / On The Boards, Seattle, USA / PICA (Portland Institute for Contemporary Art), Portland, USA / Walker Art Center, Minneapolis, USA / Museum of Contemporary Art, Chicago, USA

memorandum
Performance
"Festival de danse," Le Manège Scène Nationale – Espace Gérard Philipe, Maubeuge, FRANCE / "Festival d'Automne à Paris," Maison des Arts de Créteil, Créteil, FRANCE / Haus der Kulturen der Welt – Arena, Berlin, GERMANY / YSARCA – Teatro Albeniz, Madrid, SPAIN

2000

memorandum
Performance
"Charleroi Danse," Charleroi, BELGIUM / GRAME – Maison de la Danse, Lyon, FRANCE / Centre de Développement Chorégraphique – TNT/Théâtre de la Cité, Toulouse, FRANCE / Teatro Central, Sevilla, SPAIN / "Julidans," Stadsschouwburg, Amsterdam, THE NETHERLANDS / "tanz aus japan: international sommerfestival 2000," Tanzhaus nrw, Düsseldorf, GERMANY / "La Bâtie Festival de Genève," Bâtiment des Forces Motrices, Genève, SWITZERLAND / The Museum of Art, Kochi, JAPAN / New National Theatre, Tokyo, JAPAN / Theater Drama City, Osaka, JAPAN

OR
Installation
NTT InterCommunication Center, Tokyo, JAPAN

OR
Concert
"Palermo di Scena," S. Maria Dello Spasimo, Palermo, ITALY / Kobe Art Village Center, Kobe, JAPAN / Spiral Hall, Tokyo, JAPAN

OR
Performance
"Julidans," Stadsschouwburg, Amsterdam, THE NETHERLANDS / "EXPO '98 LISBOA, mergulho no futuro "Centro Cultural de Belém, Lisbon, PORTUGAL / "Züricher Theater Spektakel, "Theater Werft," Zürich, SWITZERLAND / "het pact," de warande stad turnhout, Turnhout, BELGIUM / "BITE 98," Barbican Centre, London, UK / Kampnagel Theater, Hamburg, GERMANY / Dansens Hus, Stockholm, SWEDEN

Sweet Memories
Working title, performance – public rehearsal
"Festival Studio Vidéo Danse," Théâtre Kallisté, Ajaccio (Corsica), FRANCE

LOVE/SEX/DEATH/MONEY/LIFE
Installation
"Fancy Dance," Artsonje Museum, Kyongju, and Artsonje Center, Seoul, KOREA

OR
Installation
"Musiques en Scène," Musée d'Art Contemporain de Lyon, Lyon, FRANCE / "Gendai: Japanese Contemporary Art – Between the Body and Space," Centre for Contemporary Art Ujazdowski Castle, Warsaw, POLAND

cascade
Installation & performance
"Stanze e Segreti," Salone del Mobile, Milano, ITALY

LOVE/SEX/DEATH/MONEY/LIFE
Installation
"vision.ruhr," Museum am Ostwall, Dortmund, GERMANY

2001

cascade
Installation & performance
"Translated Acts: Performance and Body Art from East Asia," Haus der Kulturen der Welt, Berlin, GERMANY

2002

memorandum
Performance
New Opera of Tel Aviv, Tel Aviv, ISRAEL / Museum of Contemporary Art, Chicago, USA / On The Boards, Seattle, USA / PICA (Portland Institute for Contemporary Art), Portland, USA / Walker Art Center, Minneapolis, USA / "Festival ART ROCK," La Passerelle, St Brieuc, FRANCE / Maison des Arts de Créteil, Créteil, FRANCE / "Singapore Arts Festival," Victoria Theatre, SINGAPORE / The Japan Foundation Kuala Lumpur – Istana Budaya, Kuala Lumpur, MALAYSIA

2003

memorandum
Performance
"The 22nd International Modern Dance Festival," The KCAF Theater, Seoul, KOREA / "la Biennale di Venezia," Teatro Piccolo Arsenale, Venice, ITALY / Bangkok Playhouse, Bangkok, THAILAND / "Melbourne International Arts Festival," Forum Theatre, Melbourne, AUSTRALIA / REDCAT (Roy and Edna Disney/CalArts Theater), Los Angeles, USA / Pittsburgh Dance Council, Pittsburgh, USA

2004

Voyage
Performance
YCAM (Yamaguchi Center for Arts and Media), Yamaguchi, JAPAN / Novel Hall for Performing Arts, Taipei, Taiwan / "Tanztheater 3 wochen mit Pina Bausch," Schauspielhaus, Düsseldorf, GERMANY

2005

Voyage
performance
Théâtre d'Angoulême, Angoulême, FRANCE / Le Carré des Jalles, St Médard en Jalles, FRANCE / Dansens Hus, Stockholm, SWEDEN / Bergen International Festival, Bergen, NORWAY / "International Modern Dance Festival," The KCAF Theater,

Voyage
Performance
Centre de Développment Chorégraphique de Toulouse/Midi-Pyrénées – TNT/Théâtre de la Cité, Toulouse, FRANCE / Le Parvis Scène Nationale, Ibos-Tarbes, FRANCE / Saitama Arts Theater, Saitama, JAPAN / Theater Drama City, Osaka, JAPAN / Le Maillon – Théâtre de Strasbourg, Strasbourg, FRANCE

OR
Installation
Ecole supérieure des beaux-arts, Toulouse, FRANCE

Voyages
Installation
NTT InterCommunication Center, Tokyo, JAPAN

Voyage
Performance
Deutschen Nationaltheater und Staatskapelle Weimar, Weimar, GERMANY / Biwako Hall, Shiga, Japan / REDCAT (Roy and Edna Disney/CalArts Theater), Los Angeles, USA / Maison des Arts de Créteil, Créteil, FRANCE

Voyages
Installation
YCAM (Yamaguchi Center for Arts and Media), Yamagichi, JAPAN

Seoul, KOREA / Muffathalle, München, GERMANY / Altstadherbst Kulturfestival Düsseldorf, Düsseldorf, GERMANY

OR
Installation
Tesla Berlin, Berlin, GERMANY

2006

Voyage
Performance
La Comète – scène nationale de Châlons-en-Champagne, Châlons-en-Champagne, FRANCE / Théâtre de Nîmes, Nîmes, FRANCE / Posthof, Linz, AUSTRIA / Tramway, Glasgow, UK / "Exodos Festival," Cankarjev Dom, Ljubljana, SLOVENIA / "Melbourne International Arts Festival," Melbourne, AUSTRALIA

2007

Voyages
Installation
"Body Media," Shanghai Sculpture Space, O Art Center, Shanghai Institute of Visual Art Fudan University, Shanghai, CHINA / Namura Art Meeting, Osaka, JAPAN / "Vom Funken zum Pixel," Martin-Gropius-Bau, Berlin, GERMANY

2008

Voyage
Performance
"XI Festival Iberoamericano de Teatro de Bogotá," Bogota, COLOMBIA / EMPAC (Experimental Media & Performing Arts Center), Rensselaer Polytechnic Institute, Troy, NY, USA / Montclair State University, Kasser Theater, Montclair, NJ, USA / La Filature, Mulhouse, FRANCE / Le Volcan – Maison de la Culture du Havre, Le Havre, FRANCE

2009

Voyage
Performance
O.M.M.A. (Organismos Megarou Mousikis Athinon), The Athens Concert Hall, Athens, GREECE / SEMEC (Société d'Economie Mixte pour les Evènements Cannois), Théâtre Debussy, Cannes, FRANCE

This chronology is based on the one available on dumb type's website, at www.dumbtype.com/biography.

Contributors

Stephen Barber is Professor in the Faculty of Art, Design and Architecture at Kingston University, London. His most recent book is *Berlin Bodies* (London: Reaktion, 2017). He is currently writing a book on the film projects of Hijikata Tatsumi.

Gunhild Borggreen is an Associate Professor in Art History and Visual Culture at the University of Copenhagen, where her research focuses on Japanese contemporary art and visual culture. Borggreen is the co-founder and manager of ROCA (Robot Culture and Aesthetics), an interdisciplinary research group that explores the intersection of technology, aesthetics and culture.

Peter Eckersall teaches theatre and performance studies at The Graduate Centre, City University of New York. Recent publications include *New Media Dramaturgy: Performance, Media and New Materialism* (with Helena Grehan and Edward Scheer). He is the resident dramaturg for Melbourne-based company Not Yet It's Difficult.

Shintarō FUJII is Professor of Theatre Studies at Waseda University in Tokyo. His research interests include French/Francophone theatre, European performance cultures and contemporary Japanese theatre.

FUJIMOTO Takayuki is a director, lighting designer and scenic designer and a pioneer of new media performance. His company Kinsei R&D undertakes research and the development of new artworks in Japan and globally. He joined dumb type in 1987.

Sara Jansen is a researcher and dramaturg in dance. She holds degrees in Japanese Studies (KU Leuven, Belgium) and Performance Studies (New York University) and was a Japan Foundation Fellow at Waseda University (Tokyo). Currently, Jansen is completing a PhD on choreography, history and the postwar Japanese avant-garde at the universities of Brussels (VUB) and Antwerp (UA).

KUMAKURA Takaaki is a former Professor at Kyoto University of Art and Design. His current research practice is on spirituality in the twenty-first century. He also manages a new hub for social change, "Impact Hub Kyoto."

Fran Lloyd is Professor of Art History and Director of the Visual & Material Culture Research Centre in the Faculty of Art, Design & Architecture at Kingston University, London. She has published widely on contemporary and modern visual culture, and has over fifteen years experience of collaborating on a variety of international interdisciplinary creative arts projects.

Wim Lunsing is an independent scholar specialising in Japanese society, sexuality, gender, lifestyles, discrimination and issues of sustainable development. Following his Ph.D. in Anthropology from Oxford Brookes University in 1995, he was a Research Professor of Japanese Studies at the University of Copenhagen (1997–1998) and a Japan Foundation Special Research Fellow at the University of Tokyo (2001–2002).

Katherine Mezur is Lecturer in the Department of English and Comparative Literature at the University of California, Berkeley. She is the author of *Beautiful Boys/Outlaw Bodies: Devising Kabuki Female-Likeness* (Palgrave, 2005). Her new project is "Cute Mutant Girls: Performing Sweet and Deviant in Contemporary Japan." Mezur is also a dramaturg and choreographer and directs performance workshops.

ŌTORI Hidenaga specialises in the history of ideas in Russian art. Among other roles, he was artistic director of the international theatre festival "Laookon" (Hamburg, Germany) and vice president of the Performing Arts Research Centre at Kyoto University of Art and Design. His publications include *Reverberation Machines: The Words of Richard Foreman*. Otori has also been a chief editor of numerous theatre magazines, such as *Theatre Arts*, *Chimaera* and *Performing Arts*.

Andreas Regelsberger is Professor of Japanese Studies at Trier University, Germany. His research and teaching areas focus on Japanese theater, including Bunraku, Kabuki and contemporary theatre. He is also a translator of Japanese plays.

Edward Scheer is Professor of Performance Studies and Head of School of Art and Design at the University of NSW Australia. His research interests include performance art, visual art and experimental humanities. Recent publications include *New Media Dramaturgy: Performance, Media and New Materialism* (with Helena Grehan and Peter Eckersall).

TAKATANI Shirō is a founding member of dumb type, working especially on the visual and technical aspects of their productions and events. He is a visual artist and media artist who produces artworks and collaborations globally. Recent works include: CLOUD FOREST, a collaborative installation with Fujiko Nakaya (YCAM 2010), "Camera Lucida" (Tokyo Metropolitan Museum of Photography 2013) and ongoing collaborations with the musician Ryuichi Sakamoto.

Keiko TAKEDA is an Assistant Professor in the Interfaculty Initiative in Information Studies program at the University of Tokyo.

Shinya YAMAKI is a curator and researcher working in Japan and Europe. Recent projects include "LIFE with ART: The Art of Intervention" a joint research project considering the performance *S/N* by dumb type. He currently works for Kyoto Prefecture, managing various art projects related to festivals, residency programs and archives.

YOSHIDA Miya is a curator and a postdoctoral researcher at Leuphana University Lüneburg (2012–2014). She has worked internationally with different forms of art projects and research. She has curated a series of exhibitions, "World in Your Hand" (Kunsthaus Dresden in 2010), "Labour of Love, Revisited" (Arko Art Museum, Seoul in 2011) and "Amateurism!" (Heidelberger Kunstverein in 2012).